History & Geography of Lake of the Ozarks Volume 1

Also by H. Dwight Weaver

Lake of the Ozarks: The Early Years

Lake of the Ozarks: Vintage Vacation Paradise

History & Geography of Lake of the Ozarks
Volume 1

H. Dwight Weaver

Published by:
Osage River Trails
38 Village Marina Rd
Eldon, MO 65026-5636
Phone: 573-365-1171
Email: dweaver@socket.net

Additional Copies Of This Book Are Also Available From:
Osage Valley Trader
38 Village Marina Rd
Eldon, MO 65026-5636
Phone: 573-365-1171
Email: zet@socket.net
Website: lakeozarksbookandphoto.com or lakeoftheozarksbooks.com

Above Photo: Bagnell Dam and Lake of the Ozarks. Photo by Gerald Massie, circa. 1956, courtesy of Missouri State Archives.
Cover Photo: A view of the Niangua Arm of Lake of the Ozarks at the 4-mile mark from the grounds of El Kay Motel on Hwy. 5 north of Camdenton, MO. Photo by H. Dwight Weaver, 2005.

Copyright © 2005 H. Dwight Weaver
First Edition

Library of Congress Catalog Card Number: 2005907445

ISBN 0-9772700-0-9

All rights reserved. No part of this book may be reproduced or transmitted in any form or by any means, electronic or mechanical, including photocopying, recording, or by any information storage and retrieval system, without permission in writing from the copyright owner.

This book was printed in the United States of America.

Attention Lake of the Ozarks Business Owners

This book is available at quantity discounts with bulk purchase for business use.
For information, write, email or call:

Osage Valley Trader
38 Village Marina Rd, Eldon, MO 65026-5636
Phone: 573-365-1171; Email: zet@socket.net

For my pal, Bill Pfantz,
who put in a lot of hours and miles on his boat
making sure that I got to every foot
of the Lake's 1,100 miles of shoreline.
He never once complained.

To my wife, Rosie,
whose memory of businesses and people at
the Lake is better than my own.
Her patience and prodding got
me to the finish line.

To my daughter, Karen,
whose sharp eye kept me from making some
embarrassing mistakes. She is a graduate
of School of the Osage, that's why.

CONTENTS

	page
Introduction	ix
Chapter A	1
Chapter B	11
Chapter C	31
Chapter D	49
Chapter E	59
Chapter F	65
Chapter G	75
Chapter H	91
Chapter I	103
Chapter J	110
Chapter K	119
Chapter L	125
Chapter M	139
Chapter N	147
Chapter 0	155
Chapter P	169
Chapter R	179
Chapter S	185
Chapter T	199
Chapter U-V	205
Chapter W-X-Y-Z	213
Bibliography	221
Main Entries Index	225
Business and Company Index	228
Lake Roads, Coves and Selected Geographic Features Index	235
Towns and Villages Index	239
People Index	240
About the Author	248

INTRODUCTION

HISTORY & GEOGRAPHY of LAKE of the OZARKS Volume One, is the first of a set of volumes for the person who wants to learn about the history of the Lake area and its natural wonders and curiosities. The books will highlight that period of time from the early 1800s to the 1970s, with special attention given to the 1930s, 40s, 50s and 60s, which were the decades of pioneer development at Lake of the Ozarks.

The books will explore the history of early fishing camps, resorts, lodges, and roadside cottage courts and motels. Narratives reach back in time to the origins of villages and towns that sprinkle the region, including places that have vanished, some beneath the waters of the Lake.

The books will probe the origins of place names; the history of fords, ferries and bridges past and present; the tragedy of fires and floods; and seek to unearth was lies in darkness beneath the hills and water-logged beneath the waters of the Lake.

The books will take readers on history quests along streams and rivers as well as Lake arms and coves, and describe landscape features such as unusual rock formations, bluffs, caves, springs and natural bridges.

The **History & Geography of Lake of the Ozarks** includes narratives about excursion boats, festivals, clubs and organizations, and highlights the people who came to the Lake area during the Great Depression years of the 1930s, and the World War II years of the 1940s, to invest their life savings in something new called "tourism." The Lake of the Ozarks region was so primitive and undeveloped at that time, that many fishing camps and resorts had to provide their own generators in order to have electricity for their log cabins and stone cottages. Many of the pioneer developers also had to be willing to carve their own roads out of the forest that covered the rocky hills so that tourists could find their places of business. The books will travel the highways and byways at the Lake in the 1950s and 60s when the first truly great explosion in tourism development occurred -- a time when businesses were small, family-owned, family-run enterprises -- the mom and pop years -- a time when national chains and brand names had not yet discovered Lake of the Ozarks. It was nothing like what is happening today in terms of commercial and residential development, but the 50s and 60s set the stage for what is happening now.

Controversy is revealed in Volume One, proving that while time and landscapes change, people don't. When the great Lake was yet unformed, Missouri politicians gathered to decide what the Lake's name should be, but their misguided efforts were foiled by the leader of their own political party.

The affairs of the City of Lake Ozark are no more challenging today than they were in the 1930s because in 1931 and 1932, the people of the future City of Lake Ozark could not decide what name to give their new town at the west end of the dam. Uncle Sam had to resolve the issue for them.

In 1931, the new business community at the Lake cried out for area-wide advertising and promotion for their paradise in the wilderness, lest they all starve to death for lack of trade. The Lake of the Ozarks Improvement and Protective Association was organized for that purpose, but it soon became apparent that the leader of the organization had a different agenda than the business community had anticipated.

Volume One and subsequent volumes in the set will incorporate entries from the entire Lake of the Ozarks region. The geographical boundaries for these volumes can be determined by looking at a Missouri highway map. The northern boundary runs from the junction of Hwys. 65 and 52 at Cole Camp, in Benton County, eastward along Hwy. 52 through Cole Camp, Stover, Versailles, Barnett, Eldon, and on to Tuscumbia in Miller County. The boundary then drops south through Brumley, runs diagonally through Montreal to connect with the southern boundary of Camden County, and then moves west along the Camden County line to Hickory County. There it runs north to the Benton County line, then west to connect once again with Hwy. 65, and then north through Warsaw to the Cole Camp Junction, completing the circuit.

These are the boundaries that define the Lake of the Ozarks region or area featured in this work. Any topic of interest that falls within the area enclosed by these boundary lines is considered appropriate for the **History & Geography of Lake of the Ozarks**. It should be clear then, that this is not a history of the four counties in which the Lake is located, but only a history of the corridor described above that frames Lake of the Ozarks.

Even though Lake of the Ozarks originally extended an additional 40 miles above Warsaw on the Osage before the construction of Truman Dam and Reservoir in the 1970s, that portion of the former Lake region above Warsaw will not be included in these volumes.

People often seek the location of early resorts and businesses at the Lake for a variety of reasons, but over the decades so many landscape changes have occurred, and the numerical designations of the roads have changed to such an extent, that locating the old sites can be difficult. An effort has been made to pinpoint the location of the early businesses and trace the history of lake road designations for the sites included in the text. It is recommended that the reader purchase a Lake map, one with numbered and named roads. Several excellent Lake of the Ozarks maps are currently sold in the region and most are regularly updated. The narratives in **History & Geography of Lake of the Ozarks** have been written to compliment the information provided on maps in current circulation.

Because the topics included in these books are arranged in alphabetical order, and have been written so that each entry stands alone, a certain amount of repetition in text is unavoidable, especially with regard to locational information.

The indexes will be useful to anyone seeking a subject that is not a main entry. The indexes contains many additional points of entry into the narratives.

These pages are full of the nearly forgotten past, a past that should not be forgotten. While local county historical societies do an excellent job of preserving the heritage of Benton, Camden, Miller and Morgan counties before the construction of Bagnell Dam, their historical records contain very little about the history of Lake of the Ozarks itself and the growth and development of the tourism industry. Each historical society, of course, focuses upon their own county as well they should, but little effort has been made to put that history into a regional context. **History & Geography of Lake of the Ozarks** strives to fill in this 70-year gap of regional history.

With business entries in this text, the oldest or founding name of the business is generally used as the primary entry title, but there are exceptions. A forward slash (for example - Adkin's Camp / Resort) indicates that at some point in time the name of the business was modified from camp to resort.

Only a few major federal and state highways pass through the Lake of the Ozarks area. In these books prefix designations have been eliminated and the word "highway" abbreviated (for example - Hwy. 54). Also for the sake of brevity, the words "Lake Road" are abbreviated "LkRd." Readers should keep in mind that new highway construction is scheduled through Osage Beach along Hwy. 54, and along Hwy. 5 north and south of Camdenton. When that is completed, many of the roadside businesses featured in these books, with locations given along Hwy. 54 and Hwy. 5, will then be on Bus. Hwy. 54 and Bus. Hwy. 5.

The highways in the Lake area, as well as the Lake itself, meander. Hwy. 54 is an established east-west highway but through much of the Lake area, it tends to run north and south, thus we hear of businesses in Lake Ozark being both west and south of the dam. Roadside businesses in these books are generally located according to how they set with the road they are on at their specific site, and not necessarily by the highway's established direction. The same procedure is used with businesses and features located on the shores of the Lake.

Italicized words in brackets following entry titles give the name of the incorporated town closest to the subject and the county in which the subject is located.

While some lengthy coves on the Lake are called "arms" of the Lake by residents, these volumes recognize only the following as arms of the Lake -- Gravois, Grand Glaize, Niangua and Little Niangua. In this text, the main stem of the Lake along the former Osage River course is referred to as the Osage Arm.

The history of some businesses is separated into two or more narratives under separate entries depending upon how much of the history of a subject is relevant to a particular name. For this reason, it can be helpful to follow the cross references within and following a narrative if the reader is using the book selectively, rather than reading from beginning to end.

Due to the fact that wild cave locations are generally considered proprietary information in Missouri, the locations of some wild caves mentioned in these volumes will be generalized. A person should always get permission from the land owner before entering a cave or attempting to visit a natural wonder that is on private property.

In a sense, the roots of the **History & Geography of Lake of the Ozarks** began growing more than 40 years ago when my wife, Rosie, my daughter, Karen, and I moved to Lake of the Ozarks and became immersed in "tourism." We found it wonderfully infectious and so Lake of the Ozarks became our permanent home. I very quickly became intrigued with the early history of the region and began to collect everything I could lay my hands on that provided any information -- such as old postcards, photographs, booklets, maps, brochures, travel literature and a multitude of other records. I also became active with the Camden County Historical Society. But during those years I was much too busy trying to make a living to think about committing what I was learning about the Lake's history to paper. Now that I am retired and am able to devote more time to historical interests and writing about the Lake, my collection has become the foundation of this work on the **History & Geography of Lake of the Ozarks**. And the quest for additional information continues unabated.

Because much time has elapsed since this work began, I'm sure I have forgotten the names of some people who were helpful in the earlier years, and so, if I overlook anyone in saying thank you, be rest assured, the omission was not intentional.

I am indebted to Bruce F. James of Lake Ozark for being kind enough to read every word of my original manuscript for Volume One and offer a critique. That was before I discovered that I had far too much material for one book and had to hold out many narratives to keep the book to a reasonable size. That material will come in a future volume. Bruce "buried" himself in that original manuscript. He knows the Lake, he knows its people, and his insight was invaluable. He is also a great supporter of my effort to delve into the history of the Lake and preserve priceless images and information.

Other people that I must thank, both living and deceased, include Tex Bemis, James A. Franklin, Mabel C. Hawkins, R. H. "Ollie" Ohlson, Nell Moulder, Fern Moreland, Harvey Fry, G. T. Richards, Dan Jarvis, Allen Sullivan, Lloyd Slone, Sylvia Brinkman, Dale Jeffries, James Martin, Eddie Miller, Rich Schleper, Frank Hurley, Susan Kuhn, James E. Lawrence, James Brooks, Randall Dawdy, Thomas J. Grubbels, Lynn Morrow, John Bradbury, Ollie Hibbler, Jim and Karla Thompson, Victoria Hubbel, Diane Warner, Steve Crocker, Mark Mitchell, Cathy Wright, Anita Allee, Jim Taylor, John Poehlein and Susan Dunn.

I relied heavily upon the archives of the Camden and Miller County historical societies, records of the Missouri State Archives, the Missouri State Library, and the newspaper records of the Missouri State Historical Society. The bibliography reveals other sources of information for which I am grateful.

An effort has been made to make the information in this book as accurate as possible. It is based upon published sources, oral history and personal recollections, but therein lie problems compounded by the fact that history can be illusive, facts are not always certain, documents are scarce, dates are hard to pin down, people often remember history differently and disagree on names, dates, locations, and the chronology of events. Unfortunately, time corrupts history and too many people die without leaving a written record of their life and accomplishments.

If you have old photos, brochures, postcards, written records and memories of the Lake that you would like to share to enhance future volumes, please contact me at 573-365-1171 or email: dweaver@socket.net. I am seeking long-timers to interview.

H. Dwight Weaver

Attention Lake of the Ozarks Business Owners

This book is available at quantity discounts with bulk purchase for business use.
For information write, email or call:

Osage Valley Trader
38 Village Marina Road, Eldon, MO 65026-5636
Phone: 573-365-1171; email: zet@socket.net

A. M. Pope & Sons Hardware & Lumber Company *(Bagnell, Miller County; Old Linn Creek and Osage Beach, Camden County) -*

The John Pope family came to Missouri in 1839 and settled near Passover on Route A in Camden County. The family operated a cardingmill and gristmill on Glaize Creek.

Arthur M. Pope, one of John Pope's sons, established a hardware and lumber company in Old Linn Creek and operated it until Union Electric took the property in 1930 during the demolition of Old Linn Creek for the coming of Lake of the Ozarks. [*In this book, "Old Linn Creek" refers to the original Linn Creek, at a location now inundated by the Lake.*]

The Pope family also had the Pope Hardware & Lumber Company in Bagnell, Missouri. The business had been established in 1923. It was operated by B. O. Claiborn until 1927 when Arthur Pope's son, Walter Morgan Pope, became manager. Bagnell was ravished by two destructive fires in 1931, which virtually destroyed the town but the fires did not reach the Pope business.

In 1935, Arthur Pope and his sons -- Lee, Joe and Vernon -- opened the A. M. Pope & Sons Hardware & Lumber Company in Osage Beach along Hwy. 54 just east of LkRd. 54-10, later designated 54-24 and now called Osage Beach Road. The lumberyard was on the south side of the highway.

Along the south side of the highway between LkRd. 54-10 and the lumberyard, the Osage Beach Post Office was built in 1935, and Idlewild Court in 1936. Idlewild Court was between the lumberyard and the post office. Later, a service station was built between Idlewild Court and the lumberyard.

Walter Pope, who had worked with his father at the Bagnell location, remained in Bagnell until the 1943 flood, operating a lumberyard and a tourist court. After the flood, the A. M. Pope Hardware & Lumber Company at Bagnell ceased operation and the buildings were torn down.

Arthur Pope acquired a hotel by default on LkRd. 54-10 and named it the Arthur M. Pope Hotel. As the story goes, the man who built the hotel obtained his lumber from Pope but failed to pay his bill and Pope subsequently got ownership of the hotel.

In 1944, Pope sold both the lumberyard and the hotel. The name of the lumberyard changed to Lake Lumber Company, and the Arthur M. Pope Hotel became Kirkwood Lodge. [see Kirwood Lodge]

Adam's Cafe & Tobacco Shop *(Camdenton, Camden County)* -

Adam's Cafe opened in Camdenton around 1943 and was in operation until about 1966. It was located at 119 East Hwy. 54 about one-half block from the square on the northwest side of the highway. The cafe served Ozark-style chicken, steaks and channel catfish dinners. In 1954, a customer could buy a plate lunch dinner for 25 cents. The business also featured a gift shop and sold liquor and wine.

Adam's Cafe was open day and night in its distinctive one-story building, which had a giraffe-rock veneer. For a time there was a large billboard-size map of Lake of

Adams Cafe & Tobacco Shop, *Camdenton, MO, Circa, 1940. Photographer Unknown.*

the Ozarks facing the highway adjacent to the building's northeast side. Adam's Cafe may have operated briefly as the Adam's Star Restaurant in 1967 and 1968. A portion of the building is still standing and in use by a different business, although changes have been made to the building's exterior.

Adkin's Camp / Resort *(Gravois Mills, Versailles, Morgan County)* -

Adkin's Camp was an early fishing camp on the Gravois Arm reached by LkRd. 5-8 until the 1960s when the road designation changed to LkRd. 5-20. It is now called Adkins Village Road off Route P.

The camp opened in the late 1930s near the headwaters of Mill Creek Cove, which is at the 4-mile mark on the Gravois Arm. Mel Adkins first advertised it as

Adkin's Camp, later with "Mel" in the title in brackets, and finally, by 1940, as Mel Adkin's Camp. The camp was patronized by fishermen and hunters. Bass fishing guides were avilable as well as dogs for fall hunting. What was unusual about Adkin's Camp in its day was that it had its own airplane landing strip on the uplands northwest of the camp.

By 1957 the "camp" was being advertised as a "resort" and was under the management of Len & Ruby Craft. In the early 1960s it was operated by Leah & Aaron Brown. The resort appears to have ceased operation about 1965. Early camps that were neighbors included Silver Moon Camp, Bodie's Rondavo and Jester's Camp. [see Mel Adkin's Airplane Landing Facility].

Ak-Sar-Ben Resort *(Sunrise Beach, Morgan County)* -

The advertising for this resort with an uncommon name construction, began appearing in 1951. For the first couple of years the name was spelled AkSarBen Resort. Hyphens were added later. The letters are "Nebraska" spelled backwards.

Ak-Sar-Ben Resort was located along the shores of Moonlight Bay [originally Cape Hollow Cove] at the 10-mile mark on the Osage Arm. It was reached by way of LkRd. 5-16, later designated 5-33 and now called American Legion Drive.

Ak-Sar-Ben Resort had an excellent view of the Twin Islands that sit at the mouth of the cove. The resort identified with the Hurricane Deck area and their brochure labeled their location as "one of the most scenic points on the Lake."

Neighboring resorts included Cape View Resort, Whispering Oaks Resort, Crestwood Resort and Cliff Haven Resort. In the mid-1970s, Ak-Sar-Ben Resort was owned and operated by Monte Stubblefield & Son. The resort appears to have ceased operation about 1977.

Ammon's Boat Dock & Marine Railway *(Sunrise Beach, Morgan County)* -

Ben Ammons, of Kansas City, built Ammons Boat Dock & Marine Railway in 1932 near Galena Point at the 8-mile mark on the Osage Arm. His place could be reached on LkRd. 5-16, later designated 5-33 and now called American Legion Drive.

During his second year of business, Ammons discovered that crime could seek him out, even in the Ozarks. He also learned to be more careful about picking up hitchhikers, which he called "wayfarers." He was on his way out of Kansas City one week when he picked up a wayfarer and brought the man to his resort property at the Lake. A few days later, Ammons drove into Versailles for groceries to leave with the man because Ammons planned to make a trip back to Kansas City and was going to be gone for a few days.

As Ammons "drove up in his car at the resort he was confronted with a shotgun and told to shell out his valuables, and to divest himself of his leather coat. [This happened in the month of January.] This Ammons did and then at the point of the gun he was forced to crawl under the house through a small door and not being satisfied with padlocking the door, the thief nailed two heavy boards across the door.

"He filled Ammons car with gasoline from the storage tank, loaded in all the valuables he could lay his hands on, including a typewriter and many tools, climbed in the car and bid a hurried exit from the premises," said a local newspaper account. "The loot also included the gun with which he forced Ammons to do his bidding, a watch [and] $60 in money..."

Ammons forced his way from under the house and proceeded to the nearest neighbor who took him to Versailles two hours later. In town, Ammons learned from Charley Crow, the attendant at Carl's Oil Company, that Charley had seen Ammons' car, which was a 1930 Model A of an olive drab color, go past the station and turn west on Hwy. 52.

According to Ammons, the thief's name was Archie Thompson who supposedly lived in St. Louis. The man had told Ammons that he was a landscape gardener by trade and had been in Kansas City looking for employment. The man was about 31 years old. Whether the thief was ever caught isn't known at this writing.

The name of Ammons' resort apparently changed when Ammons sold it. It was one of the first marine services of its type to locate at the 8-mile mark on the Osage Arm.

Early neighboring camps included Greer Resort and Porter's Twin Coves.

Anderson Hollow Bay / Party Cove *(Osage Beach, Camden County)* -

Generally known today as Party Cove [originally Anderson Hollow Cove], this cove is at the 4-mile mark on the Grand Glaize Arm. Its axis runs generally north by south. The cove has a length of 1.5 miles and is 800 to 1000 feet wide with 30 feet of water in the lower one mile and 10 feet of water in the upper half mile. Surrounded by undeveloped wooded hills of the Lake of the Ozarks State Park, the ridges on either side rise to a height of 160 feet above the Lake. Just opposite the mouth of Party Cove is a scenic bluff that displays a variety of interesting geologic features including a natural rock bridge at the top.

Beyond the head of Party Cove, Anderson Hollow splits into three arms. The right unnamed hollow drains the east flank of Salt Ridge about two miles away. Anderson Hollow, which is the middle hollow, continues for about three miles. The left fork, called Willow Springs Hollow, runs for several miles and has Willow Spring and Cave near its head. The cave intersects an old lead mine shaft but the cave is a watercrawl that requires a wet suit for exploration. Lead mining occurred on the hillsides of all three of these hollows nearly a century ago.

On weekends during the summer months, Party Cove is the gathering spot for thousands of party-minded boaters, hence the cove's newest name. The name "Party Cove" is actually a transplant since the party group began gathering years ago in a cove along Horseshoe Bend at the 6-mile mark on the Osage Arm. Boat racing, drinking, nudity and cannon water-balloon fights were the principal activities. As development came to the cove, the party group moved their "Party Cove" to the 15-mile mark but development eventually caught up to them there as well. About 1996, they relocated to Anderson Hollow Bay within the boundaries of Lake of the Ozarks

State Park. Here, residential development is unlikely to ever occur and the wooded hills provide a measure of privacy and confine the noise.

Anderson's Cottages *(Sunrise Beach, Camden County)* -

Anderson's Cottages, built by C. P. Anderson around 1933 or 1934, was located in the Sunrise Beach area on what was then LkRd. 5-17, later designated 5-35A [Indian Hills Road] near the 9.5-mile mark on the Osage Arm. Other groups of "cottages" soon appeared in the same general area such as Dr. Kaiser's Lakeside Apartment Cottages and Crestwood Cottages.

When first built, Anderson's Cottages had running water but no electricity, but were rapidly improved. He added a grocery store and bait shop and advertised that "we supply everything for the cottages but the eats." The name of the business changed to Barker's Cottages in the 1940s under new ownership. Other businesses that sprang up nearby included [Little] Sunrise Lodge, Ti-Sun Terrace Resort, Reeder's Resort and Thickstun's Store.

***Anderson's Cottages,** Sunrise Beach, MO, 1943. Photographer Unknown.*

Arnhold Cave *(Camdenton, Camden County)* -

Arnhold Cave is one of the better known of the many caves inundated by Lake of the Ozarks. It is located near several other historically significant sites now beneath the waters of the Niangua Arm, including Chimney Rock, Chimney Rock Cave, Stone Face [Chief Ne-ong-wah], and Arnhold's Mill. The site is marked by a few feet of the limestone cap of Chimney Rock. The tips of rock protrude above the Lake's surface about 12 to 20 inches when the Lake is at full reservoir [660-foot level]. They are about 30 feet off the south shore at the 4.5-mile mark.

Arnhold Cave is also known as Arnhold Onyx Cave or Onyx Cave [there is more than one Onyx Cave in Camden County and on the Niangua Arm]. The cave has a small entrance now beneath about 40 feet of water, but a large interior with about 1,500 feet of known passage.

In 1909, "The Onyx Quarries Company" of Boonville, Missouri, owned by F.R. Dutton & Associates, purchased the cave to quarry its onyx deposits. They cleared the property around the entrance, installed an aerial railway to haul onyx from the cave, and added a powerhouse and workshop. At that time, the onyx deposits in the cave had an estimated value of about one million dollars. Fortunately for the cave, the market for cave onyx collapsed before the company was able to do more than remove a few test samples from the cave. Unfortunately, the cave was inundated by the Lake two decades later. The cave passages are now silting and the cave's beautiful formations are being eroded and re-dissolved by Lake water. Only recently have cave divers located Arnhold Cave and explored some of its water-filled passages.

Arnhold Mill *(Camdenton, Camden County)* -

Arnhold Mill began life as the Cleman Mill on the Niangua River near the mouth of Barnes Hollow [now Barnes Hollow Cove] at the 5-mile mark on the Niangua Arm. This site is at the end of LkRd. 5-81, now called Resorts Road.

The Arnhold Mill was also known as the Niangua Mill. George Arnhold, a German immigrant to the territory, bought the Cleman Mill in 1878 and made improvements, including the addition of a sawmill. He and his wife became well known for their kindly disposition and hospitality. He was affectionately called "The Jolly

Arnhold Mill And Dam, *On the Niangua River, Circa. 1910. Photographer Unknown.*

Miller." The scenic location of the mill and the abundance of wild game and good fishing attracted fishermen and sportsmen from throughout Missouri. Word spread and the popularity of Arnhold's Mill site grew. Cabins were eventually built on the nearby hills to accommodate the large number of sportsmen who showed up in season.

George Arnhold died in January 1896. Sportsmen formed an association to collect money to build a monument in his honor. The monument was carved in Aberdeen, Scotland, and shipped to Versailles whereupon it was delivered to the mill site by wagon. On the day of dedication, June 1, 1899, more than 500 people attended the ceremony. The inscription said: "*Erected in the memory of Dorotha Arnhold and George Arnhold by many fishermen friends as a tribute to their unlimited generosity.*"

Arnhold Monument, *Versailles City Cemetery. Photo by H. D. Weaver, 2005.*

Dorotha Arnhold died May 29, 1918. When Lake of the Ozarks was formed, the bodies of George and Dorotha, as well as the monument, were moved to the southeastern part of the Versailles City Cemetery where the gravestone can be seen to this day. To learn more, see the history of "The Arnhold Family" by Neta Pope in the 1992 issue of the *Camden County Historian* published by the Camden County Historical Society.

Arrow Point Cave *(Brumley, Miller County)* -

Arrow Point Cave, originally called Wright Cave after homesteader Frank Wright, is located in Mill Creek valley off Hwy. 42 on Swinging Bridge Road [LkRd. 42-18] about 1.5 miles west of Brumley, Missouri. The headwaters of the Grand Glaize Arm and Lake of the Ozarks State Park property lie just west of the cave where two historic suspension bridges -- the Mill Creek Bridge and the Glaize Bridge --survive and are still in use.

The cave was discovered by American settlers sometime around 1842. Foklore holds that early American settlers used the cave as a place for social gatherings and occasional church services.

In 1966, the late Fred Robinett of Latham, Missouri, a descendent of Frank Wright, developed the cave for public touring. In preparing the area in front of the cave entrance for a gift shop and ticket office, bulldozing uncovered Indian artifacts. The artifacts were displayed inside the cave after it was officially opened in 1967.

Discovery of the artifacts inspired Robinett to rename his attraction Arrow Point Cave. Several weddings were held in the cave during its short commercial life. It was open to the public for only five or six years.

Arrow Point Cave has about 375 feet of walking passage and only a few short, dead-end crawlways beyond that point. As it penetrates the hill, the passage gradually narrows down to the point where tours ended. The cave features little in the way of original stalactite and stalagmite deposits.

Robinett retired in 1973 and closed the cave. The building was later removed. The entrance is walled off and the doorway locked. Entry is no longer permitted.

Arrowhead Lodge Hotel*(Lake Ozark, Miller County)* -

Arrowhead Lodge Hotel is located about 1.5 miles south of Bagnell Dam along Hwy. 54 overlooking the 15-mile mark of the Osage Arm. The lodge is on the northeast side of the highway and has a spectacular view of the Lake.

Arrowhead Lodge was built in 1935 by Arthur J. Kelly, Jr. of Kansas City. Before coming to the Lake area he was recorder for the Aarad Temple of the Shrine in Kansas City. He chose a wooded knoll with 600 feet of highway frontage for the lodge. Seven acres of land was bought from the Arrowhead Beach Club. Access to the Lake for the lodge was purchased by Kelly through the negotiations of Romney R. Gifford, with the Ward C. Gifford Realty Company. Arrowhead Lodge was built of rough timber with a stone exterior. Kelly's wife, a recognized Kansas City gardener, was responsible for landscaping. She later opened an antiques gift shop in the lodge.

In 1940, the Kellys sold the lodge to Bill Raynor, Sr. who operated the lodge until it was sold to G. Edwin Popkess in 1946. In late January 1950, the lodge burned.

Arrowhead Lodge Hotel, *Lake Ozark, Circa. 1940. Photographer Unknown.*

The fire was of undetermined origin. Only the chimney was left standing. Popkess estimated his loss at $100,000, part of which was covered by insurance. The original lodge had 20 rooms, a coffee shop and nightclub known as the Wigwam. Popkess immediately rebuilt using the original stone and his building is still in use to this day. Popkess sold to Eddie Jordan in 1975 and Jordan had it until 1992. Since Jordan's ownership the lodge has had several different owners. It is currently being advertised as "The New" Arrowhead Lodge. It is noted for its dining facilities and entertainment. The newest feature at Arrowhead Lodge is the C & R Saloon, which serves meals until 5 p.m. after which it becomes "The Pub." The slogan is "Where the Pub is the Hub."

Art Luck's Fishing & Hunting Resort *(Linn Creek, Camden County)* -

Built in 1931, Art Luck's Resort was the first fishing camp in Linn Creek Cove, which is at the 31-mile mark on the Osage Arm. The resort was located above the confluence along the northeast side of Linn Creek Cove. It could be reached by LkRd. 54-27, later designated 54-66, which became Y Road. The resort was on today's Fontana Lane.

Although the words "Hunting and Fishing" would later be deleted from the title, the resort survived for more than 40 years. In 1935, it was described as a "rustic resort of comfort and convenience offering a complete wilderness vacation service for the fisherman and hunter. Here, under shade trees, high up overlooking the Lake are completely furnished cabins, boats of all kinds, fishing license and tackle may be obtained for those who forget, groceries, ice, beer, meals, gas and oil and plenty of good fishing worms, and in the winter the cabins are heated, and you may come here

***Art Luck's Fishing and Hunting Resort Lakefront**, Circa. 1950s. The site of old Linn Creek is beneath 40 feet of water here. Photo Courtesy Camden County Historical Society.*

and enjoy hunting duck, wild turkey, squirrel, rabbit, quail and night hunting of coon, 'possum and fox. Here is the place for the sportsman to make headquarters."

People who fished at Art Luck's Resort could boast of fishing in the waters over Old Linn Creek because the inundated town site lay just off shore beneath 40 feet of water.

Aurora Springs *(Eldon, Miller County)* -

Aurora Springs, settled in the 1880s, is located just inside the southeast edge of the Eldon, Missouri, city limits on Bus. Hwy. 54. In the late 1800s and early 1900s, the two were separate towns. Aurora Springs was the largest town in Miller County in the 1890s, with a population between 600 and 900, while Eldon had fewer than 400 people.

Business enterprises in Aurora Springs included several general merchandise stores, a blacksmith shop, telegraph office for Western Union, several saloons, a sawmill, flourmill, tinsmith shop, barbershop, lumberyard, lawyers' offices, and a newspaper office. There were also two churches, and the Aurora Springs Mineral Sanitarium owned by W. A. Miller.

In 1880, Rev. William C. Downing discovered the springs that issued from the hillside along the upper reaches of Saline Creek [most of these springs no longer flow]. He believed they possessed strong medicinal qualities. A park was built encompassing the springs, and the town of Aurora Springs built up around the park. The sanitarium had four sources of water -- Bluff Spring, Round Spring, Healing Spring and an artesian well. Promotions for what was billed as the"Great Sanitarium of the West" were going fine until a legal controversy erupted over the ownership of the parcel of land at the center of the park -- a suit involving Gov. George Anthony of Kansas, and the promoters of the sanitarium. For years it put a hold on the use of the springs, which were the mainstay of the town's economy. Anthony claimed he owned 40 acres in the park area. Aurora Springs finally won in court but too late to save the town.

In addition, the town lost its bid for the Missouri Pacific Railroad, which reached Eldon in 1903 and by-passed Aurora Springs, giving birth to a site known as West Aurora.

The final blow came on Jan. 1, 1907, when the federal government's Pure Food and Drug Act became effective. It dealt a death blow to patent medicine and mineral water promoters nationwide.

Aurora Springs did not go quietly. Over the years numerous efforts were made to revive interest in the springs, to no avail. The town's merchants moved away and the town's corporate status was dissolved in 1922. Eldon residential growth eventually overtook the old town site. Only a few hillside steps and concrete ruins remain in the now privately owned park to testify to the vanished dreams of Aurora Springs.

Bagnell *(Miller County)* -

Bagnell, Missouri, is four miles downstream on the Osage River from Bagnell Dam. By road, it is about two miles north of the dam off Hwy. 54 on V Road.

For this small village along the banks of the Osage River, survival during the first 100 years of its existence was a series of "booms" and "busts."

The first settlers who arrived in this vicinity in the 1830s stayed along the fertile river floodplain. Settlement in the surrounding hills did not begin until the 1850s. By this time, steamboats were plying the waters of the Osage. It is surmised that a landing for steamboats was more feasible along the northwest side of the river, where Bagnell grew up just downstream from the mouth of Little Gravois Creek and Brockman's Island, than elsewhere along this stretch of the river. It was also possible to ford the river here when the Osage was low.

Families by the name of Kehr, Carmack, Brockman and Umpsted settled here in the 1870s when the railroad tie industry was getting a foothold in the hills along the Osage. The expansion of the railroad industry throughout Missouri and westward created a lucrative demand for ties and the woodlands along the Osage were thick with white oak, the preferred tie-making material. To exploit this resource, the Missouri Pacific Railroad built a spur line south from Jefferson City to the site of future Bagnell in 1881-1883. The Bagnell Brothers Construction Company handled construction and the Bagnell brothers -- William and Robert -- established the Bagnell Timber Company. They quickly transformed the new town into one of the largest tie shipping centers in the United States.

In 1882, Samuel Umpsted began operating a ferry across the river. The town was named for William Bagnell and the section of railroad between Jefferson City and Bagnell became known as the Bagnell Branch Railroad.

The new town experienced a "boom" between 1883 -- the year the town was platted -- and 1910. The Bagnell Post Office was established in 1884. The population grew to about 100 by the time the industry fell into decline nationwide and white oak was depleted along the river. There were two general stores, two hotels, a bank, a lumberyard, a feed store and the ferry business in Bagnell by this time. The ferry had had six different operators since Umpsted. In 1911, it was being operated by Perry O. Kehr. Most of the town was surrounded by property owned by Lewis Kehr.

Bagnell, MO, 1929. *Photographer Unknown.*

The town's decline was short lived because in 1925 the Missouri Hydro-Electric Power Company of Kansas City began activities toward the construction of Bagnell Dam, a project that was taken over by Union Electric Light & Power Company of St. Louis in 1928. By 1929, the town was booming again as actual construction of the dam got underway.

Just as the dam was nearing completion in 1931, Bagnell suffered two devastating fires that nearly wiped the town off the map. Completion of the dam rerouted Hwy. 54 across the dam, bypassing Bagnell and its ferry. The residents of Bagnell were discouraged yet some made an effort to rebuild, but then the Bagnell Post Office was discontinued in 1942. And in 1943, the Osage River brought a devastating flood, which finally convinced most of the remaining people to move to higher ground. The railroad also shortened its line by moving the depot up the valley to higher ground along the main highway. Finally, in 1954, the railroad tracks were taken up, the depot building sold and moved away, and the Bagnell Branch Railroad was abandoned. Later, there was an attempt to dissolve the town's corporate status but this was successfully fought off and the town remains incorporated.

Today, Bagnell is a quiet, peaceful little village with a noted eating establishment, a popular tourist camp, and a scattering of private dwellings and a fish hatchery. It has survived despite all the turbulence in its past.

Bagnell Branch Railroad *(Cole and Miller Counties)* -

This railroad was a spur line of the Missouri Pacific Railroad built from Jefferson City to Bagnell from 1881 to 1883. It was originally called the Jefferson City, Lebanon & Southwestern Railroad as original plans intended for the tracks to be extended to Lebanon, Missouri, in Laclede County. It took the name Bagnell Branch

Railroad after the Bagnell brothers -- William and Robert. The line passed through Lohman, Russellville and Enon in Cole County, and Olean, Eldon and Aurora Springs in Miller County. The Bagnell Brothers built the line. The tracks were improved between 1926 and 1929 so they could handle heavier trains during the construction of Bagnell Dam. The line from Eldon to Bagnell was abandoned in 1954.

Bagnell Dam *(Miller County)* -

While the physical construction of Bagnell Dam did not begin until 1929, the concept was conceived in 1912 by Ralph W. Street, then a Kansas City attorney.

In 1924, Street partnered with Walter Cravens, president of the Kansas City Joint Stock Land Bank Company, to build a hydroelectric dam across the Osage in an effort to bring cheap electricity to Kansas City, and to create a lake that would become a recreational retreat in the northern Ozarks. The two men were also ambitious to place similar hydroelectric dams on other Ozark rivers, including the Gasconade River and Current River.

On Nov. 12, 1924, Walter Cravens obtained a Preliminary Permit for Project No. 459 from the Federal Power Commission. A few days later their new company -- the Missouri Hydro-Electric Power Company -- was issued a Certificate of Incorporation by the State of Missouri.

On Nov. 20, 1924, their company was authorized to perform initial development work under the Preliminary Permit. Cravens and Street hired the Burns-McDonnell Engineering Company to survey the proposed basin area and determine how much land would be inundated by a dam 100 feet high built near Bagnell.

By May of 1925 the company had determined where they would build the dam and began obtaining options to purchase the land that would be inundated by the waters the dam would impound.

By 1926, the company had 50,000 acres of basin land under option and began exercising their options to purchase land along a 100-mile stretch of the river upstream from the dam site. They engaged the Bickel Contracting Company of Kansas City to build the dam. Bickel set to work strengthening the Bagnell Branch Railroad tracks to handle heavier trains; built a service road from Bagnell to the construction site; extended the railroad tracks from Bagnell to the dam site, a distance of 4.5 miles; built an administration building and a "clubhouse;" and built a dormitory, mess hall, powerhouse, machine shop, warehouse and hospital for their work crew.

Cravens and Street also obtained the services of Missouri State Geologist Henry A. Buehler, Ph.D., for a geological assessment of the proposed dam site.

Shortly after this phase of the project, trouble reared its head when the federal government began an investigation of how Cravens was managing the assets of the Kansas City Joint Stock Land Bank. He was suspected of misapplying $1,000,000 of the bank's funds through interlocking relationships with a group of his business enterprises, specifically the Farmers Fund Inc. and the Kansas City Finance Company; and that some of the transactions of the Farmers Fund Inc., which was handling transactions for the acquisition of lands in the Osage River valley, were questionable.

Because of the investigation, Cravens lost the financial backing of the bankers who had been interested in the dam project, in particular the Guy Houston Company. Work at the dam site and in the basin came to a halt. Street, who up to this time had been spending all of his time overseeing work at the dam site, set about trying to salvage the project by finding new funding. He spent the next 14 months at the task and finally worked out a deal with Dillon, Read & Company and Stone & Webster, Inc., who gave the Missouri Hydro-Electric Power Company a loan to partially cover their indebtedness of about $250,000.

While Street continued to try to salvage the project, Stone & Webster redesigned the project to meet the needs of the Union Electric Light & Power Company of St. Louis, and negotiated a sale whereby Union Electric acquired the project from the Missouri Hydro-Electric Power Company with the approval of the Public Service Commission.

Physical construction of the dam by Union Electric and Stone & Webster began on Aug. 29, 1929, and was complete by the summer of 1931. Ralph Street was not convicted of any wrong doing but Walter Cravens and the bank's secretary, Miss Alice B. Todd, were convicted. After a lengthy appeal, which he lost, Cravens was sentenced to five years in the federal penitentiary.

Bagnell Dam Strip *(Lake Ozark, Miller County)* -

The section of Bus. Hwy. 54 that extends from the west end of Bagnell Dam to Lake Ozark Christian Church, a distance of about three-quarters of a mile, is known as the Bagnell Dam Strip or "The Strip." This nickname originated at an early date and is a term often applied to a commercially developed corridor along a highway. The official name for this section of road -- Bagnell Dam Boulevard -- is of recent origin.

Bagnell Ferry *(Bagnell, Miller County)* -

From 1882 until the late 1930s, the Bagnell Ferry carried highway traffic across the Osage River from a landing at the end of Main Street in downtown Bagnell. The operation began with Samuel Umpsted who obtained a contract from the Miller County Court on Dec. 12, 1882. He began with the following rates: wagon with four horses or oxen, $1; wagon and buggy, 30 cents; rider on a horse or mule, 20 cents; loose horses or cattle, 10 cents per head; hogs, 5 cents each; sheep, 3 cents each; and other freight other than in wagons at 10 cents per 100 pounds.

Subsequent ferry operators included: W. S. Brockman and P. M. Carmack, 1887; W. H. Waddle, 1889; R. S. Thorp, 1892; John N. Brockman, 1896 and 1901; W. P. Martin, 1906; H. L. Moles, 1909; Perry O. Kehr, 1911; J. E. and P. O. Kehr, 1916; J. L. Howser, 1917; R. P. Howser, 1923; R. P. Howser and D. H. Rea, 1928; J. L. Howser 1932 and 1937. Contracts generally ran for two to five years.

During the early years, the Bagnell Ferry was one barge with railings along the sides and a rope or chain at each end to keep wagons and other wheeled conveyances from rolling off [gates could be put up to keep loose animals penned, such as hogs being driven to market]. These constraints, however, did not prevent some serious accidents during the more than 50 years the ferry was in operation. The most serious accident occurred July 26, 1934, when the brakes on a Star automobile failed. It was carrying six people and ran off the ferry into 25 feet of water. Three people drowned -- David Vineyard and Mrs. Henry Vineyard and her two-year old son, Wayne Vineyard.

Traffic on Hwy. 15, which became Hwy. 54 about the year 1925, used the ferry to reach Linn Creek and other destinations south and east. This route was also known as the Bagnell-Linn Creek Road. There were many years when the ferry struggled to survive for lack of business but during the Bagnell Dam construction years it was exceptionally profitable.

In the period 1923 to 1928, before the dam's construction actually began, ferry operator, R.P. Howser, said: "Sometimes on a Saturday I would hire a boy to help me run the boat. I paid him a dollar and a half a day and some Saturdays, at the end of the day, he had more money than I did, so you can tell by that that business wasn't so good."

After preparations for the construction of the dam got seriously underway in 1929, Howser's fortunes turned for the better. On weekends he would run 600 to 700 cars per day across the river and needed to add a second barge to the ferry so he could haul more automobiles per trip. He charged 50 cents per car.

During these years an effort was also made to get the highway department to build a bridge across the Osage River at Bagnell, but with no success.

Once the dam was completed, Hwy. 54 traffic was rerouted across the dam and the ferry was no longer needed except for half a dozen families who lived across the river from Bagnell. The ferry ceased operation about 1940.

Bagnell Flats *(Miller County)* -

Bagnell Flats is a portion of a stretch of Hwy. 54 about one mile northwest of Bagnell Dam. It runs from Wrights Creek at its north end to Little Gravois Creek at its south end. The highway along this stretch parallels the East Fork of Little Gravois Creek and the valley is about 800 to 1,000 feet wide. About half of the valley floodplain is still cropped.

In the late 1800s and early 1900s, the portion of this section at the south end was called Bagnell Flats. At that time, Hwy. 15 did not run the full length of the valley from creek to creek but continued west along a route generally paralleling the Bagnell Branch Railroad. It was during the mid 1920s when Hwy. 15 was designated Hwy. 54, and some new highway construction occurred, that the highway assumed its present route north through the valley between the two creeks.

Because members of the Mead family own land at the valley's south end and members of the Howser family own land at the valley's north end, this newer stretch of highway has been called both Meads Flats and Howser Flats. It is more often called Meads Flats or Johnnie's Bottoms after Johnnie Mead who had a service station in the Flats before the 1960s.

Bagnell - Linn Creek Road *(Miller County, Camden County)* -

Whether this road was called the Bagnell-Linn Creek Road, or the Linn Creek-Bagnell Road in pre-Lake days depended upon where you lived. It was also the route of old Hwy. 15, which pre-dated Hwy. 54. The road crossed the Osage River by ferry or the Elm Church Ford at Bagnell and then followed the current route of County Road D in Miller County to the junction of Hwys. 54 & 42 in Osage Beach. It continued southwest about one mile southeast of present Hwy. 54, staying on the uplands, except where it crossed the Grand Auglaize Creek, until it reached Old Linn Creek. Most of current Hwy. 54 from Bagnell to modern Linn Creek was built during the construction of Bagnell Dam. The old Bagnell-Linn Creek Road meandered back and forth across this newer route in several places between the Grand Glaize Bridge and modern Linn Creek.

Bagnell Timber Company *(Miller County)* -

This company was established by railroad builders William and Robert Bagnell in the late 1880s. By the beginning of the twentieth century it was one of the largest railroad tie businesses in the United States, according to historian Gary Kremer. Railheads along the Osage River valley included Osage City in Cole County, and Hoecker and Bagnell in Miller County.

Ties produced for the Bagnell Timber Company were cut between Bagnell and the Hurricane Deck area and floated down the Osage in long tie "rafts." The typical tie raft contained 200 to 400 ties but rafts of 1,000 ties were not uncommon. Since the railroad builders needed 3,000 ties per mile of track, there was a huge demand for ties. Hardwood white oak ties were hacked by hand using a broadax and cut six inches by eight inches by eight feet. Ties of good quality brought 15 to 25 cents each

Osage River Tie Raft, Circa. 1900. *Photo courtesy Camden County Historical Society.*

at the railhead. At times as many as 30,000 to 40,000 ties would be stacked in the tie yards at Bagnell awaiting shipment.

Men and companies who engaged in the business in Miller County besides the Bagnell brothers, included R. S. Harvey and J. S. Franklin at Bagnell; George T. Hauenstein at Tuscumbia; H. B. Merwin in Jim Henry township; and the Pyle brothers at Capps.

Bank of Brumley *(Brumley, Miller County)* -

The most significant aspect to the history of the Bank of Brumley is that it gave birth to Bank of Lake of the Ozarks, now Central Bank of Lake of the Ozarks.

The Bank of Brumley opened Oct. 15, 1906, with 18 directors that included J. M. Hawkins, E. C. Thompson, James Thompson, W. R. Carnes and James C. Warren.

The officers were J. M. Hawkins, president; E. C. Thompson, cashier; and J. C. Warren, secretary.

E. C. Thompson became president in 1908 and served until his death in 1941. J. M. Hawkins served as cashier until his death in 1934. Assistant cashiers from 1910 to 1959 included Lena C. Hawkins, Mrs. W. E. Thornsberry, Nellie Hawkins [Mrs. Loyd Pugh], C. R. [Ted] Hawkins and Mable C. Hawkins, who became cashier in 1956. Presidents after J. M. Hawkins included Lee Thornsberry, Clyde S. Thompson, Elmer Thompson, W. E. Thornsberry and C. B. Bass. The final Board of Directors included C. R. Hawkins, Mabel C. Hawkins, Kent Crane, Ralph Long and Earl A. Plemmons.

The Bank of Brumley was one of the few small-town banks in the Lake of the Ozarks region to survive the Great Depression. It also survived two bank robberies. Upon the death of C. R. Hawkins in 1959, the bank's stock was sold to the group who were in the process of securing a charter and FDIC insurance to start a bank at Lake Ozark. At the time of its purchase, the Bank of Brumley had deposits of approximately $350,000. On July 1, 1960, the bank was moved to temporary quarters in Lake Ozark with Al Elam serving as temporary president, and the name was changed to Bank of Lake of the Ozarks. The old Bank of Brumley building is still standing but has seen some modifications and is now a private residence.

Bank of Lake of the Ozarks / Central *(Lake Ozark, Miller County; Osage Beach, Camden County)* -

Bank of Lake of the Ozarks, now Central Bank of Lake of the Ozarks, officially opened July 1, 1960, in temporary quarters in Lake Ozark on The Strip. It was located just north of the Casablanca Cafe, which is now the Ozark Bar.

The Board of Directors included James A. Franklin, Sr., W. W. Atteberry, Al G. Elam, W. B. James, John Laurie, Ralph Long and Lon Stanton. After a short period of operation, Lee Mace, Carl Williams and Robert E. Mason, D.O. were added to the board.

Bank officers were James A. Franklin, Sr., president; Mabel C. Hawkins, cashier; and Mrs. L. E. Sutton, assistant cashier. The bank had a capital of $75,000 with total assets of $700,000.

The bank's first customers included L. O. Nichols, who deposited $40,000, and Linda and Donna, the daughters of Mrs. Claudius Shockley, who came in lugging an oversized piggy bank with 98 silver dollars and two folding dollars in it, for a total deposit of $100.

Even as the bank was opened in temporary quarters on The Strip, a new, permanent bank building was under construction in Lake Ozark along Hwy. 54 about 1.7 miles south of the dam just north of Mills Motel, which is now Shawnee Bluff Inn, and across the highway from Our Lady of the Lake Catholic Church. The new building was 38 feet by 60 feet in size with a specially constructed vault, lobby, work area, drive-up window, night depository, two offices and a lounge for its eight employees. They were in the new building within a year.

By 1971, with assets approaching $18 million, Bank of Lake of the Ozarks needed larger facilities. A new, larger building was constructed at the junction of Hwys. 54 & 42 in Osage Beach. This building sat on the northeast corner where Walgreen's Drug Store is located today. It served until 1984 when the institution's third bank building was erected about one-quarter mile north of where the second bank building was located. The Bank moved into their third building in March 1984 and still occupy this building, which is across the highway from Stonecrest Mall.

The bank's first permanent building in Lake Ozark is still standing although used by a different business. The second building at the junction of Hwys. 54 & 42 was demolished during the Prewitt's Point Development.

The current building was designed by Bank Building Corp. of St. Louis and has a rustic appearance and four levels. The original bank had only 2,280 square feet of work space. The current building has more than 40,000 square feet. The staff has grown from eight to more than 50. From assets of $1 million by the end of 1960, the bank grew to more than $10 million by the end of 1970, and by the end of 1988, had total assets of more than $270 million.

Bank of Lake of the Ozarks's first branch facility was opened in Lake Ozark on Nov. 27, 1973; its facility at the junction of Hwys. 54 & Route KK in 1984; its facility at the Osage Beach Super Wal-Mart in 1996; its Laurie facility in 1997; its Eldon facility in 2003; and its Camdenton Super Wal-Mart facility in 2005.

In December 1986, the bank became a part of Central Bancompany of Jefferson City, adding the word "Central" to its name. And in August 1988, Central Bank of Lake of the Ozarks purchased Camden County Bank, which was founded in 1894.

Baptism in the Lake -

Since the days of settlement it has been traditional to hold baptismal rituals in the waters of the Osage River and its tributaries. There were many places along the river's meandering course where such baptisms were staged at all times of the year. Sites were generally picked for ease of access such as at a ford, ferry crossing or bridge location.

At Warsaw, in Benton County, 171 miles upstream from the mouth of the Osage River [91 miles from Bagnell Dam], baptisms were often held near the east end of the Upper Suspension Bridge.

At Old Linn Creek, one of the favored baptismal spots was at the mouth of the Niangua River near where Aaron Crain was licensed to operate the first ferry across the Osage and Niangua rivers in Camden County beginning in 1841. Baptisms continued here after the ferry was replaced by a suspension bridge in the early 1900s.

The Niangua [locally called Big Niangua] and Little Niangua rivers, which form one of the more lengthy and highly developed arms of the Lake, were also popular baptismal waters, despite the cold, fresh-water springs. The Niangua gets much of its water from Ha Ha Tonka Spring and Bennett Spring. "Original baptismal places were once all along the river at almost every ford," said Glenn "Boone" Skinner, the author of the book *Big Niangua River* [1979].

One of the places was at Bunch Ford where the Niangua River Bridge carries Hwy. 54 across the Niangua Arm west of Camdenton. The site was named for Armistead Bunch, an early owner of the property and the cave that opens along the Niangua at this point.

It is fitting, perhaps, that the first baptism to be held in the waters of Lake of the Ozarks occurred beside the docks of the Niangua Bridge Camp that was built at the east end of the Hwy. 54 Niangua Bridge in 1931. The baptismal event took place on Jan. 17, 1932. The services were conducted by Rev. Gentry Parrick, pastor of the Baptist church at Roach, Missouri, a small village three miles west of the bridge.

Niangua Bridge Camp was a new fishing camp operated by Fernando Hanks. He gave the people permission to use the camp's cottages for dressing rooms. It is hard to believe that 20 people were willing to let themselves be dunked into the

Baptist Baptizing, Warsaw, MO, *1907. Photo by McKinney.*

Cabins at Niangua Bridge Camp, *Camdenton, MO, Circa. 1930s.*

January waters of the Niangua Arm, however, old timers claim that the waters of the Niangua are warmer in winter than the waters of the Osage because the springs that feed the Niangua discharge at a temperature of about 56 degrees year 'round. This event became the first baptismal ceremony held in the waters of Lake of the Ozarks.

Barber's Camp *(Osage Beach, Camden County)* -

Barber's Camp opened for business about 1935 along Hwy. 54 west of the Grand Glaize Bridge. Advertising located the resort 500 feet west of the bridge. The cabins were on the southeast side of the highway with an excellent view of the Grand Glaize Arm. The resort's cabins were large and comfortable, accommodating up to eight people and were either log or frame structures. Several cabins had attractive native rock porches. Barber's Camp was in business until about 1938 or 1939 when it was sold to Charles M. & Hazel Hymes who renamed it Hymes Kottage Kamp #1. This property eventually became Sherwood Resort, which is still in business at the west end of the Grand Glaize Bridge.

Barnes Hollow Cove *(Camdenton, Miller County)* -

Barnes Hollow Cove is located at the 5-mile mark of the Niangua Arm and is at the end of LkRds 5-81 [Resorts Road] and 5-78 [Owens Point Road]. It is about 2.25 miles up-Lake from the Hwy. 5 Niangua Bridge. The cove is along the east side of the Lake and runs east by west. Named for J. H. Barnes, who owned most of the land within the hollow in the early 1900s, the cove is about 3,000 feet long and 600 to 1,000 feet wide. The water is about 10 feet deep.

In pre-Lake days, the Arnhold Mill was located along the Niangua River near the mouth of Barnes Hollow. The conical hill along the south side of the cove rises more than 260 feet above the Lake, topping out at 927 feet above sea level.

The first resorts bordering this cove were built in the 1940s and 50s and included Ebert's Beach Resort [now the Blue Dolphin Resort], Schneider's Resort, Kinneston's Singing Hills Resort, Pleasure Cove Resort and Rock Village Resort. The 1960s brought Digger O'Dells Shoreline Resort and Cedar Crest Resort. The most recent addition was Val-E-Vue Resort.

Barnett *(Morgan County)* -

The village of Barnett was platted in the 1870s. It was called Barnettsville when the post office was established in 1875. In 1880, the post office shortened the name to Barnett. The post office has been in continuous operation for 130 years. Hiram McDow, the first postmaster, had the post office in his rock home, which became known as the Stone House Post Office.

The Rock Island Railroad came through Barnett in 1903 and the little village quickly became a busy cattle shipping center. By 1931, when Lake of the Ozarks was formed, the town had an ambitious, civic-minded business community who began promoting their town as "The Little Town With A Big Heart." The Barnett Community Club ads said "Barnett is the nearest approach either by rail or highway to the Lake of the Ozarks down beautiful Indian Creek valley whose pioneer homes and natural landscape attractions delight the eye of the traveler." Barnett also promoted "Shelida Hill" even though the hill, like Indian Creek valley, is located some distance southwest of town along the Gravois Arm.

Rock Island Railroad Depot, *Barnett, 1950. Photographer Unknown.*

Barnett prospered from being on Hwy. 52 and the Rock Island Railroad. Besides a bank, barbershops and several cafes, the little town had two grain and feed stores, a hardware store, a lumberyard, and the Barnett Hotel. For a brief time Barnett was even the home of the publisher of *Ozark Life*, a widely circulated magazine of some prominence in its day. Modest development did occur in Indian Creek valley six miles away but not enough to sustain the town's growth when the railroad eventually ceased operations. The town's thriving, diversified business community did not survive. Today, Barnett has a population of about 200 people who rely largely upon nearby Eldon and Versailles for services.

Berry's Lodge *(Osage Beach, Camden County)* -

Berry's Lodge was one of the earliest resorts to develop off Route KK. It and Flack Resort were the first two resorts to be built at the 21-mile mark near the point of the peninsula of land that teminates Three Seasons Road. Berry's Lodge was located along the peninsula's east side off Autumn Lane facing Miller Hollow Cove.

The lodge was established by Les Berry and opened in 1932 or 1933. The development was visited during the summer of 1934 by a reporter for the *Lake of the Ozarks News* who had the following to say:

"On the occasion of his last visit to the Berry's Lodge, the Around-the-Lake Reporter found Les up to his ears in work and the sound of the hammer was loud in the land. Some workmen were engaged in the building of Berry's new cobblestone home, others were repairing roads, and others were digging...a pit for the installation of a gasoline tank. The hunting dogs were hunting, the fishermen were fishing, and withal it was a very busy place with no chance for Satan to get any of his mischief done as there were no idle hands.

"These former St. Louis County people are getting a real camp established and not fooling around about it. Since our last visit they have completed additional cabins, a floating dock, several boats, and a log storeroom and have installed an electric plant. It has been necessary for the Berry's to turn away a great many people this summer and we believe that they should have a good autumn business. The Berry's have a wide acquaintance in St. Louis County who visit them and send their friends to the place so that eventually the camp will have to expand even faster than it is now doing if it expects to keep up with the demand. Berry has a fast runabout for pleasure rides, which was launched at Gore's Boat Yard, and he plans to establish another gasoline station at the water's edge to accommodate boat owners in the neighborhood."

An early promotion described the business in the following manner: "Berry's Lodge, just two miles off the highway on the Lake shore is another place that was built with comfort and convenience for the fisherman and hunter. In addition to the lodge there are several rustic bungalows scattered on the shady hillside. This is a place you would want to stay at least a week -- and for you hunters, here's a tip -- Mr. Berry specializes in hunting dogs and guides, so please remember this when you think of coon and fox."

Big Bend Acres *(Stover, Morgan County)* -

Between the 65- and 73-mile mark on the Osage Arm, the Lake creates Big Bend, which lies at the end of Route FF off DD from Hwy. 7. Even today, the properties of this bend seem remote but were even more so in 1931 when Chester "Chet" E. Edmonds of Kansas City began his development called Big Bend Acres.

Edmonds was no stranger to the region. During the construction of Bagnell Dam, he owned and operated a movie theater in Damsite, the construction workers town that existed one mile below Bagnell Dam from 1928 to 1931. Edmond's Theater was one of the most successful places of entertainment in Damsite and it sat between John Pepper's Cabin Camp and Harry Tanner's Filling Station & Garage. A restaurant and a barbershop sat across the street from the theater. Edmond's Theater could seat 150 people and Chet showed new Hollywood releases featuring the stars of the silver screen of that era.

Chet made good use of the profits generated by his theater business, investing the money in property. He chose land at the northern tip of Big Bend. Here he envisioned a development of substantial size that would have enough infrastructure and population to be nearly self-sustaining. It would be opposite the old town site of Riverview [see Riverview]. His only frustration was access because there was no bridge across the Lake at this point or anywhere close. The Sagrada Suspension Bridge had once connected Big Bend with the Riverview side, but that bridge had been lost to the Lake basin clearing [see Sagrada Bridge]. It wasn't practical to drive to Big Bend by way of roads on the south side of the Lake, which were in very poor condition and out of the way. And there was no ferry service, so he established a new ferry, largely to service Big Bend Acres. The ferry was operated by Keith Critton and Tip Flippin. The barge had a capacity for eight cars. He also began campaigning for a bridge over the Lake at this point [see Sagrada Bridge for more information on this subject].

Stover was just 14 miles to the north along Hwy. 52 and was serviced by the railroad. Chet had purchased 800 acres to subdivide into lots and tracts of land of different size and he anticipated a great deal of traffic. The railroad was a convenient means for bringing in building supplies that could then be trucked to Big Bend Acres. But even the road from Stover to Riverview was in poor condition.

"A number of weeks ago, C. E. Edmonds...called a certain businessman in Stover to inquire about the road from Stover to the Lake," reported the *Lake of the Ozarks News* in March 1932. "Previous to that time, Mr. Edmonds had taken a number of prospective buyers from Kansas City to Big Bend Acres, his Lake site, and spent nearly one whole day going over that 14 miles of road. To be certain this would not happen again, he asked this certain businessman to see what could be done, so that he might get through without any trouble.

"Several businessmen of Stover were called together, and immediately decided something must be done at once. The following day it rained, making the road much worse. But two days later, the sun began to shine and the businessmen forgot their personal duties and went to work on the road. In three days time the road was graveled and on Saturday Mr. Edmonds, accompanied by a large number of Kansas City people, were able to drive to Big Bend Acres without any trouble. Hardly a day passes without someone going to the Lake, and even though the road isn't completed, it's passable..."

The businessmen of Stover recognized that supporting Big Bend Acres would be good for the town. The Stover Chamber of Commerce found room to mention Big Bend Acres in their promotional literature, as well as several other new Lake developments. "A short drive over good roads quickly takes you to her various Lake resorts, such as Zora Heights, Riverview Heights, Big Bend Acres, Big Buffalo Beach, and others..." Stover ads said. So keeping the roads in good shape was essential. In addition, the Commercial Club of Stover erected markers on Hwy. 52 and along the road down to the Lake to keep people going in the right direction.

By the summer of 1932, Edmonds had sold nearly 60 one-acre tracts, 50 lots and four 10-acre tracts. Mr. L. Herring, the development's sales and building manager, had become a permanent resident by May of 1932. A filling station and garage was under construction by this time and a firm by the name of Bush & Knickerbocker opened a store at Big Bend Acres that handled a complete line of groceries, shoes and other staple merchandise. By summer, Edmonds' whole family was involved, including his mother-in-law who was in charge of selling groceries and serving good eats and cold drinks as well as fishing bait, ice, gas and oil. Before long 15 cabins had been completed and 128 sites sold for more cabins. A clubhouse and pavilion for dancing was also under construction.

Stover merchants were doing well. The Fajen Lumber Company of Stover was building 30 boats, which were for the use of Big Bend Acres cabin owners and their friends.

Chet Edmonds never got the bridge he wanted but the ferry did a fine job for the people of Big Bend Acres and the development became one of the largest of the early developments at Lake of the Ozarks.

Boat Shelter Cave *(Grand Glaize Arm, Camden County)* -

There are numerous cavities and other natural openings in the bluffs and rock outcrops on hillsides along the Grand Glaize Arm. Some cave openings are at water level and most do not lead into significant passage although two, large, well known caves are located in the hollows that provide spring-fed streams to the Grand Glaize Arm. These caves, near the headwaters of the Arm, are McDowell Cave and Ozark Caverns. The latter cave is open to the public but McDowell Cave is gated and off-limits to exploration because it is a habitat for endangered bats. Both caves are in Lake of the Ozarks State Park.

Among recreational boaters and fishermen, the most popular cave along the Grand Glaize Arm is Boat Shelter Cave at the 7.3-mile mark. Boaters caught on the Lake when unexpected thunderstorms or heavy rain occur sometimes take refuge beneath the sheltering overhang at the entrance to Boat Shelter Cave. What most are unaware of is that cave openings are always at risk for lightning strikes. Lightning is sometimes attracted to the ionized air that often flows from caves. So far, there are no known reports of lightning striking this particular cave entrance, perhaps because there is no second entrance to the cave to stimulate strong airflow, and the cave's interior isn't large enough to produce it.

The opening to Boat Shelter Cave at normal Lake level [660-foot elevation] is about 30 feet wide and 12 feet high over water at least 10 feet deep. The depth of the entrance room recess is about 35 feet so a fairly large boat can use the shelter.

At the back of the entrance chamber is a narrow opening leading to a series of small rooms with even smaller connecting passageways and about 200 feet of cave length. Driftwood and trash often makes entry difficult and since no dry land is normally available, a person must jump into the water and swim to enter the cave.

Boat Shelter Cave, *Grand Glaize Arm. Photo by H. D. Weaver, 2004.*

There is some walking passage in the cave, a good bit of crawling passage, and the rooms vary in size from those just barely large enough to stand up in to one that is 12 feet long by seven feet wide by 12 feet high. Birds often nest in the cave's entrance, Pipistrelle bats use the cave, and a variety of very tiny creatures including spiders and aquatic amphipods and isopods. The cave has little to recommend it for the adventure-seeking cave explorer but its entrance is very scenic and can be easily seen near the 7.5-mile mark across from McCubbin's Point in Lake of the Ozarks State Park.

Boot's Tavern, Super Service Station & Cafe *(Eldon, Miller County)* -

The word "tavern" was once widely used as a name for a place of fine food and lodging or a wayside inn. "In the Missouri tavern the pioneer settler and the wandering stranger were first welcomed to our soil. In this early wayside inn business was transacted, religion preached, duels decided, politics discussed and frequently settled, towns founded, courts convened, and hospitality dispensed. It served as home and mart, court and forum," said Missouri historian Floyd C. Shoemaker in 1921.

During the early 1930s at the Lake, the word "tavern" was frequently used in the names of lodges, hotels, inns and eating establishments, some of which became places of local distinction -- such as Boot's Tavern in Eldon; Musser's Ozark Tavern at the junction of Hwys. 54 & 52 south of Eldon; B. Ray Franklin's Osage Beach Tavern in Osage Beach; the Ozark Tavern Hotel and the Night Hawk Tavern in Camdenton; and the Westview Tavern at Warsaw. But during Prohibition from 1920 to 1933, the word "tavern" acquired an unsavory reputation. Taverns were often characterized as sinful places of drinking, dancing and illicit behavior. So by the mid 1930s, the proprietors of lodging and eating places began to change the word to "hotel" or "cafe." As one proprietor of the period remarked: "The definition of the word tavern has changed and a new connotation of the word has arisen in the minds of a public ever in quest for sleep. As one person put it 'a tavern is no longer a place where one goes to get good food and enjoy peaceful sleep. A tavern is one of those places along the highway where you go to get refreshments and hot dogs. It is one of those places characterized by a nickelodeon and stale tobacco.'"

But even as some businessmen were finding the word "tavern" a liability, Lloyd Boots of Eldon had other sentiments. "Lloyd [Boots] is a Miller County product," said the *Eldon Advertiser* in 1934. "He came to Eldon from the Bagnell district. He had a vision he would build a tavern, unique tavern, such as the visitor seldom sees. It would be attractive outside, immaculately clean inside and equipped with every modern convenience the tired muscles and bones of the weary traveler demands, so he built Boots Super Service in Eldon on Highway 54.

"It is a cobblestone front made of native rock as old as granite and attractive as can be. At one end of the rambling structure is his service station clean as a pin with every accommodation the discriminating motorist may desire. The remainder...is devoted to room accommodations for tourists with clean, comfortable bed and hot- and cold-water showers. Labor Day he had 120 applications for rooming accommodations beyond his capacity... Instead of turning them away, he spent the better part of six hours finding rooming accommodations for them in private homes... That's service!"

Boots also had a cafe sandwiched between the service station and the motel section. He variously advertised his enterprise as Boots' Tavern, Boots' Super Service Station, Boots' Cafe, and Lloyd A. Boots' Cottage Court.

In the 1940s he sold to Helen Randle. The establishment became Randles' Court & Coffee Shop on Aug. 28, 1947, and the cafe and motel are still in operation. The service station no longer exists.

Boyler's [Byler's] Mill & Spring *(Stover, Morgan County)* -

Boyler's Spring, which supplies most of the permanent flow for Big Buffalo Creek [which discharges into Big Buffalo Cove at the 70-mile mark on the Osage Arm] is in Benton County. It produces about three-quaters of a million gallons of water daily. It rises over an acre of ground and provides a discharge that Jacob Byler, who discovered it in 1819, decided to harness. He dug a small race, dammed the water to force it into the race, and installed an overshot wheel to furnish power for a mill. He also began making gunpowder. While no one is certain where he got the saltpeter needed to make gunpowder, he may have secured it from caves to the east in the neighboring watershed of Gravois Creek.

This Pennsylvanian German millwright was a stern, no-nonsense sort of man with few friends but he was hardworking and prosperous. After a couple of years he added a grist mill for grinding rye and corn. He developed a large patronage in a radius of more than 60 miles. In time, he added a log house tavern called Byler House to accommodate overnight guests. By adding a distillery to his operation, he was able to sell whiskey to his customers. As his business grew he added a store and a sawmill, thus it was that Jacob Byler established a settlement whose name, though the passage of time misspells it, survived to the twentieth century.

Interesting and romantic legends have been spun about the site of Boyler's Mill & Spring, one of which involves the contested marriage of Jacob Byler's daughter, Mary Maree, to Elihu Baden. Jacob refused to permit the marriage and supposedly, his daughter and her lover committed suicide on the property, leading to further tales of haunted rocks where their deaths occurred. It is said Jacob Byler and his family left the valley in 1847 and were never seen again.

A post office was opened at Boyler's Mill in 1874 and operated until 1922. The first postmaster was John H. Hunter. The village itself developed on the south side of Little Buffalo Creek. Boyler's Mill became a popular recreational spot for the residents of nearby Stover after that town was established in the late 1800s. In the early 1900s, the Boyler's Mill area was popular with Kansas City sportsmen.

Bridal Cave *(Camdenton, Camden County)* -

Bridal Cave is located off LkRd. 5-32, later designated 5-88 and now called Thunder Mountain Road. The cave is at the foot of Thunder Mountain and along the shoreline of the Niangua Arm at the 10-mile mark. The cave's scenic location and spectacular underground beauty has made it a favorite of Lake area visitors for more than half a century.

The date of the cave's discovery is uncertain but it is believed to have been known to the Osage Indians who once inhabited the region, despite the fact that the original entrance was fairly small. To enter the cave a person had to crawl in on hands and knees.

European and American settlers arrived in the 1820s, 30s and 40s. By the 1850s, some portions of the cave had been explored as proven by the name H. B. Hobson carved into the cavern walls along with the date 1856.

The cave acquired its name from a romanticized Indian legend popularized by Col. R. G. Scott around the beginning of the twentieth century. An Indian brave and maiden were supposedly married in the cave's second chamber, which became known as the "Bridal Chapel."

The famed Ha Ha Tonka State Park area lies just a few miles south [up-Lake] of the cave. When Robert M. Snyder purchased the Ha Ha Tonka properties in 1904 [long before Ha Ha Tonka became a state park], the Bridal Cave property was part of the acquisition. The cave became a popular outing spot for people who stayed at the Ha Ha Tonka Castle or rented a cottage on the shores of Lake Ha Ha Tonka.

After Snyder's death in 1906, his heirs sold the plot of ground upon which Bridal Cave lies. In 1929, when construction of Bagnell Dam began, it is said that surveyors and men clearing the basin explored the cave for a distance of about 1,000 feet and discovered two shallow underground lakes. They left their footprints in the

Underground Lake in Bridal Cave, *Camdenton, MO. Photo by Jim Vandike, 1981.*

clay floor of the first lake, footprints discovered in 1981 by divers who were exploring the underground lake. These footprints later inspired the naming of this body of water Mystery Lake.

In 1947, the cave property was purchased by B. F. Krehbiel, R. L. Wilkerson and Jim Banner, who developed the cave for public tours. Visitors went as far as the "Frozen Niagara," about 400 feet from the entrance. The cave is conveniently compartmentalized by nature and visitors tour from room to room. Every room is well decorated with formations.

One of the internal features that sets Bridal Cave apart from other show caves in the Lake area is how it originally developed along a high, narrow fracture beneath Thunder Mountain. This fracture is believed to be associated with a fault system.

Ceiling heights in Bridal Cave often reach 80 feet and the walls of the fracture have been heavily coated and festooned with spectacular cave formations. In places, the cave is nearly filled with them. Among these formations are great varieties of drapolite, which are folded, wavy, curtains of calcite. The undeveloped sections of the cave are as beautiful as those portions already open to the public.

In 1961, a group of cave explorers from Wichita, Kansas, explored beyond the cave's Frozen Niagara room and encountered the lakes discovered in 1929, only the lakes were not shallow because when water filled the Niangua River basin and formed the Niangua Arm of Lake of the Ozarks, it stabilized the water table beneath Thunder Mountain. This caused the spring [now beneath the Lake of the Ozarks], which discharged from the hillside and drained the underground lakes, to back up.

A boat was needed to explore the first underground lake [Mystery Lake]. "There is a second lake beyond this," said the news story "that the exploring party reported to be even larger but due to difficult passages they were unable to reach the end of this lake..." This expedition took the first known photographs of the underground lakes area.

In 1981, a study of the cave's undeveloped areas was undertaken by Lake Ozark Grotto, which resulted in a complete map of the cave system and a thorough examination of both underground lakes by divers. Divers exploring the second lake, later named Spirit Lake in keeping with the name Thunder Mountain and the cave's Indian heritage, discovered an underwater passage that led into a previously unknown, air-filled extension of the cave's main passage. This newly discovered passage is about 700 feet long and has a visual character unlike other portions of the cave.

The first modern day wedding in the cave's Bridal Chapel, which is the second room in the cave, was held in 1949. Since that date more than 2,000 couples have been married in Bridal Cave.

In 1982, the cave opened its Thunder Mountain Nature Trail, which winds through the wooded landscape above the cave, visiting interesting sandstone outcrops, allowing scenic views of the Lake, and a visit to Neongwah Bear Cave, a small but interesting and well decorated cave higher on the hillside. It has giant cave formations in an unusual setting. The cave is generally called just Bear Cave but the name Neongwah Bear Cave was given when the cave was mapped and recorded in the late 1970s to distinguish it from two other caves named Bear Cave in the vicinity. Neongwah is also a place name of historic value associated with this portion of the Niangua Arm.

In the 1990s, additional underground development work extended the public tour route beyond the Frozen Niagara room to Mystery Lake. Paradise Island and Spirit Lake are in the portion of the cave not open to the public.

Brill's Hill Resort & Marina *(Warsaw, Benton County)* -

Brill's Hill was the first resort to open along the shores of the Lake at Warsaw, Missouri. It was at the 91.3-mile mark of the Lake and inside the city limits on the west side of town. It was at the downstream end of the Upper Suspension Bridge that carried Hwy. 35 [Hwy. 7 today]. The suspension bridge is no longer in service but is preserved for its historic value. A new bridge now spans the Osage between the old suspension bridge and the former site of Brill's Hill.

The resort opened in 1931 shortly before G. E. Crosby, a Union Electric Light & Power Company official, cruised from Bagnell Dam to Warsaw in a 28-foot cabin cruiser and docked at Brill's Hill. The Gov. McClurg Ferry, a 45-ton ferry boat, which went into service in 1932 to ferry Hwy. 5 traffic across Lake of the Ozarks from the Hurricane Deck area to the Linn Creek-Camdenton area, was launched at Brill's Hill.

The resort had a capacity for 20 guests and individual cabins had hot and cold running water, showers and electric lights. Guests were charged $2.50 per person per day. Boat storage was available and the resort's ads said their facilities were "war department approved."

In 1944, a Mr. Moore who then owned and operated Brills' Hill Resort & Marina, sold the business to Ted R. and Helen Teeter of Kansas, who gave up their grocery store business to operate the resort. They changed the name to Teeter's Hill Resort & Marina. The new owners advertised their marine railway and added a fishing guide service. In the 1950s, they added a restaurant. They were active with the Headwaters Association and sold maps and advertisements. After Truman Dam was built, business at Teeter's Hill began to decline. Ted died in 1977 and Helen continued with the resort for awhile. This resort no longer exists. It was just south of today's Waterfront RV Park at Warsaw.

Brockman's Island *(Bagnell, Miller County)* -

This is an island in the Osage River along the east side about one-half mile above Bagnell [3.5 miles downstream from Bagnell Dam]. The island is about 2,000 feet long and 600 feet wide. It is named for W. S. Brockman who once owned the island. In the 1940s and 50s, the island was farmed by Lloyd Slone of Tuscumbia.

Brumley *(Miller County)* -

Brumley is located 10 miles east of Osage Beach on Hwy. 42 in Mill Creek valley. It is about two miles east of the headwaters of the Grand Glaize Arm and Lake of the Ozarks State Park.

The town of Brumley has a current population of 81. The town site was recorded in 1858 and during the Civil War, Union soldiers maintained a base of operations at this location called Camp Union.

A post office was opened at Brumley in 1863 and is still in operation. In 1868, Mark Lesem opened the first store and in 1877 James M. Hawkins platted the town. By 1888, Brumley had a school and a population of about 100. On Oct. 6, 1906, the Bank of Brumley opened for business [see Bank of Brumley]. The town was incorporated in 1928. By 1930, it was a prosperous community with a bank, several general stores, a garage, two churches, a Masonic Lodge, a high school and a fish hatchery.

Early fishing camps established on the Lake near Brumley included Lucas Lodge Camp in 1932 and McClain's Camp in the 1940s. In 1967, Wright Cave [Arrow Point Cave] was commercialized a couple of miles south of town.

Brumley is still home to people who make their living farming and working in Eldon, Lake Ozark and Osage Beach. The town bequeathed something unique and valuable to the Lake area -- its bank -- which became Central Bank of Lake of the Ozarks.

Camdenton *(Camden County)* -

Camdenton, like Linn Creek, was born from the ashes of Old Linn Creek, the former county seat of Camden County. Of necessity, Old Linn Creek had to be demolished for the coming of Lake of the Ozarks. The old town site is now beneath 40 feet of water.

The 500 residents of Old Linn Creek were of mixed sentiments about where to relocate. Some moved to the surrounding hills, some had their homes moved up the valley to the present location of Linn Creek [a site originally called Easterville], and others resettled at the location of Camdenton.

The site of Camdenton, at the junction of Hwys. 54 & 5, was platted by Clint Webb with the help of his friend and later partner, Jim Banner. Camdenton was also chosen to be the new county seat of Camden County.

Camdenton was the brainchild of Clint Webb, a "tall, quiet, easy-going" man. He created the 160-acre site by buying two tracts of land in January 1930 -- the Chapman farm and the Wooten farm. He sought not only to profit from his venture, but to provide relatives, friends and neighbors an alternative to living in the lowlands along the stream in Linn Creek valley.

"Few permanent houses were built in the area during most of the year 1930, so the town had the appearance of a camp site," said historian Fern Moreland. The rush began in late December 1930 and continued on into the spring of 1931 as the destruction of Old Linn Creek neared completion and the waters of the Lake began to creep up Linn Creek valley.

The first two businesses at the new town site were the W. H. Powell Lumber Company and the Sidwell Barbershop. From that beginning, each month saw new homes and businesses spring up around the town square laid out in the shape of a wagon wheel with the junction of the two highways as the axis of the hub, hence the town's early nickname -- "Hub City of Lake of the Ozarks." The Camdenton Chamber of Commerce considered this nickname as well as "Capitol City of Lake of the Ozarks." Hub City became the town's promotional tool.

Among the well known and civic-minded residents of the new town was Abbie Bankson, a young woman of unusual intestinal fortitude for a woman of her day. She had been born and raised on a farm in Pulaski, Illinois. As a child and teenager, she had developed a Florence Nightingale reputation as a person of independent thinking and strong will, and as a person with a healing touch and a winning personality. By the time she reached adulthood, she was living in Camden County, Missouri. If there was sickness anywhere, she could be counted on to help. She also had the ability to deal with death and to console those who had lost loved ones.

There was no mortician in the county but a need for one. "The doctors of the county signed a petition to the State Board of Embalmers to grant Abbie Bankson a license without the customary two years practice, citing the county's need and her experience. She passed the examination and in 1932 put up her sign 'Abbie Bankson, Mortician,'" wrote a reporter for the *St. Louis Post-Dispatch.*

Another need of Camdenton was for a coroner. Abbie filed her application in 1932 for a place on the ticket and was elected with no opposition. In addition, she married B. E. Woolery.

The new town also needed a correspondent for the *Lake of the Ozarks News* as well as a director for the town's Information Bureau. Abbie took on the challenge of both positions without batting an eye.

Thus it was that Abbie Bankson-Woolery became a mortician, county coroner, wife, newspaper correspondent and director of Camdenton's Public Information Bureau all in the same year.

"Camdenton has a Bureau of Information concerning the Big Lake and the Region surrounding it. All interested in this Ozark territory and those that contemplate a visit to the shores of this wonderful Lake, can write, wire or phone and information will be cheerfully furnished. The Bureau is located in the new Abbie Bankson Building on the north side of the Camdenton Court House. Look for the sign," said a newspaper announcement in Sept. 1932.

Abbie was so busy that her husband had to become her assistant. They became a hardworking team of morticians, coroners, reporters and information specialists. Her reports to the *Lake of the Ozarks News* kept people updated on the new businesses coming into Camdenton and the new buildings going up all while she was taking drowning victims out of the Lake and the dead and injured from highway accidents. She was even known to officiate at graveside services when a minister was not available.

In 1943, she and her husband moved into the elegant old two-story home of Dr. George M. Moore that sat on the south corner of the Camdenton square near the Courthouse. It was one of the houses that had been moved from Old Linn Creek to Camdenton in 1931. Here, Abbie would spend the rest of her life while she served her town, her people and the Lake of the Ozarks region. Over the years Abbie took 32 bodies from the waters of the Lake and local rivers. She was not a native of Camden County nor an Ozarkian but she earned the respect of those who were. In her final years she opened her home to friends and strangers, giving tours of one of the county's most historic old homes. It was filled with original Camden county heirlooms.

Camdenton has also distinguished itself over the years. One annual event in particular -- the Dogwood Festival -- not only put Camdenton on the map, but has been beneficial to the entire Lake region.

The other Camdenton claim to fame was the J Bar H Rodeo. The Rodeo began in the summer of 1952 and for the next 20 years attracted thousands of people to the Lake area each summer to see top national rodeo talent. The J Bar H Rodeo no longer exists but the boost it gave to tourism at Lake of the Ozarks in its day was unmatched by any other regional event.

Campbell's Lake House *(Lake Ozark, Miller County)* -

In 1941, the Missouri WPA Guide Book gave the following description of Lake Ozark, saying that the village was "composed of a single row of one- and two-story buildings, hotels, restaurants, dance halls, taverns, and shops...a roadside hamlet catering to vacationists. The left side of the highway, too steep to support buildings without expensive foundation construction, is unused." The observer who wrote the description was traveling west through Lake Ozark.

The lack of development on the left side of The Strip changed in 1946 with the arrival of Joseph Audell Campbell and his wife Jewel Marshall.

Audell had been superintendent of schools in Eldon for a number of years. He and his wife left the state in 1938 but returned in 1946 and began the construction of a restaurant on the left side of the road at the edge of the large parking lot at the west end of Bagnell Dam. Their building was so close to the Hwy. 54 right-of-way

Campbell's Lake House, Shagbark Room, *Lake Ozark, MO, Circa. 1950s. Photographer Unknown.*

that the boundary was just a few feet from the restaurant's front door. What materialized was Campbell's Lake House, an establishment that became legendary on The Strip. It was in operation for more than 40 years and was a family-owned, family-run operation.

In 1947, a motel was added to the restaurant, the same year that their son, William, and his wife, Margaret, joined the operation and brought some Scottish decor to the interior. But what truly made the restaurant and its various dining rooms special were the remarkable murals painted on the walls by Jewel. She was an accomplished oil painter and scenes of Lake of the Ozarks adorned the restaurant walls.

In the wake of Campbell's Lake House, development along the left side of the highway through Lake Ozark spread and had run the full length of The Strip by the end of the 1950s. Campbell's Lake House is no longer in business, its building complex having been used by several later businesses that are now gone. It is unfortunate that Campbell's Lake House, with its beautiful murals, is now just a memory.

Cannady's Cafe & Grocery Store *(Osage Beach, Camden County)* -

Cannady's Cafe & Grocery Store were in separate but adjacent buildings along Hwy. 54 in Osage Beach in the 1930s and 40s. The businesses were at the northeast corner of LkRd. 54-24 or Osage Beach Road. The buildings were erected in 1933 by Mr. & Mrs. A. B. Cannady. The Cannady's were influential in the early development of Osage Beach, taking an active role in getting the name of the post office changed from Zebra to Osage Beach. In the 1930s, they helped organize the Osage Beach Chamber of Commerce, which was initially called the Grand Glaize-Osage Beach Chamber of Commerce. According to Mrs. A. B. Cannady's "History of Osage

Cannady's Café & Grocery Store, *Osage Beach, MO, Circa. 1940s. Photographer Unknown.*

Beach," some people west of the Grand Glaize Bridge wanted their community to be called Grand Glaize. The area east of the bridge was considered Osage Beach at that time. The Chamber of Commerce often held its meetings at Cannady's Cafe.

In the late 1940s, the Cannady's sold their grocery store to Melvin Minder, who renamed it Minder's Grocery. Mrs. Cannady and Mrs. Minder were sisters. Minder's Grocery was in business until 1969.

The Cannady Cafe, which sat between the grocery store and Osage Beach Road, was sold to Dot and Harvey Garvey who renamed it the Folded Hills Dining Room. The business kept this name until about 1960 when the building became the Osage Beach Post Office. At that time the building was veneered with red brick. The post office used the building until about 1965 when it moved to a building at the corner of LkRd. 54-29.

F. C. Arnold Realty acquired the old post office building in the 1970s and opened the Arnold's Gift Shop [later called Arnold's Country Corner], which closed in 2005. These buildings have since been demolished.

The Cannadys moved to Eldon in 1953 and leased a business building at 115 Maple Street from Jim Crum for a Gambles Store. The Eldon building had formerly been occupied by the American Sales Company.

Cape Galena *(Sunrise Beach, Camden County)* -

Cape Galena was a hamlet and railroad tie-buying center that existed from about 1875 to 1910 in the southeast corner of Morgan County. It was at the mouth of Cape Hollow [now Cape Hollow Cove] near the 8.25-mile mark on the Osage Arm and about 200 feet west of the northernmost of the Twin Islands. The old town site is now beneath 30 to 50 feet of water.

Cape Galena was named by Dr. J. W. Calfee when the post office was established in 1875. He was the postmaster. The post office was housed in a store Calfee built on the west slope of the hill whose top is now one of the Twin Islands. According to folklore, he named the site Cape Galena because the hills surrounding the town were "filled with galena." The ridges that rise on both sides of Cape Hollow Cove reach elevations of 850 to 860 feet above sea level and Calfee referred to them as "lookout mountains." Galena Point lies just west of the inundated old town site and is a place name still found on most maps of Lake of the Ozarks.

Cape Hollow & Cove / Moonlight Bay *(Sunrise Beach, Morgan County)* -

Cape Hollow lies just northeast of Sunrise Beach between LkRds. 5-33 and 5-35. The cove, which local people now called Moonlight Bay, occupies more than half of the lower portion of the hollow, which is about two miles long. Its axis runs southwest by northeast. Before the Lake was created, drainage from the hollow flowed into the Osage River just north of today's Twin Islands at the 8-mile mark.

The bay portion of Cape Hollow is more than one mile long. The bay, which averages 500 feet wide, has several large coves along its southeast side and an averge water depth of about 30 feet.

Early resorts that occupied the banks of Cape Hollow Cove included Ammon's Boat Dock & Marine Railway, Greer's Resort, Island View Resort, Schreit's Lodge, Crestwood Cottages, Collins Oakwood Resort, Rock Harbor Resort, Nature's Haven Resort, Logan's Resort, Rockledge Resort and the McCoy Resort.

Caves *(Benton, Camden, Miller and Morgan counties)* -

More than 250 caves are recorded in the four-county Lake of the Ozarks region, which includes Benton, Camden, Miller and Morgan counties. The existence of these ancient caves is made possible by the presence of thick, soluble, cave-bearing dolomite and limestone formations that outcrop along the Osage River and its tributaries.

Caves in the region are very old, having been formed by the acidic action of groundwater dissolving the the rock along bedding planes, joints and fault lines in the dolomite and limestone formations. It is a process that can take millions of years. As surface waters entrench the landscape through erosion, forming hills and valleys, the old cave passages are severed, creating cave openings in bluffs and hillsides. As valleys are deepened, the water table is lowered, the caves are drained and no longer water-filled. Air enters the caves and stalactites and stalagmites and other formations begin to develop in them.

Caves both large and small are included in the cave inventory for the Lake area. Most of the caves are less than 1,000 feet long. A substantial number of them are only a few hundred feet long, although some have large rooms. About 20 caves exceed 1,000 feet in length and only one cave, east of Montreal, is presently known to have more than one mile of passage.

Numerous caves in the Lake area are noted for their secondary mineral deposits in the form of stalactites, stalagmites, columns and flowstone. Some of the more scenic caves have been developed for commercial use as show caves and are open to the public for guided tours [see Show Caves]. Caves not open to the public and undeveloped are called "wild caves."

Most of the caves in the region are wet and have an average year 'round temperature of 56 to 60 degrees. Cave life is varied and many of the caves harbor threatened or endangered species of cave life including blind salamanders and gray and Indiana bats. Cave ecosystems are delicately balanced and the life forms fragile. Over use, pollution, vandalism, disregard for their existence, ignorance of their value and surface developments threaten many local cave systems.

All of the caves in the Lake area are on private property except those within state parks managed by the Missouri Department of Natural Resources, or on land owned by the Missouri Department of Conservation.

Chet's Anchor Inn *(Osage Beach, Camden County)* -

In the late 1930s, Orville Kelly built cottages along the south side of Hwy. 54 at the east end of the Gand Glaize Bridge. The cottages had large picture windows overlooking the Lake. He called his place Kelly's Modern Cottages and charged $1.00 per day for a cottage.

Kelly put the business up for sale around 1942 and Chester "Chet" Mason Hymes, whose parents owned Hymes Kottage Kamp #1 and Hymes Kottage Kamp #2 beyond the west end of the Grand Glaize Bridge, bought Kelly's business and property.

The first structure Chet added along the highway was a small gift shop and soft drink stand. Down along the Lake shore he anchored a barge that had been used to haul gravel during the construction of Bagnell Dam. He converted part of the barge into a place for him and his family to live until better accommodations could be arranged. He and his wife, Lela, named their new business Chet's Anchor Inn.

The business grew rapidly and by the time they sold in 1953, the gift shop was a very substantial two-story structure. On the hill slope just above the Lake was a Ferris wheel and the accommodations on the barge had blossomed from "home" into a busy recreational center where tourists could take excursion boat rides, sail boat rides, a sea plane ride, or learn to water ski, or rent a fishing boat.

From 1953 to 1955, the gift shop and cottage portion of the business was advertised first as Conrad's Anchor Inn and then Anchor Inn under the operation of Herb and Mabel Conrad.

Around 1956, both the highway and lakeshore business operations at Anchor Inn were sold and became Link's Landing. New Grand Glaize Bridge construction work in the 1990s took the Link's Landing property and today no business is located on the south side at the east end of the Grand Glaize Bridge.

After selling to the Conrad's, Chet opened Chet's House of Gifts and Eats in 1954 a few blocks east along the highway, renaming it Chet's Restaurant in the mid

Chet's Anchor Inn, *Osage Beach, MO, Circa. Late 1940s. Photographer Unknown.*

1960s. Adjacent to the restaurant was Chet's Fun Spot featuring go-karts and bumper cars. These businesses were located at the junction of LkRd. 54-30, which is now called Red Bud Road. Chet's Restaurant building now houses Domenico's Restaurant.

Chief Ne-Ong-Wah / Stone Face *(Camdenton, Camden County)* -

Folklore says that Ne-Ong-Wah is the ancient Indian name for the Niangua River, "meaning under a liberal construction, Spring River." Chief Ne-Ong-Wah, also called Stone Face, is the name of a bluff feature -- the natural profile of an Indian chief's face along the Niangua River at about the 4.5-mile mark. In 1931, this landmark feature was inundated by the Lake. It was located a short distance downstream from the Arnhold Mill and was associated with another prominent riverside landmark called Chimney Rock.

Chimney Rock *(Camdenton, Camden County)* -

In several places along the Niangua, Grandglaize and Osage rivers are pinnacles of rock, usually dolomite and limestone pillars separated from adjacent bluffs by erosion. Chimney Rock is one such pinnacle of stone at the 4.5-mile mark on the Niangua Arm. It stands apart from the south end of Chimney Rock Bluff. Bold and majestic, it is about 50 feet high and "surmounted by a natural stone head and face bearing a...resemblance to an Indian Chief in his war bonnet." Early steamboat pilots named the bluff, the pinnacle, and the stone face. Unfortunately, all but a few feet of this pinnacle's top are now inundated by the Lake. [see Chief Ne-Ong-Wah]

Chimney Rock Cave *(Camdenton, Camden County)* -

A small cave passes completely through Chimney Rock at the 4.5-mile mark of the Niangua Arm. Like Chimney Rock, it is now inundated. In recent years, Chimney Rock Cave has been located and entered by divers who report that silt from the Lake waters now largely fills the cave's passages. [see Chief Ne-Ong-Wah; Chimney Rock]

Christmas Tree Court *(Versailles, Gravois Mills, Morgan County)* -

This roadside business opened in 1951 as Urlaub's Palace Cabin Court just south of Jacob's Cave on Hwy. 5 [now Route TT] about six miles south of Versailles. It was along the east side of the highway. The court had housekeeping cottages and advertised being within "walking distance of Jacob's Cave." A couple of years later, the business was sold to Dick & Ott Meyer who renamed it Christmas Tree Court & Souvenir Shop.

The principal building was a long, one-story, gable-ended frame structure facing the highway with a business sign along the front roof-line. Below the roof overhang was a red-, white- and blue-striped metal awning that protected shelves along the front of the building where colorful Ozark pottery was displayed. There was an additional open-fronted building to the left where Ozark pottery, fishing tackle and bait were sold. Cabins were located to the right of the building. In front of this building were two gas pumps that dispensed Sinclair gasoline.

Even though a new stretch of Hwy. 5 south of Versailles was opened in 1965, bypassing the location of Christmas Tree Court & Souvenir Shop and relegating the business to the lesser-traveled County Route TT, the Court managed to survive into the 1970s. People traveling down Route TT today can see no sign that this once thriving business ever existed.

Cleland's Cottages *(Osage Beach, Camden County)* -

Cleland's cottages was once located in Osage Beach along Hwy. 54. The business was about one-quarter mile northeast of Osage Beach Road on the northwest side of the highway across from today's Super Wal-Mart Center. The cottages were originally built in 1931 by J. W. Pooler and the business operated as Pooler's Modern Cottages, Store & Bus Stop. It later became Fred Cossey's Modern Camp and then Cleland's Cottages. The business closed at the end of the 1967 season. [see Pooler's Modern Cottages]

Climax Spring *(Camden County)* -

Climax Spring issues from a rock outcrop at the base of a hill in the small city park of Climax Springs, which is about 23 miles west of Camdenton on Hwy. 7. A concrete trough in the park captures the water of the spring and then releases it into the spring branch. The spring has an average daily flow of about 50,000 gallons. The recharge area for this spring has several sinkholes that provide input to the spring's water supply. Dye tests in 1970 established a water connection between Climax Spring and Climax Springs Cave. The spring and its water supply was the focal point of the town's mineral spa "boom" in the 1880s. [see Climax Springs; Climax Springs Cave]

Climax Springs *(Camden County)* -

The town of Climax Springs is located along Hwy. 7 in the northwest corner of Camden County about one mile short of the Camden-Benton County line. The town has a current population of about 100 people. Most of today's business establishments are located along Hwy. 7 but Old Climax Springs, where the town orginally grew up around a spring, is about one mile to the north. City Hall and the school are still located in the old section of town but many of the buildings that once housed businesses in Old Climax Springs are now vacant.

There are two springs in the community, one that issues from a rock outcrop in the city park, and another in Climax Springs Cave, which is entered through a sinkhole along County Road DD, the road into Old Climax Springs.

Settlement began here in 1868 with James C. Beard. In 1881, according to folklore, W. W. Hockman named Climax Springs Cave while stopping at the site during a trip. In 1882, the town was platted as "Climax" by Professor H. W. Wiley, a chemist, who analyzed the spring water and wildly stated that it was "the richest water in the world known to chemistry."

Climax Springs Hotel, *Climax Springs, MO. Photo by H. D. Weaver, 2004.*

In the same year, Craven Thompson built the first hotel. In 1883, a post office was established at Climax but in 1886, the name was changed to Climax Springs. Other merchants moved into the community and formed the Climax Springs Association to capitalize on the "healing powers" of the springs. The association's founders included Daniel T. McNiel, Milton C. Hockman, James T. Hockman and Alexander R. Jackson. They built the Climax Hotel, a three-story structure with 22 guest rooms. As a consequence, the town experienced a "boom" in the 1890s. At its height, Climax Springs probably had a population close to 500. "Climax Springs was the earliest intended resort town in the Ozarks, and one of the first west of the Mississippi River," said Robert S. Vogel [1971].

Spa activities centered around the spring in the park and the one in the cave. The spa business fell on hard times after 1907 when the federal government's new Pure Food and Drug Act became effective. Afterwards, Climax Springs struggled to survive on subsistence agriculture and the timber industry in the 1920s, 30s, and 40s.

Up to the 1950s, Climax Springs was relatively isolated from the main arteries of traffic flow in its county. There was only minimal development in its sector along the shores of Lake of the Ozarks about five miles northeast of the town [Rainey Creek Cove]. Hwy. 7 was built through the area in 1956, and instead of passing through Old Climax Springs as the people wished, it was built along the ridge about one mile to the south. Some of the commercial buildings of Old Climax Springs were then abandoned as local businesses moved south to be along the new highway.

In 2004, there was renewed interest in the spring at the park when the U. S. Department of Agriculture provided grant money to the Village of Climax Springs to study the spring water and determine the feasibility of constructing and operating a bottled water facility at the site, or create a collection and treatment center for supplying high quality water to bottling companies.

Climax Springs Cave *(Camden County)* -

The entrance to Climax Springs Cave is located about one-half mile north of Hwy. 7 just off County Road DD, which leads into Old Climax Springs. The name was bestowed upon the cave by W. W. Hockman in 1881.

The entrance sinkhole is 20 feet deep, sloping gradually downward from east to west directly into the mouth of the cave. The west side of the sinkhole drops abruptly to the cave entrance, which is six feet high and 15 feet wide. The entrance chamber is 30 feet wide, 75 feet long and eight feet high. The far end of the room contains an underground lake that siphons along the ceiling at the back side where the water is at least 15 feet deep. The spring that feeds this lake comes in from the right side of the entrance room, which actually lies beneath the county road.

The late Ernest Kumpf, who owned the cave for many years and whose house was close to the sinkhole, once used the cave as a source of water for his livestock. From about 1886 until 1907, when the Climax Springs mineral spa was booming, the cave water was used for drinking and bathing. Dye tests have shown that the water draining into this sinkhole cave flows directly to Climax Spring in the city park of Climax Springs. The distance between the two is about 900 feet.

Coakley Hollow & Coves *(Linn Creek, Camden County)* -

The mouth of Coakley Hollow is located at the 12.5-mile mark along the south side of the Grand Glaize Arm where the Lake makes a sharp bend around the Lake of the Ozarks State Park Public Beach No. 1 campground point. Jeffries Point on the opposite side of the Lake at the mouth of Coakley Hollow is the tip of a peninsula that is about 600 feet long and 400 feet wide. Little Coakley Hollow Cove is on the east side and Big Coakley Hollow Cove is one the west side.

Jeffries Point is the terminal point of an old road that leads three-quarters of a mile up Coakley Hollow to Ozark Caverns, which was called Coakley Cave prior to its commercialization in the early 1950s. The road has its own history, which is associated with the point and the cave.

The peninsula, like much of Coakley Hollow, has some interesting geological features. On either side of the old road are small sinkholes that feed into a small cave system [probably too small for human entry] that penetrates the peninsula and is believed to drain into Big Coakley Hollow Cove. On the west side of the road, the dolomite and limestone bedrock surface has been so unevenly weathered by solution that small troughs and miniature pinnacles have formed on the bedrock surface. They are nearly buried by leaf litter and forest mulch, making it very difficult to walk where they are present.

Coakley Hollow extends for about two miles in a southwesterly direction. The hollow is reasonably wide with the ridge-tops on either side rising to heights of 160 feet above the spring branch that flows down the hollow. The west side is much steeper than the east side, the west side having intermittent rock outcrops and small terrace-like bluffs. The west side, which Ozark Caverns penetrates, is host to a perched water table that is responsible for the valley's innumerable seep springs and natural fens or bogs. A somewhat impervious layer of rock floors these areas, carrying the seep spring flow out onto the valley bottom beneath accumulated layers of porous forest soils and natural debris; it is as much as two- to three-feet deep in places. The perched water table also provides the water supply for the cave's unique display of water-showing formations, an assemblage called the Angel's Shower. When the first water well was drilled in the valley near the cave in the late 1950s, the artesian flow was struck at less than 40 feet and water shot higher than the tree tops. When the surge stabilized, the well had seven pounds of natural pressure, according to the late R. H. Ohlson who owned the cave at that time.

About 3,000 feet up the hollow from its mouth on the west side of the old road there was once several houses [long gone], one of which is believed to have provided living quarters for Coakley, the miller who built a dam across the spring branch at this point in the late 1880s to form an impoundment. He then built a gristmill which had an undershot wheel. The valley saw lots of activity in the 1890s.

After Lake of the Ozarks State Park was created, a split-rail corral was erected near this location in the hollow in the 1940s to contain cattle and other stock that some locals in the vicinity would turn loose to forage free on state land. Remnants of this old corral were still present in the valley in the 1970s.

Since Jeffries Point was a private in-holding within the state park for four decades, locals would drive down the old road to swim and picnic on the point. They also enjoyed gathering wild edibles within the hollow and did it on a seasonal basis well into the 1960s. Shortly after the cave was commercialized, the cave owners had some difficulties with certain locals who used the old road that crossed the cave owners' property and went through the show cave's parking lot. A "No Trespassing" sign went up just beyond the parking lot and a chain went across the road where it crossed the Coakley Spring branch. The locals simply blazed their own road down from the ridge along the east side of the valley and it connected with the primary road near the neck of the peninsula.

The Ozark Caverns properties, which included Coakley Hollow, became part of Lake of the Ozarks State Park in 1978. The fens [marshy areas] in the valley became part of the Coakley Hollow Natural Area and wet meadows. A self-guided nature trail now winds through this area displaying its unique features such as the calcareous wet spring seeps, glades, the old Coakley dam and fens.

Coakley Spring *(Linn Creek, Camden County)* -

This is a spring located in Coakley Hollow at the 12.5-mile mark on the Grand Glaize Arm. The spring discharges from an opening that is actually three-quarters of a mile from the Lake. It issues from a rock outcrop at the base of a hill in the

Coakley Spring, *Lake of the Ozarks State Park. Photo by H. D. Weaver, 2004.*

southeast fork of the hollow at an elevation of about 745 feet above sea level. The opening is 12 feet wide and two to four feet high. A small concrete dam [about 18 inches high] was built a few feet beyond the spring mouth in the early 1930s by J. F. Hurley, Jr. to impound the water for his Coakley Springs Minnow Hatchery & Resort. The small ponds for his minnows were a short distance down the spring branch and water was piped from the spring to the ponds.

Hurley built several log cabins in the narrow valley near the spring and rented them to fishermen who generally did their fishing at the mouth of the valley in the Coakley Hollow coves. Boy scout groups were often guests at the resort. They generally were allowed to explore Coakley Cave during their stay.

The resort did not survive the 1930s and Hurley's effort to raise minnows commercially was not profitable. One of the old log cabins was still standing, though largely in ruins, as late as 1951 when it was demolished by the crew developing nearby Coakley Cave as a public attraction. This spring and Coakley Cave [Ozark Caverns] are now owned by Lake of the Ozarks State Park.

Coakley Spring has a modest perennial flow but discharges large volumes of water after heavy rain. The spring's underground course along a low, wide, bedding plane opening was explored to a distance of about 1,000 feet in 1965 by cave explorers. At no place was it possible for them to stand up and the low water crawl is extremely hazardous because of brittle and easily dislodged layers of black flint rock that cling to the ceiling.

Coakley Springs Minnow Hatchery & Resort Cabin. *Photo courtesy of Camden County Historical Society.*

Coelleda *(Camden County)* -

Coelleda is said to have been one of the earliest settlements in Camden County, its original name being Little Niangua. The town site is thought to have been located near the mouth of Prairie Hollow where the hollow hooks around sharply to the right [southeast] and again sharply to the left [northeast] to join the Little Niangua Arm at the 5-mile mark. Confusing the issue is the existence of Coelleda Hollow, which also joins the Little Niangua Arm, but which comes in from the north about one mile to the northeast.

The Prairie Hollow location is favored because of the existence of two caves, which were said to be associated with the community and its gristmill -- Prairie Hollow Cave and Prairie Hollow Spring Cave. The gristmill operated at the lower entrance to Prairie Hollow Spring Cave.

Prairie Hollow Cave penetrates Gulliver's Ridge, which rises to a height of 280 feet above the Lake and is directly north of the bend in the hook of the hollow.

Prairie Hollow Spring Cave is a natural tunnel cave with a small upper entrance on the opposite side of Prairie Hollow Cove along Prairie Hollow creek. The cave's lower entrance in Prairie Hollow Cove is submerged when the Lake is at normal reservoir level.

Settlement here came as early as the 1840s with the establishment of the Prairie Hollow Baptist Church. Sometime before the Civil War, Fredrick Gerhard settled and built a gristmill with an undershot wheel at the lower entrance of Prairie Hollow

Spring Cave. He was able to divert the waters of Eadson's Spring Branch in Prairie Hollow through the tunnel cave by way of the cave's upper entrance, to provide power for the mill at the lower entrance. The stone baffle that he built just inside the low-ceilinged lower entrance of the cave can still be examined when the cove is dry due to low water levels of the Lake. The cove dries up around the cave outlet when the Lake is at 654-foot elevation or lower.

The Little Niangua Post Office was established in 1857 but ceased operation in 1887 when the name was changed to Coelleda. The Coelleda Post Office was operated until 1930. The community that grew up around the mill had a school, a church, a general merchandise store and the post office. The Lake now floods the lower portion of Prairie Hollow at its mouth forming Prairie Hollow Cove, but as late as 1966 a few foundation ruins of the former buildings could be found above the water line just west of the two caves and close to a cavity-riddled spine of rock.

Cole Camp *(Benton County)* -

Cole Camp is located along Hwy. 52 and has a current population of about 1,054. It is noted for its vintage downtown area with buildings that reflect nineteenth and early twentieth century architecture, and for its spring and fall festivals that celebrate the town's German heritage.

Along William's Creek around 1835, about four miles southwest of Cole Camp and probably not too far from Union Church along Route F, Ezekiel Williams collected mail for his neighbors. He called his place "Cole Camp" after Cole Camp, Kentucky, his homeland. Where the town of Cole Camp sits today, other settlers built their log cabins and established stores. It quickly grew into a trading center often called Blakey Town after the Blakey Brothers.

In 1839, Ezekiel moved his unofficial post office to Blakey Town. Probably because Ezekiel was already serving as an unofficial postmaster, and perhaps through Ezekiel's influence, the U. S. Postal Service named the post office Cole Camp. The present town of Cole Camp grew from that beginning.

From the 1830s to the 1890s, German immigrants swelled the village population, bringing such names as Boeschen, Meyer, Holtzen, Brauer and Mahnken. From 1856 to 1861, Cole Camp was on the Butterfield Overland Mail route, a stage coach service that did not survive the Civil War. In 1880, the Sedalia, Warsaw and Southern Railroad, operated by the Missouri Pacific Railroad Company, came to Cole Camp, first as a narrow-gauge railroad and later [after 1902] as a standard-gauge track. By 1927, the town had a population of 889.

Cole Camp has always been a strong, independent, self-sustaining community with only a peripheral attachment to Lake of the Ozarks, which is 12 miles due south of town. After Bagnell Dam was completed, the Chamber of Commerce did not promote Cole Camp as a gateway to the Lake, like some neighboring towns were promoted. The only Lake development that has had a reasonably strong attachment to Cole Camp is Lakeview Heights at the 77-mile mark on the Osage Arm. Lakeview Heights is in the Cole Camp school district.

When the Chamber of Commerce did promote in the early days of the Lake, it was more prone to emphasize Cole Camp's strong agricultural base, its access to rail and highway transportation, its school system, industries and city utilities. If they promoted any bodies of water and fishing at all, it would be to mention local streams. "Within a few minutes drive of town are numerous streams which provide excellent recreation for those who enjoy fishing," said a 1932 promotional article. "Cole Camp Creek, Lake Creek, Turkey Creek, Deer Creek, Buffalo and Little Buffalo all yield bass, trout, channel cat, crappie and other game fish."

Cole Camp Creek & Hollow *(Benton County)* -

Cole Camp Creek is a historic tributary of the Osage River. Its 146-square-mile watershed lies in the northeast half of Benton County and almost entirely within an area bounded on the east by the Morgan-Benton County line, on the north by Hwy. 52; on the west by Hwy. 65; and to the south by Lake of the Ozarks. Since much of Benton County to the north and west is prairie uplands between 950 and 1,100 feet above sea level [north of Hwy. 52 and west of Hwy. 65], the area that comprises the Cole Camp Creek watershed is referred to geographically as the "Osage River Breaks."

Over its main channel length of about 27 miles from headwaters to discharge point into the Lake, the creek descends 385 feet. It enters the Lake east of Warsaw at the 79.5-mile mark of the Osage Arm. Major laterals of Cole Camp Creek include Ross Creek, Duran Creek, Indian Creek and Williams Creek. At the headwaters of the tributary sits the town of Cole Camp, and to the west the town of Lincoln. To the south along the shores of the Lake is Riverview Heights.

Historic old town sites associated with the Cole Camp area but no longer shown on most highway maps include Crest, Crockerville, Edmonson, Mt. Hulda, Raymond [Tahoma], Poplar and Zora. Settlement in the Cole Camp Creek watershed began in the 1830s with Ezekiel Williams after whom the largest lateral, Williams Creek, is named. Prospecting for lead and zinc occurred in the hills along both sides of Cole Camp Creek and several of its laterals in the early part of the twentieth century but was not productive.

Cole Camp Hollow Cove *(Benton County)* -

The mouth of Cole Camp Hollow Cove enters the Lake at the 79.5-mile mark with two boating entries because of an elongated, L-shaped island, most of which is submerged. The longer entry, stretching for nearly one mile, has a narrow channel 10 feet deep with emergent vegetation in the water along the island side. The more direct, shorter entry to the cove at the island's southwest end has a very narrow channel of similar depth.

The cove has a boating length of about four miles and runs 1,000 feet wide until near the 3-mile mark where, after briefly widening out, the cove narrows quickly to about 400 feet. One-quarter of a mile further, near the point where a decorative rock lighthouse stands today as a landmark on private property, the cove becomes shallow. Only canoes can go much beyond this point.

The bluffs and rock outcrops along the shoreline of Cole Camp Creek Cove are geologically interesting. Unusual piles of jumbled boulders and weathered, scalloped rock can be seen at the 2-mile mark at Wilson's Bend. The bluffs are heavily stained with manganese and exhibit colorful, striking features. A partially submerged grotto exists in the bluff along the east side at the 1-mile mark. The opening is about 12 feet wide and 15 feet high, but narrows quickly.

The Kansas City Girl Scout Camp was established on the west shore at the 1.5-mile mark in the early 1930s, and Wilson's Resort was established at the mouth of the cove on the east side. Wilson's Resort later became Lakeside Resort and is still in business. In the 1970s, Osage Marine operated at the mouth of the cove on the west side, and Shady Shore Resort was established near the 2.5-mile mark. Lake Ozark Forest was created to the west in the early days near the 81-mile mark. on the Osage Arm, and Lakeview Heights developed to the east at the 77-mile mark on the Osage.

Collin's Spring & Lake *(Gravois Mills, Morgan County)* -

This spring and lake are located about one mile east of Gravois Mills in Factory Hollow. The spring and lake have had several names beginning as Humes Spring & Lake after 1847 when the Humes brothers, Thomas and Joseph, used the spring to provide water power for mills. The gristmill was run by Joseph, and the woolenmill by Thomas.

In the 1890s, this property belonged to Asa Webster and son, who also operated a gristmill. In the early 1900s, the lake became known as Humes, Webster and Collins Lake or just Collins Lake after Andrew Collins, said to have been a former owner.

When Bagnell Dam was under construction, new development was planned at this site by then owner H. C. Mcquerter. "The lake is well stocked with trout and blue gill. Cabins may be secured here and the development plans include a golf course and recreation hall," said promotional materials. In 1939, Mcquerter named the property Troutdale Ranch and established a trout hatchery.

By 1954, the ranch was owned by Donald D. Belcher of Kansas City. In 1972, Donald Belcher, Jr., Allen A. Gates, and Elom F. Carlson became the owners of Troutdale Ranch.

At some point after the beginning of the twentieth century, the spring became officially recorded by the U.S. Geological Survey and the Missouri Geological Survey as Gravois Mills Spring.

Cove Lodge Modern Cottages *(Osage Beach, Camden County)* -

Cove Lodge Modern Cottages should not be confushed with Wood's Lake Cove Lodge, which was also in Osage Beach in the early days. Wood's Lake Cove Lodge was near the Grand Glaize Bridge. Cove Lodge Modern Cottages was established in the late 1930s at the 7.5-mile mark on the Grand Glaize Arm. It is on private property surrounded by Lake of the Ozarks State Park and was built when the state park was still known as the Regional Recreation Area.

Just east of Cove Lodge is the Kaiser Forest Lookout Tower, a landmark of the area. At about the same time as Cove Lodge was being built, the Civilian Conservation Corps was building camps in the Regional Recreation Area for the use of Boy Scouts, Girl Scouts, 4-H Clubs and other groups. Some of these camps still function so in the summer time Cove Lodge has some lively neighbors.

Cove Lodge has the distinction of being one of the few privately owned camps established on the upper reaches of the Grand Glaize Arm where most of the shoreline is owned by the state park. Cove Lodge consists of a group of fairly large housekeeping cottages made of native stone and is located in a cove along the north shore of the Lake. Early advertising for the lodge insisted that they "furnished everything but the towels" for their guests.

Cove Lodge Cottages. *Photo by H. D. Weaver, 2002.*

Damsel *(Osage Beach, Camden County)* -

When a driver leaves Route KK and turns onto Hwy. 54 in Osage Beach, it is hard to miss seeing the Damsel Dry Cleaners even though the business sits well back from the highway. It is nearly straight ahead on the other side of the road. The business name is in large block letters and the word "Damsel" is very prominent. The name of the dry cleaners preserves an old place name for this location. The village of Damsel was once at the intersection of Hwy. 54 and Route KK.

When Damsel occupied this intersection of roads before Lake of the Ozarks was formed, the intersection was called Turkey Bend Junction.

The Damsel Post Office opened in 1885 but closed in 1920 when it was merged with the Zebra Post Office a few miles northeast at the junction of the Osage and Grand Glaize. How Damsel got its French name is unknown. The word means "young unmarried woman of noble birth," but the village never grew much beyond a general store, filling station, cafe and post office. What distinguished the village was the presence of William A. Hunter, who owned most of the land on all sides of the junction and served as the first postmaster.

After Williams' death in 1925, his son, Quillie, followed in his entrepreneurial footsteps and became another legend of the Damsel area. After the Lake was created, Quillie O. Hunter earned his own colorful reputation as a shrewd, hillbilly developer and real estate promoter. To learn about Quillie and the legends of Turkey Bend, see *A Town of Two Rivers*, a history of Osage Beach by Victoria Hubbell [1998].

Damsel Cafe *(Osage Beach, Camden County)* -

Established at Damsel near the junction of Hwy. 54 & A22 [which later became Route KK] about 1932 by Quillie O. Hunter, the Damsel Cafe was advertised as the Damsel Cafe & Club Room and as the Lake Center Resort at Damsel.

In 1932, a visitor to the Lake Center Resort at Damsel said: "Here you have a camp right on the highway...a cool, shady cabin camp resort -- only a few minutes from the Lake -- and four good boat landings, two good beaches. Mr. Hunter, the owner, has a nice cafe in connection for those of you who appreciate good food, a grocery store, cold drinks, fishing tackle, boats of all kinds, and a service station for

Damsel Café & Club, *Osage Beach, MO, Circa. 1948. Photographer Unknown.*

your convenience. At night there is dancing at the cafe. There are plenty of shade trees and playgrounds for the children... Mr. Hunter will be glad to help you plan a trip or should you be interested in locating on the Lake, Mr. Hunter will gladly point out places of interest."

The service station and grocery store portion of the business was a two-story frame structure with a drive-through. Mounted on the canopy of the drive-through was a larger-than-life wooden cutout of a young "flapper" [a young woman of the period after World War I]. The building's second level had living quarters. The club portion was a long extension to the building surrounded by cedar trees. It could be entered separately.

Quillie Hunter had detailed ads that promoted other recreational offerings as well, such as tennis, riding horses, croquet, softball, horseshoes, shooting range and wading beaches.

After Hunter left the operation in the late 1940s to devote more time to his real estate business, the cafe and club were operated by Dirks and Smith. Quillie Hunter died in July 1961. The cafe and club building have been gone for more than 50 years.

Dogpatch Cafe / Village *(Lake Ozark, Miller County)* -

From the late 1930s to the 50s, one of the nation's most popular newspaper cartoons was Al Capp's L'l Abner, where the action took place in a fictional hillbilly town called Dogpatch. This theme appealed to Walter and Ada Tietmeyer, who came to the Lake in the mid 1940s with the dream of creating a unique Ozark hillbilly village on the Bagnell Dam Strip. They decided to call it Dogpatch.

In 1947, the Tietmeyers opened the Dogpatch Cafe just west of LkRd. 54-1, later designated 54-8 or Ballenger Road. There were gas pumps out front dispensing D-X gasoline. From this modest beginning the Tietmeyers built westward along the highway, adding a long, partially open structure housing a reptile gardens. At the far end was an enclosure for an African lion. At first the lion's quarters was simply a large unadorned cage but later improved with a carnival-like header at the top and a white fence in front. The reptile gardens portion was walled up along the front by 1956 and painted with an Ozark landscape scene. The gas pumps had been removed by this date.

In addition, Walt built to the rear, creating Dogpatch Village. The gift shop was located between the reptile gardens and the cafe. To see the village, for which no admission was then charged, you had to walk through the gift shop, which was integrated with the village. It was a way to entice people to buy souvenirs.

One of the first buildings in Dogpatch Village was an authentic log cabin that Walt brought from the Bear Creek area about five miles east of Lake Ozark. From that grew the village main street featuring various buildings with western facades and second floor porches. Everywhere there were mannequins dressed in hillbilly or western attire. Humor was the central theme. At one location in the crowded village was an old outhouse with a dummy dressed like a hillbilly sitting on the throne. When you opened the door, a loud recording came on with the man shouting at you to close the door and give him some privacy. In the 1950s, the display was a new novelty that could be counted on to redden the cheeks of the ladies and cause some embarrassment.

***Dogpatch,** Lake Ozark, MO, Circa. 1950. Photo by Blair Cedar Novelty.*

Walt also kept looking for that special something he could erect out front to attract even more attention. The American flag simply wasn't enough.

In the mid 1950s, Walt tried a tall rocket, which stood near the cafe, but then, as the 1960s approached, he added a giant Alfred E. Newman [of Mad Magazine fame] look-alike statue. It was exactly what he needed and it soon became the logo for Dogpatch. It was used in his advertising and the statue became a favorite place of tourists to take photos of one another. For a time, the statue held a large detached water faucet that ran a steady stream of water. It appeared as if the water was originating out of thin air when in fact, it was being pumped back up to the faucet mouth within the stream of water by way of a clear tube of plastic.

By the late 1960s, Tietmeyer had done away with the reptile gardens. Walt was becoming troubled by the fact that the visiting public was loosing interest in the Ozark hillbilly and Dogpatch themes. Times were changing. To stir up new interest, he added bumper car rides, an arcade, live artists on the grounds in the summers such as a glass blower, and installed unique gift shops behind the facades of the buildings in the village. "A Bit Of Old Missouri," "Dogpatch, Something Different," said his advertisements.

Although Walt Tietmeyer died in 1999, his Dogpatch business is still in operation. It is much changed and no longer features Dogpatch Village as it was in the 1950s and 60s, but one thing remains unchanged -- the giant Alfred E. Newman statue, somewhat weathered and no longer holding a running water faucet, still hails visitors who come his way, welcoming them to the Dogpatch complex of gift shops, food and entertainment.

Dogwood Festival *(Camdenton, Camden County)* -

When members of the Niangua Arm Chamber of Commerce met at the Palais Club at Camdenton in January 1950, and laid the first plans for staging a dogwood festival at Camdenton in the coming spring, they had no idea that five years later the Missouri Legislature would designate the dogwood tree the official tree of Missouri [designated June 20, 1955]. The idea behind the Dogwood Festival was to attract visitors and boost spring business for the Camdenton area, especially the resorts along the Niangua Arm.

The first annual Dogwood Festival was held April 20-23, 1950, with plans for a parade, queen contest, buffalo barbecue, carnival, horse show, blue grass and cowboy songs and a dog show. The event was such a crowning success that it has been held every year since with the exception of 1965 when highway construction work through Camdenton cancelled plans. Each year the chosen Dogwood committee makes an effort to stage the event during the annual flowering of the dogwood trees that beautify the Ozark hills embracing Lake of the Ozarks for a few weeks in the spring.

Dr. Kaiser's Apartment Cottages *(Sunrise Beach, Camden County)* -

Dr. A. A. Kaiser's Apartment Cottages was a Sunrise Beach area development around 1934 located at the end of LkRd. 5-88, later designated 5-18B, then 5-37 and now called Camp Branch Road. The resort had an initial guest capacity of 50 and was promoted as a modern vacation camp with a swimming pool separate from the Lake. The cabins were modern and quite handsome for the period and promoted as "superior apartments." He kept adding units until he could accommodate up to 150 people.

In 1936, Kaiser added a dining room and dance hall to accommodate large groups. The impressive building with white siding was built primarily to attract convention business, which it proved successful at doing.

In 1937, he added a music box to the dance hall that cost $1,000, and to his fleet of boats a seaplane, which guests could charter for rides. In the late 1940s, this resort became the Ellis Rod & Gun Club Resort.

Dr. Matthew's Cafe & Drug Store *(Versailles, Gravois Mills, Morgan County)* -

In the 1930s, 40s and 50s, Hwy. 5 took a meandering course through the hills south of Versailles to reach the valley of Gravois Creek and Gravois Mills. Today, it is nearly a straight shot of about six miles, the present road having been opened to traffic in 1965. The southern portion of old Hwy. 5 was then designated Route TT, which connects to Hwy. 5 a couple of miles north of Jacob's Cave and continues south to a point just northwest of Gravois Mills where it again connects to Hwy. 5. The portion of the old highway between Versailles and TT is now called Old Five Road.

In the period 1930 to 1960, a number of roadside businesses opened along old Hwy. 5 between Jacob's Cave and the Gravois Creek bridge. Most of these businesses were near the junction of LkRd. 5-3, which is now TT-1. This junction is seven miles south of Versailles on the old road.

In the 1930s, 40s and 50s, a cluster of resorts were established on Little Gravois Cove off LkRd. 5-3, which encouraged roadside businesses to develop along the highway. The early resorts included Kavanaugh's Gravois Beach Resort, Quigley's Resort, Tracy's Shoreline Resort and Blue Waters Resort.

Jacob's Cave [see Jacob's Cave] and Dr. Matthew's Cafe & Drug Store were the first roadside businesses along this portion of Hwy. 5 south of Versailles. Both were established in 1931-32.

Dr. A. A. Matthew's opened his cafe and drug store near the junction of TT-1, which is at the crest of a hill known as Matt's Hill, presumably after Dr. Matthews. A travel map for that year said: "Going south one is glad to find such an up-to-date drug store as Dr. Matthew's at Matt's Hill. Here one may stop and rest, get a cold drink or may purchase drugs, sundries, beer, sandwiches, fine wines and liquors from a new and complete stock. One stop here and you will always come back." The

Dr. Matthews Café & Drug Store, *Versailles, MO, Circa. 1930s. Photographer Unknown.*

business dispensed Cities Service gasoline. In 1936, a dance pavilion was added to the business. Afterwards, Friday and Saturday nights saw a lot of lively activity at what came to be called "Ol' Doc's Place."

As the 1930s exploded into the war years of the 1940s, Dr. Matthews sold his business and by 1945 it was called Cobb's Wayside Inn. Cobb's slogan was "Home of Good Food and Good Coffee." But within a couple of years the business had sold again and was called Manning's Wayside Inn. By the early 1950s, it was Cairn's Wayside Inn. This business appears to have closed sometime in the late 1950s and tourist literature of the period suggests that no further use was made of the building as a roadside business, although this could be incorrect.

Among the other roadside businesses near the junction of LkRd. 5-3, was the Top O'The Hill Grocery & Liquors opened about 1945 by Scottie and Gib Morgan. They stayed in business until the mid 1960s. Bert's Inn, opened by Bert Hoffman in 1946 or 1947, had a cafe and grocery. The cafe advertised steak and chicken. The Inn also sponsored dances at which they served set-ups.

By 1951, Urlaub's Palace Cabin Court had opened just south of Jacob's Cave along the east side of the highway and soon thereafter became Christmas Tree Court & Souvenir Shop.

Cooper's Antiques, established about 1948 further south, is believed to have become Bashore's Antiques by the 1960s. There was a business called Beach Combers, operated by Walt & Laverne, who had beer on tap. There was also Timberline Motel as well as the Ozark Organic Gardens.

The rerouting of Hwy. 5 traffic in 1965 had a dramatic impact upon all of these merchants. Most of their impulse business suddenly vanished. The merchants began to go out of business one after another. Christmas Tree Court and Timberline Motel survived to the 1970s. Of all the businesses that once flourished along the old highway, only Jacob's Cave survives today under its original name and method of operation, although the native stone buildings that once served as Timberline Motel are still standing. They are partially hidden by added structures and are used by Connie's Canine Timberline Etc.

Driving south today from Versailles to Gravois Mills along Old Five Road and then Route TT, it is hard to believe that so many roadside businesses once existed along this stretch of road. Even the buildings that once housed them are mostly gone.

Drum Rock *(Morgan County)* -

Drum Rock is a small island of rock in the Lake near the 6.5-mile mark on the Osage Arm. It sets about 20 feet from the shore to the left of the mouth of the Gravois Arm and rises six to eight feet above the 660-foot level of the Lake. It is round in shape viewed on a northeast by southwest axis or more oval north to south, and is about 10 to 12 feet in diameter.

Drum Rock appears to have two layers of rock due to a groove at mid-point where a prominent bedding plane [horizontal meeting point between two strata of

Drum Rock Island, *Osage Arm, Circa. 1940s. Photo by Hammond & Irwin.*

bedrock] is located. A rusted steel cable, which appears to have been in place for many years, cinches the rock at the horizontal groove. Who placed the cable and for what purpose is not generally known. A linen postcard of Drum Rock was produced during the 1940s by the Corwin News Agency of Jefferson City, Missouri, from a photograph taken by Hammond and Irwin of the Missouri Department of Resources and Development. The colorful postcard shows two women sitting on top of the rock, which was called a "Picturesque Island" by the postcard producer.

Dry Branch Cave *(Rocky Mount, Morgan County)* -

Dry Branch Cave is one of the better known caves of Morgan County and has a total length of about 1,300 feet. It is a habitat for endangered bats. The cave entrance is 80 feet wide, 15 feet high and the floor area is muddy and wet in places.

Dry Branch Cave has an active stream and numerous crawlways that must be negotiated to follow its passageways to their end. Bat guano can be found throughout the cave.

The cave's entrance passage contains three natural bridges. The 300-foot-long Formation Passage, once very attractive but long since ruined by vandals and souvenir hunters, ends in a 20-foot dome room.

The cave's Breakdown Passage is 600 feet long and has a floor area littered with breakdown boulders.

In the 1890s and early 1900s, a dance floor was present near the cave entrance and the site was the scene of many Saturday night dances with a generous amount of drinking and fighting. Eventually, a knife and gun fight resulted in the death of one participant and the dance hall operation was closed. During the time the dance hall was in operation, people were allowed to take self-guided tours of the cave.

Duck Hunting on the Lake 1932 -

As the narratives in this book indicate, the top outdoor sporting activities at Lake of the Ozarks in its pioneer decades were fishing and hunting. Walleye and bass were the reigning prizes for fishermen while ducks were the focus of hunters, even though the resort operators championed all types of game including deer, wild turkey, squirrel, rabbit, quail, possum, raccoon and fox.

The Lake was less than a year old when speculation began about duck hunting. "Will the Lake of the Ozarks prove a wintering ground for the ducks in the future? We believe it will prove to be the case," said the editor of the *Lake of the Ozarks News* in February 1932.

Until the creation of the Lake, sportsmen said there was no large body of water in this part of the Midwest available for ducks.

Walter Steininger of the Osage Development Company said there were many ducks in a wide variety in the Osage Beach district even in the early part of 1932. He contemplated sowing suitable feed such as wild rice to attract ducks. He suggested that every camp and resort establish a feeding ground for ducks. "The cost for each resort or club site or hotel, also tourist camps, would be small and the money and effort expended, would, beyond a doubt, bring more ducks..." he said.

The first big organized duck hunting promotion for the Lake began in October 1932. The season opened at Noon on Oct. 16, and ran to sundown on Dec. 15. "In anticipation of a worthwhile duck shooting season" said the promoters, "resort owners everywhere are preparing blinds, training decoys, seeing to the necessary preparations for the occasion..." *Duck Pages*, a form of advertising, began appearing in local newspapers. Resorts supporting the campaign advertised on the pages in the following way:

Chatterton's Hurricane Deck Rental Cottages, 23 miles south of Versailles, Mo. on No. 5 -- every accommodation for duck hunters; **Lake Center Resort**, Q. O. Hunter, Damsel, Mo. -- cabins, boats, blinds, guides, ammunition and supplies; **Pla-Port Modern Cottages**, Zebra, Mo. -- rooms, dining service, blinds, decoys, guides, ideally located; **Two Waters Resort**, 12 miles south of Versailles on No. 5 -- cabins, boats, blinds; **Rocky Mount Hunting & Fishing Resort**, 16 miles southwest of Eldon, Mo. -- cabins, boats, blinds, decoys, guides; **Shady Slope Camp** on Hwy. 54 south [Grand] Glaize Bridge -- cabins, boats, blinds, decoys, guides; **Indian Creek Resort**, Barnett, Mo. -- cabins, blinds, boats, groceries, ammunition; **Brill's Hill Resort**, Warsaw, Mo. -- cabins, boats, blinds, decoys, guides, protected territory; **Art Luck's Hunting & Fishing Resort** on Hwy. 54 -- cabins, boats, guides, blinds, live decoys; **Coffman Beach Resort**, Shelida Hill, 14 miles southwest of Eldon, Mo. -- cabins, boats, blinds, decoys, guides.

The First Annual Duck Shoot at Lake of the Ozarks proved to be a big drawing card said the *Lake of the Ozarks News* early in January 1933. "The cold snap that hit the Lake region a week ago, put a crimp in the fisherman's fingers and he has deserted the shoreline, but not so with the duck hunter. This fellow blazed away up to the last minute and he reported many fine bags for the last days of the season.

Duck Blind on Lake of the Ozarks. *Photo by H. D. Weaver, 2004.*

"The 60-day duck shoot on the Big Lake made itself felt as a drawing power and resort owners at every point feel it will be an annual event of much merit."

Today, the top sporting events at the Lake seem to be bass fishing and recreational boating. Very little is heard in the media about duck hunting. Nevertheless, it still occurs on a modest scale in a few isolated areas of the Lake and a few permanent duck blinds can still be found along the shoreline of Lake of the Ozarks.

Duckworth's Camp *(Hastain, Benton County)* -

In 1935, J. W. Duckworth established Duckworth's Camp on Deer Creek just up from the head of Deer Creek Hollow Cove, which enters the Lake at the74-mile mark. The camp was off LkRd. V-22 out of Hastain.

Duckworth's cabins did not have running water or electricity at the beginning but he did have a dining room where people could eat. He charged $1.50 per day for a cabin. By 1939 his cabins were furnished and had electricity and water. He also had boats for rent, a bait and tackle shop and could provide access to "competent" fishing guides.

There were two caves near his camp. One day some local boys decided to explore one of the caves. As they crawled about in the maze of passageways, their lights died and they were unable to find their way out in the cave's total darkness. Roy Drenon, a native of Hastain, rescued the boys. He said that before he arrived, other men who tried to rescue the boys had used two trot lines tied together to mark their way back into the cave for several hundred feet but had failed to locate the boys. After this incident, the cave was called Lost Boys Cave.

The cave's second name -- Booger Allen Cave -- also relates to this same incident. One far-fetched tale told about the misadventures of the boys claims that one boy was so frightened by the experience that he lost his mind, hence the word "booger" in Booger Allen Cave. The word "booger" has several meanings among them being hobgoblin or frightening apparition.

Duckworth's Camp appears to have ceased operation sometime in the late 1960s.

Ad from the 1939 Vacation in the Heart of Missouri, Lake of the Ozarks, presented by the Lake of the Ozarks Association.

E. R. Smith Ice Plant *(Lake Ozark, Miller County)* -

The E. R. Smith Ice Plant was built on the Bagnell Dam Strip in Lake Ozark in the mid 1930s. It was located just west of the White House Hotel. What distinguished Smith's structure from others on The Strip was the water tank on top of the building on which was painted in large block letters "Welcome to Lake Ozark."

E. R. Smith's Ice Plant, *Lake Ozark, MO, Circa. 1930s. Photographer Unknown.*

Easterville *(Linn Creek, Camden County)* -

Linn Creek is located two miles northeast of Camdenton where Hwy. 54 crosses Linn Creek Hollow. The town is approximately three miles from the historic confluence of Linn Creek with the Osage River at the 31-mile mark on the Osage Arm. The town site of Old Linn Creek, now inundated, was one mile up Linn Creek Hollow from this confluence.

When Lake of the Ozarks was formed, most residents from the old town relocated either to the site of Camdenton or to the site of present day Linn Creek, a site originally called Easterville. The property upon which the town was built was formerly the Easter farm. Although no record of an official post office named Easterville has been found for this site, local folklore insists that there was a post office named Easterville. It is said that the residents of the village, in an effort to capitalize on the fate of Old Linn Creek, changed the name to Linn Creek around 1930 to encourage former residents of Old Linn Creek to settle there. Many of the people not only relocated to this site but also had their houses moved to what then became briefly known as New Linn Creek [now just Linn Creek].

Ebert's Beach Resort *(Camdenton, Camden County)* -

Ebert's Beach Resort was established about 1942 at the end of what was then LkRd. 5-33, later designated 5-78 and now called Owens Point Road. The resort was on the north side of Barnes Hollow Cove at its mouth. This location is at the 5-mile mark on the Niangua Arm and about 2.5 miles from the Hwy. 5 Niangua Bridge.

When Ebert's Beach Resort was built, it had two neighboring resorts -- Brownie's Camp and Kenniston's Singing Hills Resort. Through the 1950s, Ebert's advertised complete fishing services, a covered fishing dock, a concrete launching ramp, marked crappie beds, and a safe sand beach excellent for children. The resort promoted strongly to families. In 1968, this business became the Blue Dolphin Resort operated by Marty and Betty Ernst. The Blue Dophin Resort is still in operation.

Echo Valley Camp *(Rocky Mount, Morgan County)* -

The mouth of Lick Branch Cove is located at the 5-mile mark on the Osage Arm. The cove, which stretches northward for a distance of two miles, is reached by either LkRd. W-12 [Jade Road to Jones Drive], or LkRd. Y-13 [Red Arrow Road to Jones Drive].

Three camps were developed along the east side of Lick Branch Cove by 1938 -- Echo Valley Camp, Cooper's Camp and Lillibridge Camp.

Echo Valley Camp was built in 1936-37 by I. T. Gambrel and his wife from Saskatechwan, Canada. It opened to the public in September 1937. They continued building stone cottages through 1937 and into 1938 until they had 10 or 12 cottages. The resort had 171 acres of which 16 were Lake frontage. Echo Valley Camp outlived both of the other resorts and continued in operation until the early 1970s.

Edgewater Beach Resort *(Lake Ozark, Miller County)* -

Edgewater Beach Resort, the closest resort to Bagnell Dam at its west end, was the first resort to be established on the Bagnell Dam Strip. It has benefited from being on the Lake shore and on The Strip simultaneously; its north side is on the Lake and its south side borders Bus. Hwy. 54 in Lake Ozark.

The resort was built in 1939-1940 by Harry Thomas of Chicago and operated by his daughter, Betty, and her husband, Harry Rackow.

In 1945, the resort was sold to Mike and Clara Dean from Beavercrossing, Nebraska. Their son, Bill, fresh out of military service, joined the operation the same year.

Bill Dean's Edgewater Fleet, *Lake Ozark, MO, Circa. 1950. Photographer Unknown.*

He later married Shirley, the daughter of Glenn and Francis Cromer of Osage Beach. The Cromer's had a grocery store in Osage Beach and also operated a novelty shop and the Wayside Pottery Shop in the complex of buildings on Harry Frack's Acre. Harry Frack was Francis Cromer's step father-in-law.

After Shirley married Bill, they operated the Edgewater Beach Boat Dock. By the early 1950s, the resort had 18 rustic, housekeeping cottages on the resort's wooded 5-acre tract. Advertisements said the resort had "one-half mile of rustic Ozark rock walls, patios and terraces." Bill, noted for his interest in high quality, fast boats, advertised "the fastest speed boats on the Lake and 40-mile excursion trips daily."

The Dean family retained ownership of the resort until 1994 when it was sold to Larry and Sandy Hill. The resort now has both individual one-room cottages and a condo section as well as basic motel accommodations. While many changes have occurred, the office building that a guest sees upon driving into the resort looks very much like it did 50 years ago, preserving some of the resort's architectural heritage.

El Donna Motel / Eldon Inn *(Eldon, Miller County)* -

El Donna Motel, now called the Eldon Inn, is located on Bus. Hwy. 54 at the north edge of Eldon. It was built in 1953 and owned by Bill Raynor. Connie Stewart was the first manager. The motel began with 29 rooms in two separate sections with a large courtyard complete with swimming pool and playground between the two buildings.

El Donna Motel was an award-winning roadside business and in 1959 was nationally recognized by the Duncan Hines Company as an outstanding lodging place. At the time of the award, the motel was owned and operated by the Louis Gerharts. As time passed, a residential unit was built at the west end of the motel portion that fronts the highway. A covered breezeway between the two buildings was constructed so that guests could drive up and be protected from inclement weather as they checked in and out of the motel. In 2001, new owners, Ed and MaryAnn Allen, changed the name of the motel to the Eldon Inn.

El Kay Motel *(Camdenton, Camden County)* -

El Kay Motel began life as Lake Fork Heights, which was established on Hwy. 5 about 1946, six miles north of the Camdenton square and just north of LkRd. 5-78. The business is on the west side of the highway [see Lake Fork Heights]

Lake Fork Heights was sold to El & Kay Nance about 1960 and they renamed it El Kay Motel. The Nances advertised having new deluxe housekeeping cottages and motel units as well as a new, heated, filtered swimming pool. The cottages had been air-conditioned. These owners began taking advantage of their spectacular view of the Lake and put the phrase "At the $1,000,000 view of Lake of the Ozarks" into their ads. They apparently did not operate a cafe on the grounds, as had former owners, but directed visitors to cafes nearby.

In 1965 or 1966, El Kay Motel was sold to Gerry & Thomas Robb and was operated by these individuals until the late 1970s. The Robbs put the following

***El Kay Motel** Buildings, Circa. 1940s. Photo by H. D. Weaver, 2005.*

phrase into their ads: "Enjoy a breathtaking panoramic view overlooking the Lake and then ride in comfort on our electric lift to the Lake and our covered boat dock." The view from the motel's lofty location 260 feet above the 4-mile mark on the Niangua Arm is spectacular [see front cover of this book]. Apparently, Thomas Robb began selling real estate about 1974 and operated his El Kay Real Estate business out of the El Kay Motel office.

In 1984, the motel was sold to Lloyd & Ilse Fuller of Camdenton who owned and operated the combination motel and mobile home park until 2005 when they sold to the current owners, Susan & Richard Kuhn.

The Kuhn's, who appreciate the historical character of the old lodging place, are upgrading the property and preserving two of the original buildings -- a two-story stone dwelling that houses several vintage guest rental units, and one of the original stone cottages. They have removed the old electric lift that took guests from the ridge down to the boat docks and replaced it with a road. They have also improved the adjacent mobile home park that is part of the business.

El Rancho of the Ozarks *(Eldon, Miller County)* -

El Rancho of the Ozarks, a motel, service station and convenience store combination, was located at the junction of Hwys. 54 & 52 about three miles south of Eldon from 1946 until the 1990s. A Phillips 66 gas station, convenience store and truck stop now stands where the El Rancho gas station and swimming pool used to be. Heritage Inn & Suites occupies property across from where the El Rancho cottages once stood. Only an old well house remains from the original structures of El Rancho of the Ozarks.

The El Rancho business property was previously known as Musser's Ozark Resort, which was built in 1936 [see Musser's Ozark Tavern]. The Musser business was sold to Jefferson W. and Sylvia J. Mitchell in 1945. They in turn sold to the partnership of James Lawrence, James Hannaford and Francis Biselx in 1946. The three men had just completed their tour of duty during World War II. The new partners changed the name to El Rancho of the Ozarks, a name which, in turn lent the name "El Rancho" to the junction of the two highways. Few people today who've lived in area for more than 15 years, know the junction by any other name.

Portions of the formerly extensive business property was also owned by the Phillips Petroleum Company of Kansas City who sublet their portions of it to the new partners. The property included more than 60 acres on both sides of Hwy. 54 and 52. The service station, swimming pool, and convenience store was along the west side of Hwy. 54 and individual cottages were on the opposite side of the highway.

***El Rancho of the Ozarks,** Jct. Hwys. 54 & 52 South of Eldon. Photo by L. L. Cook, Milwaukee.*

In 1950, Hannaford sold his interest to Biselx and Lawrence. In 1961, James and Martha Lawrence became the sole owners of El Rancho of the Ozarks. Martha Lawrence died in 1992 and shortly thereafter Jim Lawrence retired and sold the business.

El Rancho was noted for the elegance and charm of its brick cottages and its popular swimming pool, which attracted not only motel guests but local people. The business had its own deep well with a water tower that became a landmark for people traveling west on Hwy. 54 toward Lake of the Ozarks.

Eldon *(Miller County)* -

The early history of Eldon is the tale of two small, adjacent, competing villages -- Eldon and Aurora Springs. The latter lost its bid for prosperity and longevity through a series of misfortunes and was eventually absorbed by Eldon [see Aurora Springs].

A post office was opened at the site of Eldon in 1881, a year before George Weeks platted the town and supposedly named it after a British Lord, which makes one suspicious of the folklore surrounding the naming of Eldon. There are two legends -- one, that Weeks wanted to name it Almira after his wife but chose Eldon instead because he heard that another Missouri town was already named Almira; and two, that it was named for a railroad surveyor. Interestingly, a search of post office records shows no town in Missouri by the name Almira before 1887. Since the town's early history and the demise of Aurora Springs are both strongly linked to the coming of the Missouri Pacific Railroad in 1881, the second legend sounds more logical. If true, it would not be the only town north of the Osage River whose name originated with the railroad. An interesting narrative on the naming of Eldon can be read in *Missouri Roadsides, The Traveler's Companion* by Bill Earngey [University of Missouri Press, 1995].

In 1903, the town got a second railroad when the Rock Island designated Eldon a division point, built tracks through town on their east to west course, and established a roundhouse and some shops. In 1912, an impressive Frisco Railroad Depot was constructed and quickly became the focal point of the growing town's business community.

Eldon, MO, *Looking South on Main Street, Circa. 1930s. Photo by Blair Cedar Novelty.*

Eldon prospered from tourists following the construction of Bagnell Dam in 1931 but also relied upon farming and small industry. In 1931 the town had a population of 3, 171. The downtown was lit by a "White-Way" street lighting system. The city had issued 601 auto licenses. There was morning and evening mail delivery, the town got its water from deep wells, and a new City Hall was under construction.

Eldon had two banks in 1931. There were mercantile stores and auto salesrooms. The town boasted of having one of the finest department stores in Central Missouri. There were two hardware stores, two lumberyards, two jewelry stores, two drug stores, many shops and cafes and four hotels. The James House was well known among traveling businessmen for its meals.

The local industry included an overall factory, steam laundry, ice plant, bottling works, two bakeries, greenhouse, and shops in the elegant Rock Island Depot. The farming community had a dairy industry and strawberry and grape growing associations.

In 1931, Eldon had a weekly newspaper and an art-craft printing shop equipped for commercial printing. There were numerous civic organizations and a variety of churches. In addition, there were two movie theaters and two miniature golf courses -- the Down-Town and the Pla-Mor.

In 1931, Eldon erected a welcoming sign along Hwy. 54 at the north edge of town, declaring itself to be a "Gateway to Lake of the Ozarks." [The welcome sign is still present along the highway but no longer says "Gateway" although maps of the town produced by the Chamber of Commerce use the phrase "Gateway to the Ozarks."]

By 1950 the town's business leaders estimated that 20 percent of the money spent in Eldon came from the tourist trade. Thousands of cars flowed through Eldon on weekends and holidays with families bound for Lake of the Ozarks. In 1953 the town had 10 restaurants, two hotels and eight motels along with a tourist attraction called Tom's Monkey Jungle.

Eldon's tourist trade suffered some after new highway construction along Hwy. 54 bypassed the town in the 1970s, leaving Eldon on Bus. Hwy. 54, but the town continues to prosper in other ways and has a current population of about 4,500.

Eldon, MO, *Circa. 1940s. Photo by L. L. Cook, Milwaukee.*

Fish Haven Camp / Resort *(Lake Ozark, Miller County)* -

Fish Haven Camp, built in 1931, was the first camp to be established on the Osage River just below Bagnell Dam. It was located along the south bank of the river approximately three-quarters of a mile from the dam.

Early ads for Fish-Haven used a hyphen in the name. The word "camp" was used for several decades before being changed to "resort." Early on, the business was promoted as the "only resort located below the dam. Good river or lake fishing." Being able to use this phrase in advertising ended in the mid 1950s when Charlie's Resort, which later became Golden Rule Resort, was also built along the river below the dam. Charlie's Resort was about 1,500 feet further downstream.

Fish Haven Camp had small cottages and most were frame although the resort did have at least one, two-story rock cottage built on the hillside facing the dam. The two levels were separate rental units as the text on a 1944 Fish Haven linen postcard

Fish Haven Camp, *Lake Ozark, MO, Circa. 1950s. Photographer Unknown.*

that was mailed home by a fisherman said: "This is a real pretty place. We have a cabin on the hillside. It is a two-story...and we have the lower half."

Jacob [Jake] Gier, a long-time resident of Miller County who helped clear the basin when Bagnell Dam was under construction, built most of the cottages and other structures at Fish Haven Camp. The camp was a strong competitor for business for more than 50 years. In the late 1960s, under the ownership and management of Mr. & Mrs. Roy Smith, Fish Haven acquired an enviable reputation for the enjoyment people had fishing from the resort's Catamaran, which had Coast Guard-approved pilots. To reach the camp, guests used Lk.Rd. 54-19, now officially named Fish Haven Road. The camp no longer exists.

Flanders Cave *(Eldon, Miller County)* -

Flanders Cave was the second cave in the Lake area to be opened to the public after the completion of the dam. It was preceded only by Jacob's Cave south of Versailles, which opened in 1932.

Flanders Cave is located north of Bagnell Dam about one mile east of Hwy. 54, off what was originally called the "Old Bagnell Road." The cave is less than one mile southwest of Stark Caverns.

In November 1923, W. L. Cox of Chillicothe and James Pruitt, upon whose farm the cave was located, began preparing the cave for public visitation. "The cave," said a 1932 news story, "is in its natural state within and the management will have the beautiful display of stalagmites and stalactites protected so that they cannot be broken off and carried away as has been done in Aurora Cave [Stark Caverns]. The opening is enlarged so visitors may enter without inconvenience of crawling... Only recently was the cave named Flanders from the resemblance of the first elevation inside to Flanders Cemetery hillside in France."

While enlarging the entrance, Pruitt and Cox found barite and spar crystals containing lead and zinc. Pruitt discovered the cave about 1902 less than 100 yards from his father's house. The tract upon which the cave is located dates to 1853 when the land was entered by John Davenport.

Flanders Cave was officially opened to the public on May 14, 1933. W. L. Cox announced the opening with a novel incentive for people to visit. He said that a $5 prize would be given to anyone who visited the cave each month and who then wrote the best letter telling of the wonderful sights to be seen in the cave. He added that the more detailed the letter, the greater the chance a person had of winning the prize and that the prize would be offered on a monthly basis. During the Depression days of the early 1930s, $5 was a considerable sum of money. Since the adult admission price was only 50 cents, it would have taken quite a few ticket sales to pay for the promotion, meet operation costs and still earn a profit. We have no way of knowing how successful the offer was but the cave remained open to the public until 1942, when it closed. It was never reopened.

Only the first 250 feet of the cave passage was shown to the public. It was necessary for Cox and Pruitt to trench the streambed to gain sufficient headroom for visitors along the first half of the commercial trail. The main passage meanders considerably with an intermittent upper level. All of the cave formations are located in the portion of the cave shown to the public and while not outstanding, do offer variety. The cave has a length of about 800 feet and toward the end is the largest room in the cave, called the Boulder Room. It is about 35 feet long, 20 feet wide and 15 feet high. The floor of the room is littered with huge slabs and boulders of bedrock.

Fleetwood Lodge & Boat Dock *(Lake Ozark, Miller County)* -

Charles "Charley" Fleetwood and his wife arrived at Lake Ozark during the final days of the construction of Bagnell Dam. They assumed occupancy of the first building south of the dam and watched the lakebed fill with water.

Charley joined the old State Game and Fish Department as a conservation agent in 1932 and remained in that capacity until 1946. He became widely known among sportsmen, and his boat -- Lucky Fleet -- was a familiar craft upon the Lake, particularly the Gravois Arm.

The Fleetwoods built a camp along the south bank of the east fork of Jennings Branch Cove. They named the camp Fleetwood Lodge & Boat Dock, and referred to their boats as "Fleetwood's Fleet." They referred to their fork of Jennings Branch Cove as Fleetwood's Cove, for at that time there were no other resorts on the cove. Even today, most maps do not show a name for this cove although it was generally called "Paradise Cove" after Holsman's Paradise Beach Resort was established in the early 1950s. Now it is being called Castaway Cove.

The Oak Royal Water Ski Show, later called the Ozark Water Ski Thrill Show, also performed in this cove during the 1960s and 70s. Tex Bemis, owner of the ski show, often referred to the setting as "Paradise Cove."

In 1948, a local newspaper article reported that "it was from this camp [Fleetwood's Lodge] that the first passenger boat service was inaugurated on the Lake," although this overlooks the fact that Union Electric inaugurated passenger boat service when they launched their excursion boat service from the Union Electric Bathing Pavilion and Excursion Boat Dock at the west end of Bagnell Dam in 1933.

Fleetwood was bold in his advertising with "fish guaranteed, try us!" and "free and accurate fishing information gladly given." Charley Fleetwood settled only for the best boats of his day and became a distributor for Chris-Craft. He kept only the latest models in his fleet. The resort offered speedboat rides, cruiser trips and boat storage. Mrs. Fleetwood handled the boat excursion business and she is said to have been the first woman on the Lake and in Missouri to obtain a Coast Guard-approved pilots license for commercial watercraft.

In 1948, the Fleetwoods sold the resort and their home, which was in the Arrowhead Beach subdivision, to Mr. & Mrs. Louis Ackerman of Chicago. The excursion boat service crew and docks were moved to the shoreline behind the Lakeside Casino Restaurant. Fleetwood's Lodge later became known as Bruner's Camp.

Flood of 1943 -

Early floods on the Osage River, in the days before Bagnell Dam, were always measured by how high the water rose at Tuscumbia, the county seat of Miller County. The flood of 1844 reached 42.2 feet above flood stage at Tuscumbia. The flood of 1895 was recorded at 39.0 feet. The flood in the spring of 1922 reached 37.7 feet. No one expected the flood in the spring of 1943 to reach 48.5 feet.

This record flood was occasioned by a very wet spring and record rainfalls upon the Osage River watershed. It became the most serious flood to date in Bagnell Dam's history. It was so serious, in fact, that a force of more than 500 men, many of them soldiers and army engineers from Fort Leonard Wood in Pulaski County, were needed to keep the water from inundating the machinery in the dam's powerhouse section. World War II was raging and the electricity being generated by the dam was needed for the war industry factories in St. Louis.

By May 1943, the water in the Lake stood at 4.5 feet above the 660 full reservoir level. The water had reached within four feet of the top of the dam on the Lake side. Downstream from Bagnell Dam, at Bagnell, houses and businesses were inundated. In Bagnell Flats north of the dam, water stood eight feet deep over Hwy. 54.

On May 20, soldiers arrived from Fort Leonard Wood to help place sandbags to protect the dam from the back-flow of water. With all the floodgates wide open, the water rushed into the river below the dam faster than it could be carried away and this caused a back-flow that threatened to inundate the power plant. Some of the electricity being generated by the power plant was going through transmission lines that were actually submerged a short distance down-river from the dam. The power to those lines was shut down.

A significant problem faced by the men stacking sandbags and trying to protect the powerhouse was the huge amount of driftwood and other organic debris in the water. With all 12 spillway gates wide open, there was no way to prevent huge masses of debris from making the plunge and then resurfacing in the mad boil and torrents of water below the dam. Giant logs shot to the surface of the boiling water as if fired from cannon, and acted like montrous battering rams against the sandbag walls. They terrorized the sandbag workers.

Flood of 1943, Bagnell Dam, *Lake Ozark, MO. Photo courtesy of AmerenUE.*

At its peak, more than 240,000 cubic feet of water per second was passing through the gates, including entangled masses of debris and entire trees. The dam itself was not in any danger but the rise in the water below the dam caused the water to lap at the power generating equipment. The roof over the machines was awash for days and the 52 ventilating windows just below the roof had to be bulkheaded. A dike 500 feet long, 5 feet high, and 11 feet thick had to be built of sandbags.

Flood of 1943, Bagnell Dam, *Lake Ozark, MO. Photo courtesy of AmerenUE.*

Although U. S. Army Engineers were assisting in the work, a call was sent out for carpenters employed at Fort Leonard Wood and at the Army Air Force Base at Knob Noster. Civilian carpenters in Lebanon, Waynesville and Springfield also responded to the call, working with water streaming at them through the outside bulkheads. Fifty-seven carpenters placed inside supports for the bulkheads in 15 hours. They were soaked to the skin all of that time but they stemmed the flow of water so the pumps could carry it away. Calls were constantly going out for additional help because the work had to go on around the clock with no break. About 200 additional men responded including students from the Rolla School of Mines. More than 1,000 tons of sand was started to the dam, some of it from as far away as St. Louis. Other sand came from dumps of the Missouri State Highway Commission and the recreational area at Kaiser. Constant vigilance had to be maintained to keep the heavy diftwood from battering in the window bulkheads and from washing away the sandbags. Dikes had to be rebuilt again and again.

The great number of men involved in this effort were fed and sustained by the people of the Lake community, especially those of Lake Ozark.

Most of the cabin camps and hotels were filled with workers and the problem of feeding the men was solved when the women of the community went to work in nearby restaurants that were unable to get help quickly enough. The women made an average of 1,500 sandwiches and gallons of coffee each night in addition to the regular meals served. The problem of obtaining supplies was a material one because war rationing was still in effect. The Missouri State Highway Patrol at one pont radioed Lebanon for bread and sandwich meats to tide over an emergency and the sheriff of Lebanon routed merchants out of bed in the early morning hours to accommodate the workers at the dam.

The great flood of 1943 was a full week of hell but the powerhouse machinery was saved and did not have to be shut down. It was a flood to remember.

Folded Hills Dining Room *(Osage Beach, Camden County)* -

The Folded Hills Dining Room was once located along Hwy. 54 in Osage Beach at the junction of LkRd. 54-10, later designated 54-24 and now called Osage Beach Road. It was in a building formerly housing Cannady's Cafe, which was established in 1933. The Cannady's sold the building to Dot and Harvey Garvey in the 1940s and they renamed the cafe the Folded Hills Dining Room. It was an attractive building with a steeply pitched roof having red shingles. The siding was light blue and the windows had red- and dark-blue- striped awnings over them.

The Garvey's sold the building about 1960, it was again renovated, given a veneer of red brick, and became the Osage Beach Post Office.

The post office used the building until about 1965 when the post office moved to a new building at the corner of LkRd. 54-29.

F. C. Arnold Realty acquired the red brick building in the 1970s and opened Arnold's Gift Shop [later called Arnold's Country Corner], which closed in early 2005. This building and several adjacent buildings were demolished in the spring of 2005. [see Cannady's Cafe & Grocery Store]

Folded Hills Dining Room, *Osage Beach, MO, Circa. 1940s. Photographer Unknown.*

Forrester's Beach Resort *(Osage Beach, Camden County)* -

The story of Forrester's Beach Resort, which was built in 1932 on Darby Cove at the end of LkRd. 54-17A, later designated 54-43 and now called Forrester's Beach Road [at the 19.2-mile mark on the Osage Arm] is also the story of a skilled architect -- Thomas H. Forrester, Jr. Some people called him Tom but his parents and best friends called him Tommy.

Tom was born in 1904, the son of Thomas Senior and Ida May Forrester of St. Louis. He attended Westminister College in Fulton, Missouri, and then Washington University in St. Louis where he earned his degree in architectural engineering. A few years later he assisted in the design of Bagnell Dam and as soon as Lake of the Ozarks was formed, he began designing cottages and summer homes for people who owned Lake property. Rustic buildings made of native materials were popular in the 1930s and 40s and Tom specialized in rustic designs.

At about the same time, Tom bought land bordering Darby Cove just west of the Grand Glaize Bridge and began building cottages for his own resort, as well as summer homes in and about Zebra [Osage Beach], which he put up for sale. One such home was a two-story cobblestone house, which he sold for $2,500.

In the spring of 1932, L. A. Kelly, who had purchased the old Zebra property at the end of LkRd. 54-30 or Red Bud-Lighthouse Road, hired Tom to build his Pla-Port Resort cottages and lighthouse. The Pla-Port Lighthouse would come to stand upon Observation Heights overlooking the confluence of the Osage and Grand Glaize Arms, and become a local landmark.

Although Forrester advertised some in local newspapers, most of his business came by word of mouth and his reputation earned him the unofficial title of the "Lake Architect."

Tom opened Forrester's Beach Resort in late 1932, offering all the comforts and amenities of the best resorts then at the Lake for rates of $1.50 to $5.00 per day. His cottages were large and made of a mixture of native materials including stone,

Forrester's Beach Resort, *Osage Beach, Mo, Circa. 1933. Photographer Unknown.*

log and frame. By the 1940s, the resort had a large two-story lodge designed for convention groups. He advertised a "pavilion for sun lounging, safe sand beach and playground for children."

By 1954, Forrester's Beach Resort was under new ownership. Al & Vera Rieder chose to keep the name Forrester Beach. In the 1960s, the resort sold again, this time to Bill and Del Ulkus. And in 1967, sold for a third time and became Te-To-Bo Resort & Motel. This resort no longer exists.

Tom's wife, Helen R. [Rockwell], who he married in 1947, died Aug. 14, 1984. Tom lived to the age of 91 and died Feb. 8, 1996. He and his wife are buried in the Conway Cemetery in Osage Beach.

Forth View Resort / Marine *(Hastain, Edwards, Benton County)* -

When this Benton County lakeshore business was established in the early 1930s by G. J. Forth, the name "Forthview" was spelled as two words and it was called Forth View Camp. The camp is located off Hwy. 7 at the end of LkRd. M-26. Route M is 2.1 miles west of Edwards on Hwy 7 or 5.5 miles east of Hwy. 65 on Hwy. 7.

G. J. Forth built eight cabins for which he charged $1.50 to $4.00 per day rental. He also had a store and gas station. Advertising stated that his camp had a capacity for 30 people and he promoted fishing and swimming in both the Lake and Deer Creek.

When Forth sold the camp in the 1950s, the new owners-- Gordon Jones and H. L. Davis -- kept the original name and modified the spelling so that "Forth View" became one word.

During the first few years of the camp's operation, Forth advertised in promotional materials published by the Lake of the Ozarks Association but ceased doing so by the 1940s. In contrast, the other resort on Deer Creek Cove -- Duckworth's Camp -- continued to advertise and many maps published through the years by the Lake of the Ozarks Association and the Headwater's Association, showed only Duckworth's Camp on Deer Creek Cove. Ironically, Duckworth's Camp closed in the late 1960s and never reopened but Forthview continued in operation and is still open to the public, now as Forthview Resort & Marine.

Frack's Acre *(Osage Beach, Camden County)* -

In the mid 1930s, Harry Frack bought an acre of wooded land along Hwy. 54 in the heart of Osage Beach. The acre fronted the highway along the south side about halfway between today's Bluff Drive and Jo-Jo Lane.

"His friends all thought that he was crazy or something to buy just a strip of woods," said his wife in the late 1950s. But Harry envisioned a busy road in the days ahead. On that acre he put up some of the most interesting and unique building to be seen in the Lake area in his day. He named his complex of businesses "Frack's Acre." After buying the land, Harry told his friends that he was going to put as many businesses on that acre as possible and proceeded to do just that.

Frack's Acre & The Wayside Pottery Shop, *Osage Beach, MO, Circa. 1940s. Photographer Unknown.*

At the west end, he built a small white frame building that became the Frack Barber Shop. At the east end he created a rustic rock building with a pure "hillbilly" look to it. It became the Wayside Shoppe selling Ozark pottery both wholesale and retail.

Between the Wayside Shoppe and the Barber Shop, were three bildings, two of which had large arches at the front facing the highway and the arches were anchored to native rock pillars. One of these buidings became Cromer's Meat Markt and Grocery [Baby Beef Market], and the other housed Frack's Cafe. Between these two buildings was a smaller building where ice could be purchased and cold storage was available. Harry sometimes referred to his operation as "Frack's Garden" but most generally as "Frack's Acre."

One of the items of merchandise that Harry added to Frack's Acre, which caught the eye of passing tourists, were miniature lighthouses. They were sold at the Wayside Shoppe and also became part of its ornate, folk-art architecture. Harry's wife was particularly fond of lighthouses.

In the early 1950s, the Wayside Shoppe building, which had been an open building without conventional windows and a standard doorway, was remodeled so the building could be secured during the hours when the shop was not open and less vulnerable to inclement weather. It took on a more conventional look but its walls still had much of their unique native rock character. It then became Otto's Gift Shop.

After Harry's death, his widow continued Frack's Acre for a number of years. The buildings of Frack's Acre no longer exist but old postcards preserve the images of this one-of-a-kind Osage Beach memory.

Frank's Resort / Motel / Peaceful Valley Hatchery *(Osage Beach, Camden County; Lake Ozark, Miller County)* -

In 1934, Frank and Margaret Frudeger of Des Moines, Iowa, moved to the Lake and built Frank's Resort near the end of LkRd. 10A, later designated 54-24 and now called Osage Beach Road. Frank, an avid fisherman, became the resorts "expert fishing guide."

In 1946, the Frudegers closed their Osage Beach resort and moved to Lake Ozark where they built a new Frank's Resort close to where Christ the King Lutheran Church stands today along Bus. Hwy. 54 just north of Hidden Acres Road. They made a road to the Lake behind the cottages and created a shallow swimming beach and a dock with boats. Their ads hinted at some problem wth unauthorized use of their beach facilities because the old ads say "beach for customers only."

Resorts that came to be neighbors while the Frudegers were there included Oak Hill Resort and Mountain Terrace Resort on their side of the highway, and Rockwood Court on the other side of the highway.

In 1958, the Frudegers sold the resort property and moved west along Hwy. 54 to a site just southwest of Orchid Motel and just northwest of the Miller-Camden County line. Their new locaton was on a short road that has since been named Frudeger Road.

At first they had some accommodations for tourists and advertised their new place as Frank's Motel. This operation was apparently unsatisfactory. By 1962 it had become Frank's Minnows. By 1964, it was Frank's Peaceful Valley Hatchery. Frank also worked at Missouri Aquarium, which used to be located just south of the current location of Lake Ozark McDonald's and LkRd. 54-10 or Hidden Acres Road. Frank died in 1971. Margaret died in 1994.

Frank's Resort, *Osage Beach, MO, Circa. 1930s. Photographer Unknown.*

Gladstone *(Laurie, Morgan County)* -

The old town site of Gladstone was inundated by Lake of the Ozarks in 1931. It was on the Gravois Arm at the mouth of Gladstone Cove at the 3-mile mark where Mill Creek joined Big Gravois Creek. The town once sat on the south bank of the Big Gravois, a site now beneath 70 feet of water.

The Gladstone Post Office was opened in 1886 but settlement in the vicinity of Gladstone began in 1820 when William Poor built his home on a hill overlooking the creek about half a mile from the confluence of Mill Creek and the Big Gravois. In 1865, Peter Sidebottom bought the Poor property and the house stood until well beyond the year 1900. Peter died in 1909 and his wife, Emeline, continued to live there for many years. It was the oldest dwelling in Morgan County when the Lake was formed.

Other settlers came here in the 1870s, one of them being Josiah B. Riffle who built a store, established a sawmill and erected a hotel. One account gives the name of the hotel as the Seven Seas Hotel, but the J. S. and R. T. Higgins Morgan County Map of 1880 calls it the Riffle Inn, which was beyond the settlement on the road to Cape Galena. Members of the Riffle family soon owned most of the land and the village that grew up became known as Riffletown. It kept this name until the post office was established as Gladstone in 1886. By the time the post office was established the town also had a blacksmith shop, two general stores, grade school, high school, Presbyterian church and a resident physician. The post office was discontinued in 1931.

When the Lake came, all the town's buildings were demolished. Material salvaged from the Gladstone Presbyterian church was taken to Irontown where another church was built with the salvaged lumber.

In the early days of Gladstone the town site was considered a very desirable location for a settlement. Even the Osage Indians favored the area for on the north side of the creek, where the "Osage Indian Trail" led westward [this trail later became the Harmony Mission Trace], and on hilltops overlooking the Gladstone area, there once stood the Chieftain Village of the Osage Indians. For reasons unknown, it was vacated by the Indians some time before the passage of the Zebulon Pike Expedition near here in 1806.

Glaize Bridge *(Brumley, Miller County)* -

The Glaize Bridge should not be confused with the Grand Glaize Bridge. They are separate bridges. The Grand Glaize Bridge carries Hwy. 54 across the Grand Glaize Arm in Osage Beach. The Glaize Bridge is located off Hwy. 42 on Swinging Bridge Road 2.8 miles southwest of Brumley and crosses Grandglaize Creek.

The Glaize Bridge is an example of how place names, in this instance a man-made structure, can be changed or influenced by common usage. Most articles written about this bridge by contemporary writers call it the Auglaize Bridge, but therein lies a nomenclature problem.

The late Robert L. Ramsay, a Missouri place names authority, believed that a respect for history demanded that a person find out, if possible, when a place was founded or a structure built, then consider what light is thrown upon the name by contemporary events. He insisted that a historian collect all variants of the name and put them in chronological order.

The 1893 U. S. Geological Survey (USGS) topographic map for this locale calls the stream that passes beneath the bridge Grand Auglaize Creek, but at some later date, the cartographers who create USGS maps renamed the stream Grandglaize. This is evident by looking at maps that came after the 1893 version.

The Grandglaize Creek forms about seven miles upstream from the bridge where the Dry Auglaize Creek and the Wet Glaize Creek merge to form the Grandglaize.

We know precisely when the Glaize Bridge was built -- 1931. It behooves us then, in this search for the proper name, to determine what the people of 1931 called the bridge and the stream beneath it. For this information we turn to the *Miller County Autogram* newspaper published at Tuscumbia. From this source it is apparent that the natives of Miller County called the creek not Auglaize nor Grandglaize but Glaize Creek. The text of numerous articles are consistent and the headlines written when the bridge was under construction, consistently use the term Glaize. "*May Decided to Build Bridge on Glaize Creek*;" "*Court Employs J. A. Dice to Build Glaize Bridge*;" "*Glaize Creek Suspension Bridge Is a Marvel of Wire and Steel Construction.*"

When the Haer Missouri Historic Bridge Inventory was compiled in the 1980s, the compilers registered the bridge as the Glaize Bridge and it is the name by which the bridge is officially recorded in the files of the Missouri Department of Transportation. It is the name used in this book.

The Glaize suspension bridge, which is still in service, is maintained by the Missouri Department of Natural Resources as a historic structure within Lake of the Ozarks State Park. The bridge has a span length of 414 feet and a total length of 500 feet. The roadway is 12 feet wide and the bridge is a steel cable suspension bridge with steel cable towers. The substructure has concrete tower pedestal abutments, wingwalls and piers. The deck is plank over timber stringers. The supporting towers have two channels with lacing; single strand, straight cables in concrete deadmen. There are guardrails.

The Glaize Bridge was built in 1931 by Joseph A. Dice, a noted suspension bridge builder from Warsaw, Missouri.

In January 1931, Louis H. Egan, president of Union Electric Light & Power Company, the owners of Bagnell Dam, at the request of the Miller County Court, granted right-of-way over the company's premises for relocation of the county roads impacted by the Lake. The company paid the county court $17,200 to be used in relocation of the Glaize Creek crossing at the Greenberry Pope place. In April 1931, the Miller County Court made a deal with J. A. Dice to superintend the construction of bridges over the Glaize and Mill creeks.

Glaize Bridge, *Brumley, MO. Photo by H. D. Weaver, 2005.*

Mill Creek joins the Grandglaize close to the present day Glaize Bridge. Approximately $14,500 was made available for the two bridges of which $11,500 was spent on the Glaize Bridge and $3,000 on the Mill Creek Bridge [see Mill Creek Bridge]. A delegation of farmers from Miller and Camden County had petitioned for the bridges. The remainder of the original settlement funds was spent on road relocation as the road had originally crossed the Glaize a short distance downstream from the present location of the Glaize Bridge and that crossing was to be inundated by the Lake.

Both bridges were completed in August 1931. The Glaize Bridge used 100,000 pounds of steel, approximately 200 miles of wire and 15,000 feet of lumber. The Mill Creek Bridge used about one-fifth of the material that was used in the Glaize Bridge. The Glaize Bridge was opened to traffic in September 1931.

Gore's Boat Yard *(Lake Ozark, Miller County)* -

Pogue Hollow Cove is located at about the 16.8-mile mark on the Osage Arm along the Lake's east side. It is the first cove to the east up-Lake from the Community Bridge and by road is at the end of what is today Holiday Lane. It was along here that the Arrowhead Beach Club subdivision was established in 1932. The following summer Mr. & Mrs. W. W. Gore of Madison, Wisconsin, and the Gore's son, G. W. "Jud" and his wife, Florence, established themselves here and built Gore's Boat Yard.

"The site of the boat yard looked like a wilderness to the two Gore ladies, but they managed very well during the pioneer period while homes, boat shops, docks and boat storage sheds were being built," Jud and Florence said nearly 50 years later. The original building sat at the head of a crowded inlet and had a cobblestone foundation on top of which was a two-story frame building. Living quarters were on the second floor. Well into the 1940s, a visible gas pump sat on the lakeside corner from this building.

Gore's Boat Yard, *Lake Ozark, MO, Circa. 1940. Photographer Unknown.*

The Yard's boat docking facilities further out in Pogue Hollow Cove grew with each year. Facing the Lake on top of the dock was a large sign that said: "Gore Boat Yard Company." Ads for the business were simple but effective and in 1936 ads on maps produced for Lake of the Ozarks said: "Lake Ozark Yachting Association headquarters. Boat Storage & Service. Boats built, launched and serviced. Marine railway and repair yard. Boats to rent."

In 1946, the Gore's sold the boat yard to Jack and Pee Wee Rutledge who continued to operate the business as Gore's Boat Yard until about 1960 when they changed the name to Port Arrowhead, which is still in business.

The Gore's did not leave the area but went on to establish the Ozark Woodcrafts, to own and operate the Gov. McClurg Showboat, and to build Gore's Marine, a boat sales service in Camdenton.

Gov. McClurg Ferry *(Camden County)* -

The creation of Lake of the Ozarks had a substantial impact upon roads and highways that ran north and south in the counties most affected by the Lake -- Benton, Camden, Miller and Morgan -- but none quite as bad as Camden and Morgan counties. A number of suspension bridges across the Osage were removed during the basin clearing work, severing roads of major concern to local people. As the waters of the Lake rose, these and other arteries of travel connected by low-water slabs and fords were also severed. The only provisions initially made by Union Electric or the State of Missouri to restore the connections were to build new bridges on Hwy. 54 in Osage Beach and west of Camdenton, and Hwy. 65 at Warsaw.

The Missouri Highway Department chose not to build bridges immediately to reconnect Hwy. 5, the primary route that connected Morgan and Camden counties. It was the department's plan, at least for awhile, to reroute Hwy. 5 traffic onto Hwy. 54 over Bagnell Dam. The plan did not please the residents of the two counties, nor did it sit well with many people from northern and southern Missouri who routinely used Hwy. 5 to reach destinations beyond Lake of the Ozarks. The people who depended upon Hwy. 5 launched a campaign to get bridges built as soon as possible across the Osage and Niangua arms, an effort that was eventually successful but for a period of five years, traffic on Hwy. 5 had to depend upon a private motor ferry service to get across the Lake.

Formerly, Hwy. 5 traffic had crossed the Osage River on the Linn Creek Toll Bridge at the end of what is today Route F and the location of Green Bay Terrace. The Allton brothers, John and Tom, of Columbia, Missouri, secured a permit to operate a ferry at this location. It was on the Floyd farm, connecting Route F with what is today LkRd. 5-89 just north of historic Lovers Leap and the site of Gov. McClurg's old mansion, which, in the 1920s and 30s was being operated as the Osage Inn.

Preliminary work on the ferry boat was done by Samuel Edwards of the Grafton, Illinois, Boat Works. Finish work was done by the Ozark Boat Company of Warsaw. Since the Warsaw boat works was a quarter-of-a- mile from the Lake, the Seibert Contracting Company of California, Missouri, was hired to move the boat and spent nearly a week doing so. Reports regarding the boat's cost vary from $20,000 to $25,000. Operating papers for the boat were issued by the U. S. Coast Guard on May 25, 1932. It was launched on May 28, 1932, at Brill's Hill Resort & Marine at Warsaw.

Accounts vary as to who piloted the boat on the 70-mile trip from Warsaw to Green Bay Terrace. Some reports say Frank Miles and others say C. E. Bailey. Some accounts put the boat's capacity at 19 automobiles, others at 20. The boat displaced 45 tons, had a passengers' cabin at the rear, was powered by a 100 hp Fairbanks-

Gov. McClurg Ferry, *Circa 1930s. Photographer Unknown.*

Morris diesel engine and could travel 10 mph. The ride across the Lake was a mile-and-a-quarter long according to ads produced by the Gov. McClurg Ferry Lines. The boat's operating hours were from 6 a.m. to 9 p.m. every hour seven days a week. Major holiday weekends were difficult because the boat was often inadequate to handle the amount of traffic on the road and large queues of waiting vehicles would develop at either end.

The Gov. McClurg Ferry boat was largely trouble-free until the spring of 1936 when some repair work was being done on the boat's hull. One end of the boat had been weighted down to permit work on the other end and the boat keeled over and sank. Attempt after attempt during the summer of 1936 to bring the boat up failed. The ferry company finally hired Clarence Miller of Keokuk, Iowa, who was an expert in raising sunken boats. Where others failed he succeeded. The boat was then taken down-Lake to the Pistol Club for restoration, a process that took about one month.

"This was one of the finest ferries operated in this section of the country and its sinking last spring was a serious handicap to trade on Hwy. 5 out of Versailles and towards Camdenton as it broke the connecting link," said the *Lake of the Ozarks News*. "Many people received the impression from reports in various papers that the ferry sank while in service. Such was not the case as the boat had been pulled in close to the bank..."

As early as 1934 there was speculation as to what would become of the Gov. McClurg Ferry once the Niangua and Hurricane Deck bridges were complete. Often affectionately called Ferry 5, this grand boat was more than just a convenience and connecting link for two sections of Hwy. 5. People also took the ferry to go sightseeing on the Lake because it was in such a scenic and historic location. People became fond of Ferry 5 and did not want to see it scuttled when it was no longer needed to connect the highway. Suggestions were made and appeared in newsprint.

"The changing of the Ferry 5 end of Highway 5 and the construction of the two new bridges...raises the...question of what will become of the magnificent steel Ferry when the highway is open across the two bridges?" said the editor of the *Lake of the Ozarks News*. "There are few places in the...United States that present a more picturesque environment and is more inspiring..."

One offering was a firm opinion that "the boat...remain on the Lake."

A second suggestion was that "should a need develop for a ferry elsewhere, such as the construction of a 'farm-to-market' road from 54 to the vicinity of Gladstone, that need might demand a modern ferry to connect the south shore of the Lake near the Pistol Club. Another highway might run through Rocky Mount down Shelida Hill to the vicinity of Coffman Beach and connect with the 'farm-to-market' road from 54."

And a third suggestion: "What the Lake is in dire need of and which to date it has not obtained is a sizeable excursion boat, provided with facilities for dancing and other entertainment with a first class restaurant and other accommodations. The No. 5 Ferry boat is admirably adapted to be converted to such use."

When the Hurricane Deck Bridge and the Hwy. 5 Niangua Bridge were finally opened in 1937, the ferry was out of business. It was later taken down-Lake to be converted into a showboat, a destiny that brought a lot of smiles and satisfaction to the local people. [see Gov. McClurg Showboat]

Gov. McClurg Mansion *(Linn Creek, Camden County)* -

When the Lake of the Ozarks basin was cleared during the construction of Bagnell Dam, very few structures of historic significance were left standing in the basin or close to the shoreline, which was cleared to a distance of 15 feet above the 660-foot elevation. Two exceptions were the old Iron Smelter in Bollinger Creek Cove at the 44-mile mark on the Osage Arm, and the Gov. McClurg Mansion at the 31-mile mark on the Osage Arm at the mouth of Linn Creek Cove and the Niangua River.

When Union Electric Light & Power Company set their line for the formation of the Lake, the projected waterline came almost exactly level with the front porch of the McClurg mansion. It was thought that at times water might actually enter the old mansion, but after the Lake formed and reached the 660-foot level, the water was actually one foot below the porch. Because of its historic value, the building was left standing, the only house permitted to remain on the 660-foot contour.

Joseph W. McClurg built his house on this site about 1851 when he arrived to join his brother-in-law, John Jones, who had opened a store there along the Osage River. The first house was a two-story weather-board dwelling with a two-story covered deck or front porch that looked out upon the Osage River valley. As the years passed, the dwelling was improved, enlarged and veneered with cobblestone. The second level porch was removed and large front porch added at ground level running the full length of the house. Cobblestone pillars supported the porch roof. The mansion had walnut staircases and was built of the best materials then available.

After McClurg's death in 1900, ownership of the old mansion changed several times. Owners included J. P. Jeffries, Dave Moulder, Col. R. G. Scott and finally Ab Witt.

In the late 1920s, the old mansion was operated as the Osage Inn. A description of the operation at that time said: "In an hours drive from Versailles, south on Highway No. 5, the traveler may see the old plantation home of Joseph W. McClurg, one time congressman and governor of Missouri. This rambling gray stone building, which is almost covered with ivy, is perched upon a hill, with a splendid view of the river and hills from its piazzas. It is now known as the Osage Inn and here hot biscuits, southern cornbread, fish, frog legs and fried chicken may be had. Here the antique lover will revel in the quaint furniture, rare dishes and pottery, which have been preserved for generations."

The Witts were the last to own the property. The Witts turned the old mansion into a tourist attraction after the Lake arrived. In the fall of 1938 and spring of 1939, the Witts improved and redecorated the rooms and added dining room service. On Sunday morning, July 16, 1939, hotel guests were awakened when the mansion caught fire and was totally destroyed. Fortunately, the Witts and all guests escaped injury. The flames spread so rapidly almost nothing was saved. It was theorized that the fire was started by a cigarette carelessly thrown into a group of oil mops in one of the washrooms.

Disastrous fires, unfortunately, are a reoccurring theme in the history of the early years of Lake of the Ozarks. Many historic structures have been lost to flames.

Gov. McClurg Showboat *(Osage Beach, Camden County)* -

In 1937, John and Tom Allton of Columbia, Missouri, owners of the Gov. McClurg Ferry Lines, changed the name of their company to the Lake Ozark Amusement Company. They then took their ferry boat -- the Gov. McClurg -- to Gore's Boat Yard at the 16.8-mile mark on the Osage Arm to have it converted into a showboat. [see also Gov. McClurg Ferry] While this task was underway, they built a dock and clubhouse for guests on the south side at the west end of the Grand Glaize Bridge and called it Bridgeport, which later became Churchill's Bridgeport. Today, Bridgeport Boat Rentals is at this location.

With a new lease on life, the ferry boat began service at Bagnell Dam as the Gov. McClurg Showboat and was promoted as "the largest excursion boat on the Lake." The service it provided was detailed in a local paper: "The nightly trips take the excursionist from the Casino dock near Bagnell Dam, each night at 9 o'clock, for a 15-mile tour of the Lake, lasting three hours. The boat is strictly modern, being equipped with powder rooms, rest rooms, dancing floor, refreshment and drink stand. The floor is waxed and music is furnished each night. In addition to the regular excursion runs each evening, the boat is available for special occasions..."

After a short stay at the Casino docks, the boat was moved to the west end of the Grand Glaize Bridge and the Bridgeport docks. The boat's strongest competitor was the Idle Time Excursion Boat, which docked at the east end of the Grand Glaize Bridge at Chet's Anchor Inn in the early 1940s. The Gov. McClurg Showboat had a capacity for 150 people. The adult fair for an excursion ride, when it opened was 50 cents.

"With music, dancing, refreshments and sightseeing in an atmosphere enjoyed by young and old, wile away the hours in most pleasant surroundings. Explore the most beautiful part of the Lake in luxurious comfort," said the ads. Guests had a choice for one of the daily or nightly trips and charter trips could be arranged. The pilot of the boat was Frank Miles. The ads listed J. M. [Tom] Alton [sic] as president of the company.

In late fall of 1939, W. W. Gore of Gore's Boat Yard purchased the boat. Some sources of information suggest that it wasn't until after Gore's purchase that the boat was called the Gov. McClurg, but ads that appeared before this date called it the Gov. McClurg.

The boat sold again in 1945, and in 1968, it was purchased by the Lodge of Four Seasons and renamed "The Seasons Queen." New work was done on the boat and it began launching from the marina at the Lodge with Captain Graning in charge.

During the 1940s and 1950s, the Gov. McClurg was one of the two most popular excursion boats on Lake of the Ozarks. It became a favorite for students on their high school senior trips.

Grand Glaize Arm of the Lake *(Camden County)* -

The Grand Glaize Arm of the Lake is notably scenic. Its beauty is enhanced by largely unblemished, undeveloped shoreline, which has been preserved in a natural state by the existence of Lake of the Ozarks State Park. The park borders much of the Grand Glaize Arm on both sides and has nearly 90 miles of shoreline.

The Grand Glaize Arm meanders upstream from its junction with the Osage Arm for a distance of 15 miles. The channel runs 50 to 70 feet deep for the first seven miles and 30 feet deep for the next four miles. There are many tributary coves.

The portion of the Arm on either side of the Grand Glaize bridges, which carry Hwy. 54, has long been considered one of the most scenic crossings at the Lake. It is also one of the most highly developed. Boat traffic between the mouth of the Grand Glaize and Party Cove [Anderson Hollow Bay] at the 4-mile mark is so heavy on weekends during the summer months that the entire stretch is a marked "no-wake" zone during weekends between Memorial Day and Labor Day.

Traveling upstream on the Grand Glaize, natural features of special interest begin near the 4-mile mark where a natural rock bridge high along the north shore has a commanding view of the mouth of Anderson Hollow Bay. Bluffs here are up to 50 feet high and as the Grand Glaize sweeps upstream in a great curve to the right, the bluff to the left arches out over the water, white and gray rock streaked with mineral stain. The channel then crosses to the right side where another sweeping curve is pock-marked with cave openings.

To the left at the 5-mile mark is a cove where Camp Clover Point, used by Scouts and other groups, has boat docking and swimming facilities. Some of the best cave-riddled bluffs along the Arm are found between the 6- and 8-mile marks. The

***Natural Rock Bridge Or Eye of the Rock,** Grand Glaize Arm. Photo by H. D. Weaver, 2002.*

bluffs on the right just beyond the 6-mile mark are unusual. Boat Shelter Cave, on the left just beyond the 7-mile mark, has an opening large enough to shelter a boat [see Boat Shelter Cave]. Little Boat Shelter Cave is also nearby. Here too, is the entrance to Honey Run Hollow Cove where the Fort Leonard Wood Recreation Area is located.

There are some developed areas along the Grand Glaize Arm because of in-holdings [privately-owned acreage] that were not purchased by the state when the park was created in the 1930s and 40s. But in-holdings with shoreline are limited. At the 9-mile mark, a well carved, colorful, towering, man-made totem pole [probably made by a youth group] can be seen high on a hill to the left.

Just beyond the 10-mile mark is McClain's Point, a privately developed area that has one of the oldest resorts on the Lake. More cave openings can be seen between the 11- and 12-mile marks. At 12 miles is Public Beach No. 1 and just beyond it, opposite the park's campground point, is Jeffries Point at the mouth of historic Coakley Hollow [see Coakley Hollow & Coves; Coakley Spring; Ozark Caverns].

Grand Glaize Bridge *(Osage Beach, Camden County)* -

In pre-Lake days a bridge was located approximately one and three-quarters mile due south of the confluence of the Grand Auglaize Creek and the Osage River. It was on the Bagnell-Linn Creek Road and would have been to the south of today's twin Grand Glaize bridges. A large, floating "no-wake" sign is in the middle of the Lake not far from where this bridge once existed. The point of Malibu Road aims directly at where this bridge was once located.

The Bagnell-Linn Creek unpaved road originally carried Hwy. 15, which later became Hwy. 54. The road approached from the northeast down the center of Watson Hollow, veered south and then west to cross the Grand Auglaize Creek [later called Grandglaize Creek] at a narrow place a little over one mile due south of the present day Grand Glaize bridges. The road then left the valley and gained the upland by what is today Malibu Road.

The bridge in the valley was called the Zebra Bridge because it was one and three-quarters of a mile upstream from the little village of Zebra. The bridge was a relatively new steel truss bridge when the construction of Bagnell Dam began in 1929 [having replaced a suspension bridge at the same location], but with the coming of Lake of the Ozarks it would have to be replaced with a much larger, higher bridge at a different location. The Zebra Bridge as well as two miles of the old highway would be inundated by 60 to 70 feet of water.

On June 18, 1929, Union Electric entered into contract with the Missouri State Highway Commission to build the new Grand Glaize Bridge. Money was provided by Union Electric, supervision by Stone & Webster Engineering, and Sverdrup & Parcel, Consulting Engineers of St. Louis, were awarded the contract for bridge design.

Even before the bridge design was on paper, it was obvious that the location of the new bridge would be unusually scenic once the Lake had formed, so a design was selected that would not impede the view of vehicle passengers. To accomplish this, the design of the 1,630-foot-long bridge called for trusses beneath the deck instead of overhead, a rare design feature that gave the bridge an "upside down" look, hence its later nickname as the "Upside Down Bridge." A few years later Sverdrup and Parcel would go on to design the Hwy. 5 Niangua Bridge and the Hurricane Deck Bridge, which also spaned the Lake and had similar design features.

The construction contract for the Grand Glaize Bridge was awarded to the Pioneer Construction Company of Kansas City; the contract for the bridge approaches was awarded to the C. P. O'Reilly Construction Company of St. Louis; and the Stupp Brothers Bridge & Iron Company of St. Louis was awarded the contract for the superstructure. Construction work began in March 1930, using a work force of 40 to 50 men borrowed from the construction work at Bagnell Dam. Equipment and supplies were delivered to the dam area by the Bagnell Branch Railroad and then trucked to the Grand Glaize Bridge site.

The old highway and the Zebra Bridge were officially abandoned on Jan. 14, 1931, and the Grand Glaize Bridge and its new section of highway were opened to traffic at the same time and without a dedication ceremony. For awhile, many of the local people called it the Zebra Bridge. There are even old postcards made during this period that label it the Zebra Bridge.

The Grand Glaize Bridge was opened to traffic nearly six months before Bagnell Dam was finished and before Lake of the Ozarks formed. The total cost of the project was $295,440.00. The picturesque location of the bridge and its unusual design won the hearts of millions of people in the following decades. Over the years, scores of different scenic view postcards have featured the bridge.

By the 1960s, the bridge had aged to the point that it needed replacement. In 1983, a companion bridge, one of contemporary steel stringer/multibeam design, was constructed parallel to the Upside Down Bridge on the north side. The old bridge was closed to traffic in 1985. The two bridges, one vintage with deteriorated concrete and complex trusses, and the new one of sleek and much simplified design, sat side by side for 10 years before the old bridge was demolished and replaced with a twin of the newer bridge. During those 10 years, local people lighted the old bridge railings each December with Christmas tree lights, and also placed other lighted holiday attractions on the deck, showing their affection for a bridge that had served them well as a travel link and also as a promotional attraction. Its image can be found on just about every kind of advertising and promotional literature that Osage Beach and its businesses produced from 1932 to 1985.

The same company that built the companion bridge in 1983 -- the Massman Construction Company of Kansas City -- was awarded the contract for demolishing the old bridge. Demolition cost $3.5 million. All equipment was trucked in and assembled on site because the barges needed to hold the cranes were too large to be moved over the highways. The old bridge was dismantled piece by piece, not dynamited and allowed to sink into the Lake. The bridge that replaced it was built in 1995. The old Upside Down Bridge may be gone but it will be remembered for a long time to come and its image has been preserved on thousands of different postcards that will still be in circulation long after everyone alive today is deceased.

Grand Glaize Cafe *(Osage Beach, Camden County)* -

In 1931-32, the Hultsman Oil Company built a filling station 500 feet west of the Grand Glaize Bridge on the north side of Hwy. 54. Its location brought substantial business and the filling station was doing well until the spring of 1933 when it caught fire and burned to the ground.

Following the fire, the property was bought by a Mr. James of Springfield who built a sandwich shop and cold drink stand where the filling station had formerly stood. He was in business by June 1933. Folklore circulated years later hinted that the cold drink stand had been part of a fisherman's shack that had once been in the Grand Glaize Creek bottom before the Lake was created. Supposedly, this shack was moved to higher ground before the basin was filled and James used the lumber from it to build his cold drink stand.

By 1940, the sandwich shop had been enlarged by new owners -- Roy Jeffries and Alta Monte -- and named the Grand Glaize Cafe. The cafe sat on the edge of a 40-acre tract of land belonging to N. D. Jeffries. This tract ran along the north side of the highway from the Grand Glaize Bridge to LkRd. 54-15A, later designated 54-37 and now called Jeffries Road.

A short distance up Jeffries Road, the Jeffries home sat along the roadside on the west side overlooking the Grand Glaize Arm. Part of the Jeffries tract had been sold to Union Electric and was beneath the water near the bridge. The Jeffries family also built a commercial boat dock and fishing barge [see Jeffries Boat Dock] at the west end of the Grand Glaize Bridge, and a cottage camp on the hill west of the cafe along Jeffries Road.

The Grand Glaize Cafe became a well known cafe. The words HOT FISH were painted white in large letters on its pitched roof, leading people to call it the Hot Fish Cafe. That portion of the building on the east side had two stories facing the highway but being on a hillside, it also had a walk-out basement level where "The Cool Spot" Glaize

Grand Glaize Café, *Osage Beach, MO. Photo by L. L. Cook, Milwaukee.*

Rathskeller was located. Alta Monte [a woman] operated the cafe and Roy Jeffries operated the rathskeller.

On the west side was an attached one-story building facing the highway that also had a lower unseen basement level. As the years passed and the 1950s arrived, signs began to proliferate on the building and property. The words "Air Conditioned" were added, then in large letters "Fishing Tackle" and "Permits" and "Ski Belts," and then a white picket fence that ran to the west along the parking area. On this fence was a sign that read "Marigold Glass Hand Blown" and another sign nailed to two posts that announced HOT BISCUITS. The cafe served Pevely ice cream, Coca Cola and was open from 6:30 a.m. to 9:00 p.m. daily except Tuesday, when it was closed.

In the 1960s, the large, two-story building saw some remodeling, the peaked roof was removed, and the building was given a flat roof, which lowered its profile.

In 1976, the Grand Glaize Cafe was sold to Joseph H. Boer. Boer came to the United States in 1956. He went to culinary school in Switzerland and served as an assistant chef at the home of a Belgian ambassador. After serving in the U. S. Army, he worked as a manager of several restaurants in Kansas City before coming to Lake of the Ozarks. He operated the Mai Tai Top Deck Restaurant under a lease for awhile and also owned Lefty's Little Chef Steak House. He then bought the Grand Glaize Cafe and renamed it The Potted Steer. Boer also owns the Blue Herron Restaurant on Route HH just off Bus. Hwy. 54 in Lake Ozark.

Gravois Arm of the Lake *(Morgan County)* -

The Gravois Arm has a main channel length of 10 miles, with at least 11 miles of additional channel in its tributaries [branches and coves]. Water 30 to 70 feet deep extends all the way to the confluence of the Gravois and Little Gravois. Beyond that, in the area approaching Gravois Mills, the maximum depth is 10 feet when the Lake is at full reservoir.

A plan view of the Gravois Arm looks like a leaning tree with numerous branches, each branch covered with large thorns [triangular coves formed by steep-sided hollows]. Major branches of the Gravois Arm along the east side include Raccoon Hollow Cove, Cedar Creek Cove, Bogue Bay, Indian Creek Cove and Little Gravois Cove. Major branches entering from the west include Gladstone Cove, Mill Creek Cove and Soap Creek Cove. Indian Creek Cove is the most extensive tributary cove along the Gravois Arm with at least three miles of channel.

At the mouth of the Gravois Arm at about mid-point beneath 70 feet of water lies the site of Mining Port, one of the oldest settlements in this part of the state. It was established about 1819 and survived to 1837 when a great flood on the Osage River and the Gravois, washed the small village away. The people moved upstream about three miles to the mouth of Gladstone Hollow Cove to establish the village of Riffletown, which later became the town of Gladstone, a site now also beneath the Lake.

Well before the arrival of European and American settlers, and even the Zebulon Pike Expedition in 1806, there was a large Osage Indian encampment [known as the

Sky Lodge Chieftain's Village] along the northeast side where Indian legends surround the "balds." Folklore claims these "balds" were Indian ceremonial sites.

Mill Creek Cove just above Gladstone Cove is fed by North Mill Creek and South Mill Creek, which merge just above the headwaters of the cove. Along South Mill Creek was the village of Bonds Mines, which had a post office from 1872 to 1879. The settlement grew up around the Globe Mining & Smelting Works operated by the Bonds family. The little village had a general store, blacksmith shop and sawmill.

The Gravois bottomlands near the mouths of Gladstone Cove, Mill Creek Cove, Cedar Creek Cove and Bogue Bay were heavily settled in the latter half of the 1800s. The people were an industrious bunch. At the mouth of Soap Hollow was a "soap factory" where women rendered lard, obtained through butchering, to manufacture soap.

Many of the families who settled here before the Civil War had negro slaves. The slaves lived largely in Possum Hollow opposite the mouth of Soap Creek Hollow [Cove]. Six miles up the Gravois Arm at the mouth of Indian Creek Cove the Lake covers a negro slave graveyard and the site of the old Rastofer School, which was demolished when the basin was being cleared.

Indian Creek was named for an Indian burial mound on the hill near the mouth of the cove. A lot of lead prospecting and some mining occurred along Indian Creek in the late 1800s. The Indian Creek Mines were among the better known. And just beyond the headwaters of Indian Creek at an elevation of 820 feet along what is today Route W, is the site of the former Stover Coal Mine. It was once considered one of the largest coal mines in the region. Its slag piles and pits have since been cleaned up and the landscape returned to its original appearance.

In the hills of the Gravois Arm where the Stephenson Riders and Cotton Band Raiders created havoc during the Civil War, there was much commercial timber. The early stands were largely destroyed from 1880 to 1910 by tie hackers who floated their ties downstream on the Gravois and Osage to Bagnell. But not all of the giant trees that once grew along the banks of the Gravois were totally gone by 1931. On the land of John Rastofer there stood a sycamore tree seven feet in diameter. The first eight feet were hollow with a shell six inches thick. An opening in the tree would allow six men to stand inside the tree with space left over. The old tree was often a refuge for John's boys when they were plowing or harvesting and a storm would come up.

Uncle John used the tree to register high water marks when the Gravois overflowed its banks. When the water reached its height, it would leave a white foam line on the tree trunk and there Uncle John would carve a mark and add the date. When the men who cleared the basin for the Lake came upon this old tree to fell it, they found a record of dates from 1878 about five feet above the ground. Bad floods on the Gravois and Osage that preceded Uncle John's marks included 1823, 1837, 1844, 1851 and 1875. Unfortunately, Uncle John's grand old sycamore record tree was lost to the Lake and so was his record of flood dates from 1878 to 1931.

Gravois Beach Resort *(Gravois Mills, Morgan County)* -

Gravois Beach Resort was built in 1931-32 by C. W. Kavanaugh about one-half mile up-Lake from the mouth of Little Gravois Cove, which is at the 9-mile mark on the Gravois Arm of the Lake. It was along the west side just beyond the first bend of the cove. The resort could be reached by way of LkRd. 5-7, which is now Anchorage Road off Route TT, or old Hwy. 5. Anchorage Road is just over two miles north of Gravois Mills.

Kavanaugh called his place Kavanaugh's Gravois Beach Resort. He had 18 log cabins with electricity and running water by 1934, and added two additional buildings, one for a gas station and the other for the Bass Head Tavern & Grocery. Some of the cabins were built along the hillside facing the Lake. One structure was large enough to be called a "hotel."

Kavanaugh operated the business until 1939 when he sold to Carl Schmidt who dropped Kavanaugh's name and continued it as just Gravois Beach Resort. Schmidt promoted the resort as the "first and finest beach resort on Highway 5." He also advertised having modern apartments.

In 1951, the resort was sold to Fred M. Ward who advertised an "outdoor dance floor." By 1952, the resort again had new owners, this time Nolder and Goering.

The resort's neighbors by 1953 included Quigley's Resort and Baska's Peaceful Valley Resort upstream on Little Gravois Cove, and Tracy's Shoreline Resort and Blue Water Resort down-Lake. A year later Quigley's Resort became Lightfoot's Resort. And in 1954, Fred Ward opened Gravois Beach Anchorage adjacent to Gravois Beach Resort on the upstream side. Ward advertised having 400 feet of dock space, modern cabins, and that his new resort was the "Home of the Ozark Rambler Speed Boat." He offered daily trips to Bagnell Dam and had other boats for charter.

By 1957, Fred Ward and his Gravois Beach Anchorage had ceased operation but within a couple of years it became Jeff's Anchorage Resort and in 1962, Nolder left the Gravois Beach Resort operation, which remained the charge of Vic & Lorett Goering. They advertised having a campgrounds with a modern trailer park. Tracy's Shoreline Resort down-Lake became Leaches Shoreline Resort while Jeff's Anchorage, under the ownership of Jeff & Lavonne Jeffrey changed the name of their place to Jeff's Anchorage & Mobile Home Park.

Today, the operation is called Anchorage Resort Park and the Bass Head

Gravois Beach Resort, *Versailles, MO, Circa. 1930. Photographer Unknown.*

Tavern & Grocery is the Anchorage Pub & Grill. One of the more outstanding log homes probably built here in the 1930s is one block east of the Pub & Grill.

Gravois Mills *(Morgan County)* -

Gravois Mills, originally known as "Gravi Mills," is at the head of the Gravois Arm on Hwy. 5 about nine miles south of Versailles. It sits at the mouth of Wilson Hollow where Gravois Mill Spring branch comes tumbling out of Factory Hollow to discharge into Lake of the Ozarks.

Before the Lake's arrival, this was the confluence of the spring branch with Gravois Creek where settlement began as early as 1811. A gristmill and a log building were erected here in 1835. The log building was sometimes used by the county court. The post office was established in 1860 and has been in continuous operation since that date.

The village of Gravois Mills was platted in 1884 by John Humes. What brought settlers to this location was the abundance of spring-fed streams. Sawmills, flourmills, woolenmills and gristmills sprang up all around the area in the late 1800s. Mills of one type or another were operated by the Humes, Veulemans, Websters, James and Collins families.

The first or French half of the village name "Gravois" was borrowed from the creek and means "gravel." The second half of the name came from the presence of so many mills in this vicinity. The largest spring -- Gravois Mills Spring -- originates in Factory Hollow about half-a-mile above Gravois Mills. It has a daily discharge of three to five million gallons of water. In 1932 a trout hatchery was begun at the spring and is called Troutdale Ranch.

The Gravois Mills community has long been a favorite of Kansas City fishermen. Early resorts associated with the Gravois Mills area included Adkins Camp, Cedar Dale Springs, Clear Water Camp, Curtright Springs Camp, Happy Days Resort, Twin Bays Resort, Two Waters Resort and Washburn's Resort.

In 1932, H. B. Hart built one of the most impressive and unusual fishing piers on the Lake at Gravois Mills. It extended some distance out into the headwaters of the Gravois Arm, which is relatively shallow here and usually less than 10 feet deep.

The population of Gravois Mills in 1884 was 30. The year-round population today is barely 100. Lake of the Ozarks, it would seem, has not had a significant impact upon the town's population, but most of the people who come here end up staying not within the city limits, but at one of the fishing camps or resorts. Even today, life moves at a slower pace in Gravois Mills than in most places around the Lake. Although Bagnell Dam was generating electricity by 1931, electricity didn't reach Gravois Mills until rural electrification came in 1937-39. Street lights didn't show up in town until 1974. And while a few merchants in town would like to see things liven up in this little fisherman's village, there are other residents who like things just the way they are --laid back and quiet.

Happy Days Resort *(Gravois Mills, Morgan County)* -

Happy Days Resort was one of the early resorts on the Gravois Arm. It was located along the shore of what is today Gibson Point at the 4-mile mark at the end of County Road P. Mr. & Mrs. H. H. Boulden opened the resort in 1937 as Happy Days Resort after buying and renaming Trail's End Camp, which had opened in 1935.

The resort had a dozen or more modern and semi-modern cottages. The Bouldens advertised "clean, cheerful cottages and courteous treatment to a selected clientele."

Neighboring resorts during the 1930s included Two Waters Resort and Washburn's Point up-Lake near the mouth of Soap Creek Cove, and Jester's Camp and Mel Adkins Camp along the north shore of Mill Creek Cove. Gibson Point and Cedar Point mark the points on either side at the mouth of Mill Creek Cove.

Mr. Boulden died in the early 1940s and Mrs. Boulden continued the operation until selling it in 1944 to Jo & Ed H. [El] Hensiek of Kansas City. They advertised "modern and semi-modern cottages, cold and hot water, groceries, ice, minnows, motors and guides, safe beach, no hills," capitalizing on the fact that so many shoreline properties along the Lake, including many on the Gravois Arm, rise steeply from the water's edge.

Resorts proliferated in their area as the 1940s progressed. Keys Resort developed north of them, and Snell Groves Resort, Mill Creek Resort, Silver Moon Resort and Bodie's Rondavo developed along the shores of Mill Creek Cove.

By 1951, Happy Days Resort was again under new ownership, this time that of Don & Iris Firoved who added the words "on level, well-shaded point" to their ads. In the 1950s they built two large cottages that would accommodate 10 people each.

In 1959, the resort again had new owners, this time Bill & Viola Gibson, for whom this point on the Gravois Arm is probably named. By 1965, Happy Days Resort was no longer in operation. While resorts often change names when they change owners, Happy Days was an exception. It retained the same name for 28 years, despite having changed owners four times during that period.

Hastain *(Benton County)* -

The village of Hastain in Benton County is on Route V a few miles north of Edwards, which is on Hwy. 7. Hastain grew up around a nineteenth century general store operated by Lewis B. Thomas, and a gristmill and sawmill operation at the mouth of Picnic Hollow and Turkey Hollow where they enter Deer Creek. The post office was established in 1884.

Hastain is about four miles upstream from the headwaters of Deer Creek Cove, which enters the Lake at the 74-mile mark. Before the Lake was created, the little village saw substantial farm traffic because it was on the old Climax Springs-Stover-Cole Camp Road. The ferry at Duroc carried this traffic across the Osage River. Once the Lake was formed, resort activity on the banks of Deer Creek Cove brought fishermen through Hastain. In the 1930s and 40s, when Duckworth's Camp was thriving, much of the camp's traffic passed through Hastain. But the demise of this resort and other developments on and near the Lake hurt the village. Today, only one resort -- Forthview Resort & Marine -- continues at the mouth of Deer Creek Cove.

The Hastain Post Office closed in 1951. Only half a dozen buildings now remain at the location and two of them are small, rustic log cabins. Along the north-west edge of the village is the wide, wooded valley of Deer Creek, which is scenic at this location. Along the west side of the valley are low bluffs that are riddled with inviting cave openings, several of them large enough to attract attention. The largest one has about 100 feet of passage. In the 1940s and 50s, the property owner -- Roy Drennon -- who was an amateur archaeologist, excavated several of the caves and found many Indian artifacts.

Hawkeye Modern Cabins *(Osage Beach, Camden County)* -

This Osage Beach business was in operation for a brief period during the 1940s. It stood along the south side of Hwy. 54 about one-quarter mile northeast of LkRd. 54-24 [Osage Beach Road] between the Wal-Mart Supercenter and Rockway Center. Hawkeye Modern Cabins also sold Texaco gasoline.

Heckerman's Cottage Camp & Service Station *(Lake Ozark, Miller County)* -

In the period 1932-33, Les Burd operated the Lake Ozark Service Station selling Mobilegas. It was the service station closest to Bagnell Dam along the north side of The Strip. There were also four log cabins just west of the service station. Shortly thereafter, Gordon's Drug Store was built on the north side of the service station by Paul Gordon. V. "Red" Moore built a cafe between the cabins and the White House Hotel. Two gift shops were also located in this area.

By 1934, the service station had a new sign that said Heckerman's Cottage Camp. By 1935, the business had 11 cabins renting for $1.25 per day and advertised the availability of fishing guides and boats. The rental cabins had a total capacity for 38 guests. H. H. Heckerman kept adding to the business and built an apartment building that was air-conditioned. Each room had a radio.

On Dec. 14, 1939, a fire broke out that destroyed the V. "Red" Moore cafe and spread to most of the cabins and business structures between the service station and the White House Hotel. Bob Cunningham's Souvenir Shop and Oliver Payne's Souvenir Shop were among the buildings that were lost.

Following the destructive fire, Heckerman built a large, two-story sandstone-veneered building just north of the service station. This building became the Copper Kettle Cafe. Where the log cabins had been, a new, one-story, native stone building was erected parallel with the highway. It had three matching gable roof sections facing the highway and six rental units. It was known as Conrad's Cabin Court. Between it and the White House, two additional buildings arose, one that housed Bob's Place Souvenirs, and the other, Spalding's Liquors & Gifts.

All was well until July 20, 1944, when once again, fire ravaged this side of The Strip. It destroyed the Copper Kettle Cafe & Gift Shop, Heckerman's Service Station, and Gordon's Drug Store & Restaurant. The fire broke out at 3 a.m. in the Copper Kettle Cafe. Mrs. Howard Heckerman and son, Junior, were sleeping in their apartment on the second floor. They were forced to jump from the second floor to the cab of a truck because flames had cut off their escape by stairway. She suffered severe shock during the episode.

Hildebrand's Camp / Resort *(Osage Beach, Camden County)* -

In 1935, Reinhard Hildebrand, an electrical engineer who graduated from a school of engineering in Stuttgart, Germany, and was, for many years, the Chief Engineer of the Diesel Engine Department of the Fulton Iron Works in St. Louis, built Hildebrand's Camp. It was near the end of what was originally LkRd. 54-24, later designated 54-59 and now called Swiss Village Road. At that time the community around the junction of Hwy. 54 & Route KK was called Damsel.

At the entrance to his Lake road, Hildebrand built a stone arch over the roadway. The arch stood for many years and was used as a directional tool in Hildebrand's advertising. To reach Hildebrand's "drive through the arch at Damsel," he advertised.

In his ads, Reinhard also took advantage of the resort's spectacular view of the Lake and the Palisades, the latter the name of a bluff that hugs the east shore of the Lake in a great curve on the Osage Arm between the 27- and 28-mile mark. "Visitors are welcome to view the Palisades and this broad expanse of exotic beauty. Here is peace, contentment and recreation," he said.

Hildebrands Resort Cabins, *Osage Beach, MO, Circa. 1938. Photo by Wayne Box Paper.*

The camp's rustic housekeeping cottages could be rented for $1.00 per person per day. A cafe and grocery store were on the grounds and boats, bait and tackle were available. Among other amusements and facilities available to guests on the grounds besides hiking, boating, swimming and fishing, were dancing, archery, badminton, table tennis, shuffleboard and bowling. Like many of the resorts, he promoted to families.

Hildebrand's Resort opened for business in 1936. Shortly afterward the editor of the *Lake of the Ozarks News* visited the camp and later wrote: "I visited the Hildebrand Camp...and was rewarded by some of the most beautiful scenery I have seen on the Lake. Mr. Hildebrand settled here before 'the rush' and bought 40 acres of wonderful sites. The Palisades are to the right of the camp and lend a very pretty border to the large coves in sight. Mr. Hildebrand has made an Indian-like path from the camp to the Palisades. All along the path there are steps up or steps down leading to beauty spots. These beauty spots were all equipped with comfortable benches. I can image the delight they will bring to honeymooners and those people who desire a quiet nook to read [and] think while enjoying the superb beauty of the place..."

There was bus service to Damsel in those days and Hildebrand advertised that the resort "will meet guests coming by bus at Damsel." His camp was open all year.

The camp, built along a natural terrace about 100 feet higher than the Lake, was about 1,000 feet north of Blue Springs Branch Cove, which is fed by a spring. Many of the fishermen who patronized the resort fished in the cove. "Hildebrand's offers a delightful fishing area where the fish are attracted by the cool water of the famous Blue Springs of the Ozarks. Here one can find bass, crappie, pike, jack salmon [walleye], catfish, perch and others of the finny tribe."

An added attraction in the late 1930s was the camp's floating swimming pool and fishing dock. Since the resort was perched at some elevation above the Lake shore, a very long flight of steps led straight down to the floating dock. The enclosed swimming area was 20 x 50 feet in size with a gently sloping bottom ranging from 15 inches in depth to slightly over five feet. Around the pool were covered seats for the convenience of the guests.

Although water skiing did not become a common recreational activity on the Lake until the 1950s, it actually began at Hildebrand's in 1937. At that point in time, water skiing and water skis were in their infancy. The sport originally evolved from snow skiing, which began in Europe around 1900. Water skis as we known them today were first developed in the United States in the mid 1920s but were still experimental well into the 1930s. Even the term "water skiing" was generally unheard of when Hildebrand built his resort. He had some of the early, primitive water skis available at the resort for brave guests to try. He also had an inflatable, cane-like invention of his own, which he demonstrated on the Lake July 27, 1936. Used with the skis, it allowed him to cross the water as if walking. He called it "water walking," but his invention apparently didn't catch on.

Reinhart's unmarried sister also worked at the resort. She was a former art teacher and an accomplished oil painter. Her beautiful paintings added to the attractions at Hildebrand's. Many of her paintings were also available as "art cards" that guests could buy and mail home.

While the word "camp" and "resort" sometimes appeared in their ads, by and large, the business was simply known as "Hildebrand's." The Lodge and Office as well as the cottages were handsome log structures. Extensive rock retaining walls were eventually built along the Lake shore where fishing, swimming and boating took place. In 1967, the resort had new owners -- John and Clara Hohn -- who continued the operation in its former style. Hildebrand's Resort, which no longer exists, survived to the early 1980s.

Holiday House *(Lake Ozark, Miller County)* -

A lodge called Holiday House, once stood on the crest of the hill overlooking Bagnell Dam at its northeast end. The building was constructed in 1925 by the Missouri Hydro-Electric Power Company that initiated the Bagnell Dam project. An early announcement regarding the design of the building said it would have "eleven rooms, a large living room, large dining room, kitchen and six toilet rooms. It is being constructed with a large corridor 36 x 6 feet on the second floor... The entrance porch is 16 x 16.6 feet from which a view of the river and surrounding scenery is very beautiful. There are two cobblestone fireplaces on both the first and second floors for comfort and coziness and the building will be wired throughout for electric light and heat. A Delco plant will be installed for the lighting system and the current from the hydro-electric power plant when it is ready for service. The building will be modern throughout with all the conveniences that can be provided. The building is being erected entirely out of oak and elm, sawed from timber in that locality. A hickory floor will be laid over the concrete...

"The special features of this building were the large lounging room with fireplace, dining room, large hall and bed rooms. The furniture is of natural wood design and the style generally of the modern club house architecture and arrangement. This building will be known as the contractors' clubhouse."

After the dam project was taken over by the Union Electric Light & Power Company, this building was used by Stone & Webster Engineering during the dam's con-

Holiday House Hotel, *Lakeside, MO, Circa. 1950s. Photo by Sylvia Brinkman.*

struction. Upon completion of the dam, this building and an adjacent building that served as a dormitory for some employees, were acquired by the Union Electric Land & Development Company, remodeled and transformed into a luxurious hotel called Holiday House.

Holiday House & Cottages formerly opened to the public on July 1, 1932, with Mrs. Merle Williamson in charge. "Holiday House, operated on the American plan, was built to meet the needs of those who demand the better things in life -- who prefer not to sacrifice the comforts and conveniences of home while visiting this beautiful section of the Ozark country," said the advertising. The various accommodations of the hotel, often described separately in promotional materials, were detailed:

The Veranda - a half-circle screened-in porch affords a spectacular view of Bagnell Dam. "Cool , comfortable wicker chairs abound, with card tables for foursomes desiring a game of contract; also dining tables for those choosing to have their meals in the open." At night, the veranda was illuminated by ship lanterns suspended from the ceiling, supplemented by indirect bridge lamps.

The Bedrooms - each had twin beds, decorated in a restful shade of pale green, the furniture and drapery being of bright yellow. Each room had a private bath. A very attractive overhead lighting fixture with parchment shade hung in the center of each room and each bed was equipped with a small reading light. All the rooms had electric fans.

The Lounge - an airy, spacious room that was decorated in pale green. At one end was a large fireplace of cut stone. Above the hewn oak mantle, superimposed on a panel of white stucco, was an open-work design of wrought iron in silhouette form. Indirect lighting fixtures hung from the ceiling, shedding soft, shadowless illumination. Draperies on either side of the fireplace as well as on the French doors leading to the veranda were of yellow material with clusters of roses as the motif. The rugs blended with the furnishings. On the walls were pictures of birds native to the Ozarks. A Windsor table, together with brass and copper flower vases and ladder-back chairs, gave the room a distinctively Colonial tone.

The Hallway - between the lounge and the dining room, ran the width of the building. At one end was the main entrance to Holiday House and at the other was the door to the veranda. The stairway to the upper floor was said to be a charming creation in and of itself.

The Dining Room - was off the hall, opposite the lounge. The room had attractive Windsor tables with chairs to match and would accommodate 60 guests at one time. By special arrangement, the number of accommodations could be doubled. The walls of the dining room were decorated with a pastoral panorama of fields and trees symbolic of the Ozark region. The light fixtures, draperies, china and silverware complimented each other.

The Kitchen - which adjoined the dining room, was well lighted and ventilated. The equipment was electric and the kitchen was always open to the guests for inspection.

The Cottages - were adjacent to Holiday House amid the trees. There were six fully furnished cottages and each cottage had a living room, two bedrooms, a bathroom and screened porch. The furnishings were of the same order as those found in the Holiday House.

Holiday House was operated by Union Electric Land & Development Company until the company was dissolved whereupon the hotel became a private operation. Holiday House and its cottages have been gone from the hill now for many years.

Hopi Camp / Modern Cottages / Motel *(Camdenton, Camden County)* -

Where First National Bank stands today along Hwy. 5 just north of the square in Camdenton, Mr. & Mrs. C. Fred Hansen built Hopi Camp in 1935. The main building, which housed living quarters on the second floor beneath a steeply-pitched four-gabled roof, had native rock walls up to the second story. The square building, about 30 feet wide on each side, was the office for a filling station, cabin rentals, and the location of Mrs. Hansen's beauty shop. The architecture matched that of the individual cottages.

The housekeeping cottages at Hopi faced Hwy. 5 but were set back fronting a private access road that ran parallel to the highway. Each cottage was nicely appointed and had a fireplace.

Proud of his cottages and their setting, Hansen made sure that his advertising stressed the fact that his cottages were made of "native stone," which characterized the rustic Ozark theme typical of the Lake area in the 1930s and 40s.

Hopi Camp, *Camdenton, MO, Circa. 1936. Photographer Unknown.*

The sign Hansen erected out front said: "Hopi Camp" but for some reason, by 1937, he had changed it to Hopi Modern Cottages. In front of the office building were two gas pumps dispensing Marathon gasoline. The tall, calculating pumps, introduced by Marathon in 1929, had clock face gauges. Interestingly, many of the early cottage courts along the highways of the Lake area had gas pumps because tourist cottage courts originally evolved from the auto camps of the 1920s. It was traditional at that time for a cottage court to have gas pumps.

In 1941, the camp was sold to Mr. & Mrs. E. A. Arnold of Slater, Missouri, who later sold to Leon Ellis who, in turn, sold the business to Floyd and Vera Nellans about 1951.

Roadside courts began to do away with their gas pumps in the 1950s and by the late 1950s, Hopi Modern Cottages had done away with theirs, turning the old pump site into a small landscaped island beneath their business sign.

By 1959, ownership of the business had changed again, this time to John P. White who changed the name to Hopi Motel. The word motel came into vogue in the 1950s. During this period a swimming pool was also added for the convenience of guests. Hopi Motel went out of business in the late 1960s.

Horseshoe Bend *(Lake Ozark, Miller County)* -

Horseshoe Bend is the northernmost part of Camden County but isolated from the larger landmass of Camden County because of the irregular boundary between Camden and Miller counties and the existence of the Lake. Until the new Community Bridge was built at the 16-mile mark, you could get to Horseshoe Bend from Camden County only by water or by driving through a corner of Miller County.

The best way to visualize the great Horseshoe Bend is to look at a map of Lake of the Ozarks. Between Bagnell Dam and the 24-mile mark on the Osage Arm are two great bends in the Osage. The Lake forms an elongated "S" facing east. The interior of the upper segment of the "S" is Horseshoe Bend and the interior of the lower segment of the "S" is Shawnee Bend. These two bends are among the crown jewels at the heart of Lake of the Ozarks and until the 1990s, when a new bridge was built across the Lake at the 16-mile mark, Shawnee Bend was the unpolished jewel. It had only modest development with nearly half of its landmass undeveloped woodlands. Today it is undergoing a rapid transformation and is becoming an enclave of luxury homes and up-scale development. But Horseshoe Bend, because of its proximity to Bagnell Dam and Lake Ozark, was the first to draw the attention of private developers even though at first they were denied access.

In 1931, all 5,400 acres of Horseshoe Bend belonged to Union Electric and its future was in the hands of the Union Electric Land & Development Company. The peninsula has 100 miles of shoreline and is 6.5 miles long from the neck of the bend to its point. The great bend almost became an island with the creation of the Lake because at its neck, the bend is only 1,600 feet wide. At its widest point it is more than two miles wide.

Spectacular Scenery From "The Rock" On Horseshoe Bend, *Lake Ozark, MO, Circa. 1950. Photo by L. L. Cook, Milwaukee.*

Men of vision have eyed the commercial potential of Horseshoe Bend for more than a century. Well before Bagnell Dam was even conceived, men talked of tunneling through the bend at its neck to draw water from the Osage River on the bend's south side. The tunnel, if it had been created at the 15-mile mark above the dam, would have sent water plummeting downward to the headwaters of today's Jennings Branch Cove, which has its mouth at the 1-mile mark above the dam. The fall of water would have made it possible to generate power, much as was done more than 70 years ago along the Niangua River at Tunnel Dam near the southern boundary of Camden County.

Many a covetous eye was newly cast upon the wooded, hilly landscape of Horseshoe Bend after Bagnell Dam was built but substantial development was delayed because even the Land & Development Company couldn't decide on its future. Much thought was given to transforming it into a hunting preserve and at least one area near the point of the bend was designated a wildlife refuge. While it pondered the development of Horseshoe Bend [whose name originated long before Bagnell Dam was built], the Land & Development Company proceeded to build Holiday House, a luxurious hotel on the bluff overlooking the dam; to build the Lakeside Casino Restaurant at the west end of the dam; and to build the Union Electric Bathing Pavilion & Excursion Boat dock at the west end of the dam.

The scheme for Horseshoe Bend, according to the *Kansas City Journal Post*, was "to include hotels, summer camps, private estates, and other attractive features." But they delayed too long for in the early 1940s the Union Electric Land & Development Company was dissolved by edict of the federal government. Union Electric had to divest itself of all enterprises not having to do with hydro-electric power generation. At the time, the holdings of the Development Company were sold to private investors. So actual development of Horseshoe Bend, except for the creation of Horseshoe Bend Road to provide access to the area, was delayed until after the end of World War II. Private resorts then began popping up all along its shores and exploded in the 1960s with the coming of the bend's first large development -- Lodge of the Four Seasons

Horseshoe Bend Road *(Lake Ozark, Camden County)* -

In the spring of 1933, the Union Electric Land & Development Company, owners of the 5,400 undeveloped acres of Horseshoe Bend, sent a crew into the bend to construct a road. "The hard-surface highway will extend from the neck of the bend to its toe, six and one-half miles westward," said a news story.

On Sept. 9, 1933, a news story said: "To Missouri's really impressive list of scenic attractions was added last week a completed 7-mile road that makes the most of the heretofore veiled beauty of Horseshoe Bend... Horseshoe Bend has some ten square miles of wooded Ozark hills, deep inlets that multiply and vary its Lake shoreline... U. S. Highway 54 skirts the narrow neck of Horseshoe Bend peninsula and from the highway the new drive has been carried westward, for the most part a hill drive, but dropping into valleys for variety. Where necessary the forest is being thinned or cleared to give vistas... The present intent is to leave the new scenic road

Horseshoe Bend Road, *Lake Ozark, MO, Circa. 1935. Photo by Estes.*

and its laterals open to the public, but Union Electric officials say the continuance of such a policy will depend on how the property is treated by the visitors who are given unrestricted access. If redbud and dogwood are stripped of branches and watermelon rinds [sic] left behind as a sorry payment, the result will be restrictions such as are maintained on many similar northern and eastern resorts or estate properties.

"Some of the first persons to drive the length of the new road pronounce it the most beautiful drive in Missouri... A common regret from Lake of the Ozarks visitors the last few years has been the fact so few views of the Lake are afforded from the approaching highways. Some day a great circle drive around the Lake will remedy this...but the new 7-mile drive open this week will serve to add new interest to short visits to the dam site and the head of the big lake."

Heavy development has consumed Horseshoe Bend in recent years and new road construction has bypassed the first and perhaps one of the most scenic sections of the old Horseshoe Bend Road. It formerly left Hwy. 54 just west of the new Community Bridge and followed the rim of the bluffs, circled around the hill crowned by the Blue Herron Restaurant, reclaimed the bluff edge and continued due west in a roller-coaster fashion to then curve inland to where Bank Star One is today just west of Duckhead Road.

The remarkably scenic beginning of this road [now bypassed by newer road construction and abandonded] passed by a prominent Lake overlook known informally as "The Rock." This was one of the spots along the road where vegetation was thinned by the road's builders to allow a scenic view and people were able to pull off on the opposite side of the road and park so they could walk across the road to view the Lake and take pictures. Commercial photographers have been especially fond of this spot and postcard views of the Lake taken here have been a staple of Lake of the Ozarks postcard sales and promotions for 70 years.

The other especially scenic portion, referred to as the roller-coaster segment, and also a photographers' favorite in the early years, is now Bluffs Circle and a private drive lined with luxury homes.

The south side of Horseshoe Bend is noted for its scenic bluffs, which make sightseeing and photography from boats most enjoyable between the 13.5- and 16-mile marks of the Osage Arm.

The "common regret from Lake of the Ozarks visitors...[that] so few views of the Lake are afforded from the approaching highways," which was a complaint of vacationers of the 1930s, is even more true today. Few public overlooks of the Lake along highways and roads exist and little or no real effort has been made by state or local authorities or public officials to set aside such treasures for public use. Dense roadside development as well as lakeshore condominium development is rapidly relegating scenic views to the private domain of the fortunate and to business enterprises. Unfortunately, the scenic circle drive around the Lake that many people once hoped for never materialized.

Hymes Kottage Kamp One & Two *(Osage Beach, Camden County)* -

Charles M. & Hazel Hymes came to the Lake area in 1936 from Ottawa, Kansas. They built Hymes Kottage Kamp off Hwy. 54 just west of the Grand Glaize Bridge near the end of what was then LkRd. 54-A15, later designated 54-37 and now called Jeffries Road.

Hymes Kottage Kamp, with its clever use of the letter "K," sat on the west side of the narrow peninsula of land that carries Jeffries Road and faced the mouth of Harpers Hollow Cove. It was the first resort built near the end of the Lake road, its nearest neighbors then being Iris Park off LkRd. 54-A16, and Forrester's Beach at the end of LkRd. 54-A17.

About 1939, the Hymes purchased Barber's Camp, a roadside camp along Hwy. 54 just west of the Grand Glaize Bridge and renamed it. At that time they assigned numbers to their two camps, which had identical names. The camp on Harper's Hollow Cove became Hymes Kottage Kamp Two, and the one along Hwy. 54 became Hymes Kottage Kamp One.

About 1941, they sold the lakeshore camp, which was then renamed Lake Edge Resort by new owners. This resort is still in business.

The Hymes family continued to operate Hymes Kottage Kamp One along Hwy. 54 until Charles died in 1948. Hazel Hymes then sold the business and moved to Camdenton where she lived until her death in 1968. The new owners of Hymes Kottage Kamp One renamed it Sherwood Resort, which is still in business.

Charles and Hazel's son, the late Chet Mason Hymes, established his own business at the east end of the Grand Glaize Bridge in the mid 1940s. [see Chet's Anchor Inn]

Hymes Kottage Kamp No. 1, *Osage Beach, MO, Circa. 1945. Photographer Unknown.*

Idle Days & Gala Resort *(Osage Beach, Camden County)* -

Idle Days Resort was established about 1950 at the west end of the Grand Glaize Bridge, on the north side of Hwy. 54, on the first broad, rounded point between the first two coves. Easy to see from the Grand Glaize Bridge when traveling west, the resort was also easy to reach. It was just off LkRd. 54-37 [Jeffries Road].

The resort formed a semi-circle of individual cottages wrapping around the nose of the point. Guests had a "wonderful view" of the Grand Glaize Bridge recreation area. The resort was in one of the busiest tourist areas of the Lake. It was owned and operated by Curley and Vi Halloman who sold to Opal Davis in the 1960s.

At some point in the early 1960s, Gala Resort was established higher on the hill, near where the private road for Idle Days Resort left the Jeffries Road, by a member of the same family. The ownership and operation of the two resorts was merged after several years. At first, two separate ads were published. Eventually, both resort names appeared in the same ad. The use of the two names was not consistent from year to year, some ads saying Idle Days & Gala Resorts, other ads reversing it to Gala & Idle Days Resorts. Now and then Gala would be dropped and the name would just be Idle Days Resort.

Through the 1970s and 80s, when the resort was owned by Paul and Helen McGuire, ads generally referred to it as just Idle Days Resort. As late as the year 2000, however, ads appeared that still called it Idle Days & Gala Resort. Hopefully, people looking for accommodations were never confused by such inconsistency. The resort had 800 feet of shoreline, covered fishing docks and luxurious cottages and motel

Idle Days & Gala Resort, *Osage Beach, MO. Photo by H. D. Weaver, 2005.*

units with large windows and picturesque views of the Lake. The playground for children occupied a central knoll within the motel portion of the resort, which was higher on the hill than the lake-front units. Walkways and roads leading to cottages, pool, lakeside and elsewhere on the property featured extensive native rock retaining walls. Idle Days & Gale Resort closed at the end of 2004. The buildings no longer exist.

Idlewild Court / Cabins *(Osage Beach, Camden County)* -

In 1936, Idlewild Court was built on a knoll on the south side of Hwy. 54 in Osage Beach across from the junction of Hwy. 54 and LkRd. 10, later designated 54-24 and now called Osage Beach Road. The Court faced Cannady's Cafe and Grocery Store, which were on the south side of Hwy. 54. The Osage Beach Post Office was adjacent to Idlewild Court on its west side.

Idlewild Court was owned and operated by Lee Gunnison who apparently did very little advertising during his tenure of ownership. He did see that his Court was listed on some of the early Lake of the Ozarks tourist maps. The world "Idlewild" sometimes appeared as two words -- Idle Wild -- in tourist literature.

The one-level Court had an unusual design. The log cabins, whose backs were to the highway, were connected with partially enclosed breezeways with wood lattice at the end facing the highway. The appearance of it was reminiscent of early American dog-trot houses. Each cabin had one window on the highway side. Some people likened the Court's appearance to that of a log fort.

Tourists interested in inquiring about accommodations could park along the rock retaining wall down near the highway and climb a flight of stairs to reach the office, or drive around to the other side [what appeared to be the back side]. Other

Idlewild Court, *Osage Beach, MO, Circa. 1936. Photographer Unknown.*

cabins not attached to the connected front row of cabins were available. For a number of years the logs were unpainted but by the 1950s they had been painted white.

The operation of Idlewild Court seems to have been interrupted several times after 1939. In 1968, the property was bought by George & Vi Strickland who built a Texaco station at the Court's east end. Their ads appeared as either Strickland's Texaco Service & Court or Strickland's Cottages. In February 2005, this property and the adjacent Lake Lumber Company property were cleared for a boat dealership.

Indian Burial Cave *(Miller County)* -

Indian Burial Cave is located high on a hillside overlooking the Osage River facing Bagnell Dam and about two miles due east of it. The cave is on D Road at an elevation of about 720 feet, placing it more than 100 feet above the Osage River valley bottom.

The gently arched entrance of Indian Burial Cave is about 35 feet wide and 7 to 10 feet high on a terrace where the hillside forms a bluff. The entrance chamber, wide, fairly dry and accommodating, made an ideal shelter for the Woodland Indians who used the cave more than 1500 years ago.

According to the descendents of J. A. Atkisson, who settled the property prior to the Civil War, the cave was discovered in the early 1800s by government surveyors. There are two cave openings nearly side-by-side in the bluff. The surveyors called one opening Little Mouth Cave and the other Large Mouth Cave. In essence, they are simply two openings to the same cave inside the hill.

According to folklore, Atkisson hid in the cave to avoid conscription when the Civil War broke out and remained there until a guerrilla band terrorizing the community chose the cave for a rendezvous point. For a time, Atkisson found it healthier to hide someplace else. Around the activities of this marauding band of guerrillas a tale of buried treasure is woven. The treasure, supposedly consisting of $15,000, is said to have been unearthed near Big Mouth Cave in 1894 but no documentation has been found to support either the treasure story or the treasure find.

In 1959, James F. Atkisson, the great-grandson of J. A. Atkisson, discovered Indian artifacts and burials within the cave entrance. The burials were exposed and the cave floor improved to accommodate visitors. Atkisson opened the cave to the public by creating a switchback road down to the entrance and buying several jeeps to take people down to the cave and return them to the small office and gift shop building on top of the hill.

The cave's entrance chamber is roughly circular in outline with two passages leading from it. The left passage leads to the second entrance [Little Mouth Cave]. The cave's main passage, which carries the cave stream, leads straight into the hill. To make the Little Mouth Cave passage available to the public, a trench was dug through the archaeologically fertile cave fill. Near this trench, as it leaves the entrance room, two complete Indian burials were found side by side. Atkisson also trenched into the main stream passage for a distance of about 150 feet for a tourist trail. All Indian artifacts and burials were displayed beneath glass. Atkisson operated the cave for several seasons and then leased the cave to Lee Mace of Ozark Opry fame, and Al Lechner of Lake Ozark.

Indian Burial Cave. *Photo from an Indian Burian Cave brochure, Circa. 1960s.*

The new operators installed an inclined cable car down the hillside to the cave opening, removed much of the fill in the cave's entrance passage back for a distance of around 200 feet to let the cave stream form a small lake, housed in the cave entrance to protect the artifact site and enhance its commercial presentation, and provided a pontoon boat ride on the new underground lake. Many additional Indian artifacts of the types created by Indians of this region thousands of years ago were added to the displays to make them more interesting.

In the years that followed, Lee Mace promoted the cave nightly to the audiences of his Ozark Opry show along Hwy. 54 in Osage Beach, which resulted in large crowds of visitors to the cave. The cave attraction thrived until Lee Mace died in a plane crash in 1985 and Al Lechner left the operation. Business declined afterward and the cave was closed about 1990. In 2002, the old gift shop building on top of the hill was destroyed by fire believed to have been set by vandals. The cave is no longer shown to the public.

Indian Burial Cave actually has more than 1,500 feet of passage along its underground stream course, however, the passage is a low, rocky, hazardous water crawl with few places to stand erect except at the very end where there is a series of high dome-roofed chambers.

Iron Smelter / Furnace *(Climax Springs, Camden County)* -

One mile up Bollinger Creek Cove at the 44-mile mark on the Osage Arm stands the remains of the old Iron Smelter, a relic of the 1870s when the Osage Iron Works Company was in operation. The base of the iron smelter stands in the waters of the cove close to the shore. It is the only historic structure that was left standing in the basin when it was cleared for Lake of the Ozarks. [see Osage Iron Works; also Irontown]

Irontown *(Climax Springs, Camden County)* -

The site of old Irontown is now inundated by the Lake. It was located about one mile up Bollinger Creek Cove from the 44-mile mark on the Osage Arm. It is covered by about 30 feet of water.

Irontown was established in 1872 when a Dr. A. Condee and Alex J. Campbell formed the *Condee & Campbell Company* to mine and process iron ore in the hills bordering Bollinger Creek. The name of the company was changed to *Osage Iron Furnace* and then *Osage Iron Works* all within the time frame of one year [see Osage Iron Works].

The Irontown Post Office was established in 1872 as Osage Iron Furnace but changed the same year to Osage Iron Works with Abram E. DeLozier as postmaster. Although the mining company got off to an impressive start and built some substantial mining and iron smelting facilities in Bollinger Creek valley, the company folded rather quickly.

The town that grew up around the company site had a population of about 250. The Irontown Ferry was a busy operation and the steamboat landing was the port of call for a number of steamboats that plied the Osage River in the last two decades of the nineteenth century.

After the company collapsed, tie hacking became the industry that kept the town alive. Still, its population dwindled and by 1900 the local timber resource was all but exhausted. In 1904 the town's last business closed but enough citizens remained in Irontown homes to keep the post office open until 1931.

Irontown may have had a short and unfortunate life but it is the only inundated town site beneath the Lake with a surviving monument -- the impressive ruins of the old Osage Iron Works smelter, which still sit along the shoreline of Bollinger Creek Cove. To learn more about life in old Irontown and the interesting people who once called it home, see the 1992 issue of the *Camden County Historian* published by the Camden County Historical Society. It contains a complete and well researched history of the Osage Iron Works and Irontown by Neta Pope.

Irontown Ferry *(Climax Springs, Camden County)* -

The Irontown Ferry was established in the 1880s on the Osage River at what is today the 45-mile mark on the Osage Arm. By today's coordinates, it would have docked on the Lake's north side at the end of LkRd. 5-25N or what is now Camp Hohn Drive off County Route RA out of Laurie. Because there was an island in the river in the old days, the ferry docked along the south side of the river at the downstream end of the island off what is today Osage Trails Drive at the end of Bollinger Creek Road off Hwy. 7.

The old ferry was originally built for horse, buggy and wagon traffic and was therefore rather small. It was simply a short barge with wooden railings along the sides and was poled across the river. The ferry operator repeatedly had problems losing the ferry during high water. On one occasion it broke mooring and was swept downstream by floodwaters all the way to Old Linn Creek, a distance of 14 miles. Eventually, the ferry went to the cable system. In the early 1900s, after cars arrived, it was discovered that the barge could accommodate only three vehicles.

The owner of the ferry was John White, an Irontown merchant who hired Lindsey Capps to run the ferry. According to Neta Pope's history of Irontown, John built fenced lots near the ferry landings so that livestock could be penned up for the night. White provided lodging in his home for travelers using the ferry. As Irontown began to fade from existence, John White was soon the only merchant left in the valley. When Union Electric bought John out in the late 1920s, he was in his 70s and so attached to his home that he had to be present when the men clearing the basin came to burn down the old homestead. Although John White would no longer have a ferry service at this point along the Osage after Lake of the Ozarks was created, a ferry service was re-instated here in the early 1930s.

In the spring of 1934, what could have been a very serious ferry accident occurred with the new ferry. "The presence of mind of a young woman and the quick action on the part of another passenger on the Irontown Ferry...resulted in the saving of the life of the young woman after she and a young companion had fallen from the bow of the ferry into the Lake of the Ozarks at a point where the water is approximately 70 feet deep," said the *Versailles Leader* May 4, 1934.

"Miss Gene Perry, teacher in the Climax Springs schools, and her companion had accompanied the Gospel Team of the Missouri Valley College at Marshall, from Climax Springs to the ferry and were riding across the Lake with the six members of the team and their chaperones. When the ferry reached the middle of the Lake, Miss Perry and her companions walked to the end of the "apron" on the ferry, which operates on hinges for the loading and unloading of cars and passengers, and which, ordinarily, is fastened securely. As they reached the end, the apron gave way throwing them into the Lake directly in the path of the ferry. The young man, who could swim quite well, soon appeared above the surface of the water, but Miss Perry, who could not swim, did not. Arthur Biley, Missouri Valley College student, dived from the ferry in search of Miss Perry, swam completely under the boat but found no trace of her. A few seconds later, seemingly hours to those on the boat, Miss Perry's hand appeared above the water as she pulled herself hand-over-hand from the cold water with the aid of the tie-up cable which she by chance came into contact with soon after falling into the water. Her friends...pulled her from the water. Other than being chilled...Miss Perry was none the worse because of the accident. When she came into contact with the cable, she realized it was her one and only chance, held her breath and began her climb to safety."

J Bar H Rodeo *(Camdenton, Camden County)* -

The J Bar H Rodeo arena was built along Hwy. 5 South at the edge of Camdenton in 1951-52 by Harry B. and Jean Nelson. Rodeo Road, across Hwy. 5 from the Camdenton school, memoralizes this former attraction. The rodeo property is now the location of the Camdenton Public Library and the Department of Health buildings.

The rodeo arena, capable of seating thousands of people, was built under the supervision of Joe Sam Libby, a well known Camdenton carpenter of the 1950s who was active in rodeos.

The J Bar H Rodeo opened in 1952 for a three-day run with livestock from the Roberts Rodeo Company Ranch of Strong City, Kansas. The dedication address by Missouri Governor Phil M. Donnelly and a parade complete with cowboys, floats and music preceded the event.

The first year's three-day event attracted 26,000 people. On Saturday night, July 11, 1953, the program included the following: *Event No. 1* - Grand Entry & Introductions of Officials; *Event No. 2* - Wild Horse Race; *Event No. 3* - Budweiser Eight White Mule Hitch; *Event No. 4* - Bareback Bronc Riding Contest; *Event No. 5* - Gone to the Dogs; *Event No. 6* - Calf Roping Contest; *Event No. 7* - John Lindsey & His Mule; *Event No. 8* - Missouri State Log Chopping Championship Elimination; *Event No. 9* - Saddle Bronc Riding Contest; *Event No. 10* - Rose-Bud Sioux Indians; *Event No. 11* - Beeswax and Moore Family; *Event No. 12* - Steer Wrestling Contest; *Event No. 13* - Curtiss Candy Pony Hitch; *Event No. 14* - Lake of the Ozarks Square Dance Team; *Event No. 15* - Brama Bull Riding Contest.

For this particular rodeo there were 80 contestants representing the states of Oklahoma, New Jersey, Kansas, Texas, Missouri, Arizona, Wisconsin, Illinois, South Dakota, Colorado and California. Every night of the rodeo was an occasion of drama, laughter and excitement. Each year the rodeo's attendance grew until by its twelfth year more than 100,000 people attended a nine-day rodeo. Nelson billed his attraction as a "World Championship Rodeo," and brought top national rodeo talent as well as Hollywood and television stars to entertain the crowds. People came to see Rex Allen and his horse Koko, Lassie, Clint Eastwood, Glu Gulager, Doug McClure, Fess Parker, the horses from the movie Ben Hur, stars from the Beverly Hillbillies and many more.

In the mid 1960s, a series of heart attacks forced Harry Nelson to discontinue his participation in the operation. A leasing arrangement was not successful. The rodeo sat silent for nearly 10 years and then re-opened July 29, 1975, under new ownership for an operational run that extended into the 1980s. The J Bar H Rodeo is gone but its memory lingers of a time when rustic architecture, rough and tumble rodeo activities, performance water skiing, square dancing and hillbilly themes characterized the Lake entertainment scene.

Jack Salmon -

In the 1930s you heard a lot about fishing at Lake of the Ozarks. The two fish that scooped most of the headlines were "bass" and "jack salmon." But at the Lake today you rarely hear the words "jack salmon" because this popular game fish has another name -- walleye. In fact, it has more than one name. What early day fishermen called it depended largely on where the fisherman came from and where he caught the fish.

G. M. Kirby, chief of hatcheries for the old Missouri Game and Fish Department revealed some of the names this fish went by for *Lake of the Ozarks News* in 1932.

In the north half of the state it is known by its proper name of 'wall-eyed pike,'" he explained. "In south Missouri...it is known as 'jack salmon'... In Pennsylvania it is called 'Susquehanna salmon'... In eastern states, it is called 'pike perch,' 'perch pike' or 'glass eye'... In the Ohio valley and western North Carolina it is called the 'Jack'... and in some parts of Ohio valley 'white salmon.'"

For the most part, the Lake's early fishermen probably didn't concern themselves with what the fish was called. It tasted good and it put up a good fight. That's all they cared about.

Jacob's Cave *(Versailles, Gravois Mills, Morgan County)* -

Jacob's Cave is located about six miles south of Versailles off Hwy. 5 on Route TT or 2.5 miles north of Gravois Mills. Not only is it one of the most beautiful show caves in the Lake area but has the distinction of being the very first cave in the Lake region opened to the public after Lake of the Ozarks was created. The history of Jacob's Cave has been well research by its current owner, Frank Hurley.

The cave was discovered in 1875 by Jacob Craycraft, a lead miner. Exactly how he discovered the cave, however, has become the grist of folklore. Minor details vary according to who is telling the tale. In general, Craycraft is said to have been digging test pits in search of lead when he and his associates stopped for lunch. They saw an animal disappear into a small hole and tossed some rocks in after it. They could see nothing in the hole and proceeded to toss in a larger rock that rolled some distance, then fell and landed with a "thunk." Curious, they proceeded to dig the hole larger and thereby discovered a cave chamber beneath the hillside. That room gave access to an extensive, highly decorated cave. Craycraft's signature and date Aug. 9, 1875, can still be found in the cave, preserved in flowstone near the cave's old original entrance.

Entrance to Jacob's Cave, *Circa. 1940s. Photographer Unknown.*

Although there is no documentation to show that Craycraft ever owned the cave, he apparently explored it thoroughly and would guide people through the cave on lantern tours for 25 cents each. The land upon which the cave lies has an interesting and checkered ownership history prior to its commercialization in 1931-32.

The cave was opened to the public in 1932 and ads for the cave appear in the 1930s issues of *Lake of the Ozarks News*, and in other publications of that period that promoted tourism in the Ozarks. Tours of the cave, however, only went at far as the Elephant Head formation, which is near the half-way point of today's tour.

Jacob's Cave was often used for apple storage in the 1920s and 30s. A news item in the *Eldon Advertiser* on Oct. 12, 1933, said: "The Versailles Orchards Company, operators and owners of one of the largest apple orchards in the state located south of Versailles, are storing a portion of their crop in Jacob's Cave... About 1,500 bushel baskets have been placed in a part of the cavern and more will be put in later. The cave has a year 'round temperature of about 60 degrees and makes an ideal storage place for fruits."

The operation of the cave at this time was fairly low key and in 1935 it was being managed by Mr. & Mrs. Eli Hays and their son, who used gas lanterns for the tours.

An interesting incident that occurred not long after the cave was opened to the public, but which did not come to the attention of the local people or the operators of the cave at that time, came to light only in 1998.

Mr. George H. De Lapp of Kansas City told of his experience at the cave when he was a boy scout in 1931. At the time, he was living in Brunswick, Missouri. In August 1931, the Rev. Morris Bailey, pastor of the Christian church at Brunswick, took a group of six boy scouts to see Bagnell Dam and the new Lake of the Ozarks. De Lapp was one of the six boys. Today, only three of that original group are still living. De Lapp tells the following story:

"We traveled on Hwy. 5, coming south from U. S. 24. We were not far from Bagnell Dam when we made a comfort stop. In doing so, we found a wooden walkway, with railing, that led around the edge of a hill and back to an old log cabin. It had a sign for "A Cave." An elderly man lived there and we asked where the cave was and how much it cost to go in...it was a nickel or a dime per person, which we paid and he said just follow the walk around the hill to the cave.

"The cave entrance was nearly big enough for us smaller kids to stand up and walk in. The others, including the scoutmaster, had to crawl.

"We entered [all had flashlights] and found a huge room like 60 to 70 feet long and 40 to 50 feet wide with a high dome. To the right was a lake with water that ran in from the left and exited from the right.

"The more adventurous of the troop used their lights and fishing cord to crawl back into some of the tunnels and crevices. But there was one boy who was scared and sat on a big rock just inside the entrance. He was swinging his foot back and forth kicking the fine dust and we began scratching through the same. Eventually, we dug up a complete human skeleton that had a 45 caliber hole in the forehead of the skull and the back of the skull was blown off...

"We put all the bones in a sack and brought them back to Brunswick and they were displayed in the front window of the town's paper for a long time..."

De Lapp visited Jacob's Cave in 1999 to visit with Frank Hurley and get a look at the cave where the skeleton had been found. He also asked the editor of the Brunswick newspaper why the story of the bones didn't get into the paper. He was told that the editor at the time probably deleted it for fear that publishing the story might get them into trouble.

Elephant's Head Formation *in Jacob's Cave, Circa. 1950s. Photo by Hammond & Irwin.*

The old man who let them explore the cave, wasn't around when they exited the cave, so they took the bones home with them. Was the skeleton the remains of a murder victim? If so, it would have had to have occurred after 1875. Was it the remains of an Indian who had been shot and buried there long ago? This hardly seems possible since the cave was probably not accessible to anyone, including native Americans, before 1875. No one knows the answers to these questions and the bones and skull are long gone. It's a Jacob's Cave mystery that may never be solved.

New commercial development took place in Jacob's Cave after 1947 when the cave was purchased by Russell P. Hall, a realtor of Versailles. Underground development was taken beyond the Elephant's head to the Soda Straw Room and into areas where cave chambers are nearly filled with exquisite cave formations. The developers discovered Snow White's Bower, a once water-filled cavity in the rock that is lined with pink crystals. It is one of the largest and most beautiful geodes to be seen along the walkways of an American show cave.

During the early years of Hall's operation of the cave there was a lighted neon sign at the highway entrance along old Hwy. 5 (Route TT) welcoming tourists to the cave as late as midnight. Show caves are rarely if ever open so late in the evening.

Hall traded the cave property for a large piece of lakeshore property and the cave became the operation of Mr. Jesse Whaley who later went into partnership with Mrs. Frances Castle. In 1965, the current owners, Frank and Jane Hurley, bought the cave.

Not all of Jacob's Cave is open to the public but those portions that are, display a vast array of beautiful cave formations and fascinating bedrock features sculpted by underground water flow. Some of the rooms are quite large, the cave is nicely lighted, and guided tours are along paved walkways with no steps, so the cave can be toured by people in wheelchairs. The bones and teeth of prehistoric animals have also been found in the cave and are on display along the tour route.

Jeffries Boat Dock, Fishing Barge & Cottages *(Osage Beach, Camden County)* -

The first ads for Jeffries Boat Dock & Fishing Barge appeared in mid 1930s. The barge sat below the Grand Glaize Bridge at its west end on the north side close to the first pier. At this point in time there was no development along the south side of the highway close to the west end of the bridge. There was room along the shoulder on the south side for vehicles to park. On the outside of the curve on the north side there was no guardrail as there is today, but there was a row of white wooden posts installed by the highway department to keep vehicles from going over the edge.

Beyond the highway on the north side was a long steep slope leading down to the Lake. A narrow road and a path with some steps led from the highway to a small wooden building that served as the bait and boat motor shop. There was a small covered boat dock where a fisherman could rent a boat and a motor. The dock and bait shop were not far from the head of the cove below the Grand Glaize Cafe.

To reach the fishing barge, a narrow road led along the cove's shoreline next to a high concrete retaining wall that held back the steep slope going up to the highway's edge. Many fishermen simply walked to the barge since parking at the end was very

Jeffries Boat Dock, *Osage Beach, MO, Circa. 1930s. Photographer Unknown.*

limited. The barge was very close to a high, steel, Union Electric utility tower, which still exists.

The Jeffries boat dock and bait shop were operated by William Derrick Jeffries and his sons, Tolliver, Frank and Leland. The Jeffries fishing barge was managed by Valonia, Wilma and Nellie Jeffries. On tourist maps and in publications these businesses were generally promoted as Jeffries Camp & Fishing Barge, or Jeffries Camp & Boat Dock, or Jeffries Cottages. The cottages were located on the hilltop just west of Jeffries Road.

Fishing was especially good near the Grand Glaize Bridge in the 1930s and 40s and the success of the Jeffries Fishing Barge business brought some unwelcome neighbors. The *Lake of the Ozarks News* carried the story on July 15, 1934:

"For some time past barges and rafts have been tying up to the piers of the [Grand] Glaize Bridge, or anchoring in the immediate vicinity and their owners and assistants are reported to be soliciting tourists and others on the highway to fish from them, charging a fee for the privilege. At first there was but one of these rafts or barges, but as the business became profitable on a small scale, others came to participate, and then others, until at times as many as five of them have been engaged in the rivalry in solicitation for patronage on or near Hwy. 54.

"At first but little attention was paid to them but as the number of barges increased certain menacing features began to develop. Those making complaint state that the sanitary conditions are such as to create a serious situation. Toilets are located on these rafts or barges, polluting the Glaize river [sic] at this point. Cleaning fish and dumping the refuse into the [water]...does not add to the sanitary condition of...the Lake or nearby shoreline.

"The first hazard is said to be...serious, both as to the occupants of the barges and to the bridge structure, since the rafts are anchored or tied up just beneath it.

"Neighboring resort owners have protested to the United State's engineers office in Kansas City. [They] claim the War Department has no jurisdiction in the matter and suggested it be taken up with the Attorney General of the State. Early this week a delegation of resort owners visited the State Capitol and presented the situation to several departments, among them the Highway Department, since the bridge across the Glaize is said to be menaced, and also with the Board of Health. Later, it is expected to ask the Attorney General to take charge of the situation if there has been no relief in the meantime.

"This seems to be the first instance in the history of the Lake where a situation of this kind has come up for attention of the State departments in suppressing what is said to be a threat to the sanitary conditions of a considerable area of the waters in the immediate vicinity of the main body of the Lake. The resort owners are also concerned about the danger to life in the event any of these rafts should burn or sink since the water is deep and the means of conveying a number of people in a short time to the shore is considered inadequate. A tragedy of this kind would reflect on the entire Lake area."

It is presumed that this issue was resolved shortly thereafter. The Jeffries Boat Dock and Fishing Barge continued in business until the late 1960s. [see Grand Glaize Cafe]

Jeffries Ozark Cafe *(Osage Beach, Camden County)* -

The Jeffries Ozark Cafe was opened in 1935 by Robert Jeffries along the south side of Hwy. 54 about one half mile west of the Grand Glaize Bridge. It was about 500 feet from LkRd. 54-47 where today, Hawk's Nest Road leaves the highway. In 1935, Hawk's Nest Road did not exist.

A 1935 advertisement for the cafe said it had dining room service and meals served family style or a la carte. It indicated they catered to tourists and patrons of the cottage camps in the area. About 1940 this cafe became Turrin's Cafe, then Neely's Cafe about 1946, and finally, Lakeview Cafe in 1953. This cafe does not exist today.

Jenn's Point Comfort *(Osage Beach, Camden County)* -

This resort, with a name that makes one think of an alcoholic drink, was short lived. It was one of the early resorts off Route KK on Turkey Bend near the 21-mile mark of the Osage Arm. It was somewhere near the end of Three Seasons Road and a neighbor to Berry's Lodge and Flack Resort. Jenn's Point Comfort was a resort of the late 1930s and may have been on the shoreline of Miller Hollow Cove or the adjacent Chimney Cove.

Jester's Camp *(Gravois Mills, Morgan County)* -

In 1937, Harry G. Jester and his wife built Jester's Camp on the Gravois Arm of the Lake. The camp was located at the end of what was then LkRd. 5-8, later designated 5-78, then Route P, which ends at Gibson Point at the 4-mile mark on the Gravois Arm.

Jester's Camp was off to the right along the shoreline of Mill Creek Cove and their neighbors were Happy Days Resort and Silver Moon Resort.

About 1951, the resort sold to R. B. Hatcher who renamed it Mill Creek Resort, taking his cue from the cove upon which the resort was located. Today, these three resorts are remembered in the names of roads near the end of Route P. Silver Moon Road leaves Route P and extends to the shoreline where the resort was once located. Hunter Road, nearby, leaves Route P and branches into Happy Days Road and Mill Creek Marina Road.

R. B. Hatcher advertised his place as "a clean camp for clean people." Mill Creek Resort had cottages with electricity and hot and cold showers. Not all camps and resorts developed in the 1930s were fully modern with cottages that had electricity and plumbing. Some camps and resorts did not become fully modernized until the 1950s.

By 1953, Mill Creek Resort also had lighted docks. In 1956, guests were paying $5.00 for two people per day for a cottage. Around 1959, the resort sold to Harry and Betty Benne who operated the resort into the 1970s. By this time the resort had covered boat docks, covered fishing docks and an enclosed swimming area. Neighbors included EEBCO Marine, Char-Mar-Cove Resort and Captain's Fancy Resort. The operation of Mill Creek Resort continued through the 1980s into the 1990s, eventually becoming Mill Creek Marina.

Johnson's Snug Harbor *(Osage Beach, Camden County)* -

In 1940, M. P. Johnson built Johnson's Snug Harbor Resort in Osage Beach in the first cove on the north side of Hwy. 54 at the east end of the Grand Glaize Bridge. The only other resorts on the cove at that time were Wood's Lake Cove Lodge and Kelly's Modern Cottages, which were on the opposite side of the cove along Hwy. 54 from the east end of the Grand Glaize Bridge.

Johnson's Snug Harbor Resort was on the south bank of the cove and reached by first taking LkRd. 54-13, now called Passover Road or Old Post Office Road and then what is now Windjammer Drive and, near the end of the drive, taking a right turn onto the resort's private road.

Johnson's Snug Harbor Resort had eight completely furnished, gas-heated, housekeeping cottages. Most of the cottages were frame but a few were veneered with native stone below the window level. Johnson kept adding recreational features to the resort besides swimming, boating and fishing and started advertising that he had horseshoes, croquet and shuffleboard for adults and a playground for children. In 1955 a covered fishing dock was added.

Johnson's Snug Harbor Resort, *Osage Beach, MO, Circa. 1940. Photographer Unknown.*

In 1959, Johnson sold the resort to Gordon C. Fender who kept the name as Snug Harbor Resort. It wasn't until the 1970s that Fender began to promote it as Fender's Snug Harbor Resort. Upon buying the business, Fender added three new cottages, built a new covered boat dock, a new floating swimming pool, a new launching ramp, a gas pump on the dock, and created crappie beds. By 1984 the word "marina" had been added to the name. This resort no longer exists, having closed around the year 2000.

Joyce Motel *(Lake Ozark, Miller County)* -

Joyce Motel was built along Hwy. 54 in Lake Ozark one-half mile west of Bagnell Dam on the north side of the highway in 1952; it opened in 1953. The motel sat about where the Lake Ozark Fire Station Headquarters is located today about half-way between Hidden Acres Road and Route HH.

The motel was owned and operated by Mr. & Mrs. Kenneth Owings. There were about 10 to 14 connected units sitting well back from the highway, each with rustic, knotty-pine interiors that had exposed rafters overhead. The motel had electric heat, air-conditioning, and featured air foam mattresses.

East of the Joyce Motel was Deer Motel and then Frazee's Modern Cabins. There was no business immediately adjacent to Joyce Motel on the west side between it and LkRd. 3A, now called Stanton Road.

In 1954, Joyce Motel was sold to Lester Estes and Bud Henderson, who are cousins. The motel was operated by Lester and Hazel Estes until 1971. During this period of time, improvements were made to the motel including the addition of a swimming pool. The motel closed in the late 1970s.

Joyce Motel, *Lake Ozark, MO, Circa. 1960s. Photograph by L. L. Cook, Milwaukee.*

Boating at Lake of the Ozarks, *Circa. 1960s. Photograph by Gerald R. Massie.*

Kaiser *(Miller County)* -

Kaiser is about one mile southeast of Osage Beach on Hwy. 42. "New" Kaiser has grown up along both sides of Hwy. 42 between School of the Osage and Blue Ridge Road. The original site of Kaiser is about one-half mile south off Hwy. 42 on Kaiser Road.

The village of Old Kaiser began with a blacksmith shop and gristmill, which formed the nucleus around which the village grew at the beginning of the twentieth century. The post office opened in 1904 in the same building that housed a general merchandise store. A second store was opened in the village in the late 1940s.

Old Kaiser was a lively center of agricultural commerce during its first couple of decades. In the late 1930s and early 40s, when the National Recreation Area, which later became Lake of the Ozarks State Park, was being created, the village saw a lot of business generated by the Civilian Conservation Corps men who worked on the park's construction. The village declined after the park was completed because the Kaiser to Passover Road that went through the village was not chosen by state officials for an official entrance to the state park. Since this county road was also severed by the Lake, it left Kaiser on a road to nowhere of significance. The state chose to send park visitors to an entrance about one mile further east on D Road, which later became Hwy. 42.

Old Kaiser, MO, Post Office, *Circa. 1936. Photographer Unknown.*

The last store in Old Kaiser closed in 1971 but by the 1960s, new development had begun along Hwy. 42 near the junction of Kaiser Road, renewing the town and stimulating growth. The post office was moved to a location along Hwy. 42 at new Kaiser. By the mid 1980s, Kaiser could boast of having an ornamental sign company, gas company, marine supply, auto shop, lumber company and general store. Following that came a second lumber company, School of the Osage, several service stations, and a variety of other businesses.

From the tourist viewpoint, Kaiser was the location of Bob Nolan's Country Music Hall in the 1960s, which was followed by Chuck Watkin's Ozark Jamboree in the same building. Today, a church occupies this property.

The old general store and post office building is still standing on Kaiser Road but now vacant.

Kalfran Lodge *(Osage Beach, Camden County)* -

Kalfran Lodge, named for K. K. Schopp, whose nickname was "Kal," was built about 1947 off LkRd. 54-15A, later designated 54-37 and now called Jeffries Road. This road runs down the ridge line of a peninsula a little more than one mile in length separating the Grand Glaize Arm of the Lake from Darby Hollow and Harper's Hollow coves, which are accessed at the 19.5-mile mark on the Osage Arm. Kalfran Lodge is near the mouth of Darby Hollow on the west side of the peninsula on Kalfran Drive.

Kalfran Resort was operated by K. K and Gladys Schopp from Webster Groves, Missouri. At first they had just a few stone cottages on a terraced hillside. Their side of Darby Hollow Cove has an inlet, which allowed the resort to, in time, "wrap around" this indention at the water's edge. For a brief period at the beginning, people wanting to rent a cottage in advance had to write to the Schopp's home address in St. Louis. It wasn't until the early 1950s that Kal moved Gladys and their four children -- Tom, Kym, Steve and Pat -- to the Lake.

Kal and Gladys divorced in 1958. Gladys continued the operation of the resort after the divorce and then in 1960 made a business trade with Dick Jasinsky -- he took over the operation of Kalfran Lodge and she took over the operation of Lakeside Courts in Lake Ozark. Gladys, a teacher by profession, went back to teaching at School of the Osage after selling Lakeside Courts in 1963. Kal Schopp died in 1966. Gladys taught until she retired in 1977.

Kalfran Lodge began small like most mom and pop businesses of the early days, but it grew rapidly, spreading along its shoreline property until the operation

Waterfront at Kalfran Lodge, *Osage Beach, MO, Circa. 1950. Note the undeveloped hillside in the background of this early view at the resort. That same background is in the next photo. Photographer Unknown.*

covered most of the original 11 acres that Kal Schopp bought. The resort's success was also reflected in its advertising. The first ads were small in Lake of the Ozarks Association annual guidebooks. By 1953, their ad was consuming one-third of a page. In 1955, it went to half a page and then to a full page by 1956. In 1957, only Kirkwood Lodge in the Osage Beach area had a guidebook ad as large and prominent as the one for Kalfran Lodge. All color ads came in the 1960s and an artist sketch of their lakefront and facilities was replaced with full color photos. By this time the resort was advertising "ultra modern beachside cottages" and an elevated swimming pool along the lakefront. In 1970, they advertised rustic rock cottages by the Lake, motel rooms with a superb view and spacious waterfront apartments. By 1980, the resort had 50 units in their combination of condo-type apartments, motel rooms and lakeside cottages. They also had two swimming pools, covered boat docks and a recreational hall. Kalfran Lodge is still in business on the shores of Darby Cove.

***Kalfran Lodge,** Osage Beach, MO, Photo by H. D. Weaver, 2005.*

Kavanaugh's Gravois Beach Resort *(Gravois Mills, Morgan County)* -

In 1931-32, C. W. Kavanaugh built Kavanaugh's Gravois Beach Resort about one-half mile up-Lake from the mouth of Little Gravois Cove. The resort was accessible by LkRd. 5-7 [now TT-1]. This portion of Hwy. 5 is now called Route TT and the resort road is called Anchorage Drive. The resort was built along the west side of the cove just beyond the first bend.

Kavanaugh constructed 18 log cabins, installed electricity, and had running water in them by 1934. He added a gas station and grocery store building that also doubled for the Bass Head Tavern. He operated the business until 1939 when he sold to Carl Schmidt who advertised it at Gravois Beach Resort. [see Gravois Beach Resort]

Kaysinger Bluff *(Warsaw, Benton County)* -

Along the Osage River and the Lake are many impressive bluffs, sometimes named for events but more often named after a former landowner. Kaysinger Bluff just north of Warsaw is one such bluff but time has corrupted the spelling of its name. German immigrants named Kaysingle lived near the bluff in the nineteenth century and used the caves and crevices in the rock to burn wood into charcoal for sale.

Kaysinger Bluff stretches for nearly half-a-mile along the northeast side of the Osage River. Before the constuction of Truman Dam, it was a feature along the shoreline of Lake of the Ozarks. In the 1970s, Truman Dam, which created Truman Reservoir, was built at the southern terminus of this bluff.

The bluff rises some 200 feet and was a landmark for early day steamboat pilots. It was a favorite of early day photographers and numerous images of the bluff, and the scenery from its top, appear on postcards, some as early as the year 1900.

The U. S. Army Corps of Engineers, who built Truman Dam, have a visitors center at the bluff's highest point and the center houses a museum that chronicles the construction of Truman Dam, and has exhibits that highlight the cultural and natural history of the area.

Kellerstrass, Ernest *(Gravois Mills, Morgan County)* -

Many interesting personalities have been and are associated with Lake of the Ozarks. One of the early ones was Ernest Kellerstrass of Kansas City.

Earnest Kellerstrass, *Circa. 1940. Photo card produced by Kellerstrass.*

Kellerstrass made his fortune early in the twentieth century raising and breeding chickens on a farm where Central High School was later built in Kansas City. He was known as the originator of the Crystal White Orpington Chicken, and also noted for his bass fishing promotions at Lake of the Ozarks in the 1930s and 40s. During the same period of time he and his wife bought a summer house on the Lake in the Gravois Mills area.

Both Ernest and his wife were avid bass fishermen. In the early 1930s, Ernest created a series of black and white real photo postcards that featured him, his wife, his boats and their fishing activities at the Lake. He said he created the cards for his friends. He handed them out wherever he went and used them as a means of advertising his services as a fishing guide on the Lake. On every card is the letter "K" inside of a circle. It stood for his name and was his unofficial trademark. He even put the symbol on his aluminum fishing boats. A picture of Ernest Kellerstrass, made from one of his postcards, began appearing on the Lake of the Ozarks Association maps in 1936, showing him standing in a boat, holding a large bass in both hands, and wearing not only a three-piece suit, but a bow tie. His photo appeared on many subsequent maps produced by the Association well into the 1950s.

"If you want to know how to catch big bass, the kind that weigh five, six and seven pounds -- just ask Mr. and Mrs. Ernest Kellerstrass. They know and they'll tell," said the *Versailles Leader* Sept. 10, 1937. "Mr. and Mrs. Kellerstrass, by the way, are Missouri's nominees for championship man and wife team of bass fishermen. They carried their claim to the title at the opening of this year's bass season when they caught 20 bass weighing 117¾ pounds in Lake of the Ozarks."

Kinds 'O Fishin' -

An entertaining article titled "Kinds 'O Fishin' appeared in the February 1933 issue of the *Lake of the Ozarks News* as a prelude to the "Lake of the Ozarks News Fishing Club Contest For 1933." Parts of it are reprinted here:

"There are almost as many 'kinds of fishin' as there are fish and that is a great many... And the fact that almost all kinds may be and often are practiced on Lake of the Ozarks simply proves what a fisherman's paradise the Lake really is.

"There's '*fly fishin*' for silver bass that fight like a fish five times their size and their even sportier [sic] and gamer cousins, the black bass.

"There is '*troll fishin*' and the many outboard enthusiasts on the lake can testify that there is seldom anything finer than the purr of a Johnson Single carrying them to the height of the afternoon's ambition -- a strike.

"There's good old '*bamboo fishin*' and the more elaborate '*rod and reel*' variety. There's -- oh at least a hundred kinds of fishing... *Cat fishin*' -- now there is a real genuine, 100% comfortable fishin.' First you dig for worms...then you go to the lakeshore being careful...to choose a shady spot... Cut yourself a pole, tie a string on to it, your hook on the string, a worm on the hook and toss the worm end...into the lake. Sit down with your back against a tree, pull your hat over your eyes and then let nature take its course...

"There are several different kinds of cat fishin' -- I remember in Florida we used to catfish with nets -- we called it "*scoop fishin*.' In some parts the fishermen substitute '*trot-line fishin*' for cat fishin'... Trot-line fishin' is no more exciting than belonging to a joint stock company...

"Yes, there are these and many other kinds o' fishin' but the kind I really prefer over all others is '*jug fishin*.' To properly jug fish you need a sunny day, a boat...to get you to a peaceful cove...and a jug with the proper fluid. No, you don't even need a line and pole to jug fish -- after a few minutes they are entirely unnecessary for by then you can jump in and catch them with your bare hands!"

The article's author was anonymous. You need to read that last part again and think about it if the meaning escaped you on the first reading.

Kirkwood Lodge *(Osage Beach, Camden County)* -

Kirkwood Lodge began life around 1940 as the Arthur M. Pope Hotel. It was on LkRd. 54-10, later designated 54-24 and now called Osage Beach Road. The road runs down the spine of the peninsula. Kirkwood Lodge is adjacent to the cobblestone-veneered Osage Beach Hotel built in 1931-32 by B. Ray Franklin on the north side of the peninsula.

Kirkwood Lodge Reservation Confirmation Card, *Osage Beach, MO, Circa. 1950s. Printed for the Lodge by Ray Printing.*

Pope did very little advertising and, in October 1944, sold the hotel to two retired Army colonels, Lawrence Kirkman and John D. Woodmansee. The new owners crafted the name "Kirkwood" by using parts of their names.

Kirkman and Woodmansee operated the Lodge for one season and sold it to Dr. A. J. Amick, a neighbor to the Lodge. About this time Bill Hagadorn, a Colorado native, became acquainted with the resort while on a business trip during a brief stopover at the Lake to visit with a friend, Vic Blakely, who met him at the Lodge. The two men liked the Lake area and tried to buy the Osage Beach Hotel, but were unsuccessful. Later, Bill and Amick negotiated and Bill ended up leasing Kirkwood Lodge with an option to buy. Bill's parents joined the operation and the Hagadorns bought Kirkwood Lodge in 1946.

Innovative and progressive in his operation, Bill probably deserves much of the credit for getting graduating high school seniors from states like Illinois, Iowa and Kansas to begin coming to Lake of the Ozarks for their senior trips. The success of Kirkwood in attracting such school groups in the 1950s was also beneficial to neighboring resorts such as Kalfran, Kapilana, Temple and several others, which were also patronized by high school senior groups. In the 50s and 60s, thousands of seniors showed up at the Lake in April and May, getting package deals with the resorts, which included lodging and entertainment for several days and nights. Their entertainment could include any combination of dances, lake cruises, trail rides, and trips to country music shows, show caves, and water ski performances as well as all of the attractions that could then be found on the Bagnell Dam Strip.

Bill Hagadorn was also instrumental in making the area popular with square dance groups. In 1972, the Hagadorns sold Kirkwood Lodge to their entertainment director, Marshall Flippo.

Klinger Cave *(Eldon, Aurora Springs, Miller County)* -

Klinger Cave is located east of the site of old Aurora Springs and Eldon in a hollow along the southeast side of Saline Creek. The cave is also known as Ancient Grotto and Vernon Cave. The name Klinger originated with William Klinger who owned the property in the 1890s. He had a watch repair shop in Aurora Springs during the town's boom days. He was the inventor of a patent eyelet hook in general use when high top shoes were in vogue. He sold his invention for a reported $1,200 to $1,500 and thought he had done well, however, the new owners of the eyelet hook promoted it widely and became quite wealthy. The passage of time has corrupted the spelling of the name and the cave is sometimes listed as Klinner Cave. It has also been called Kemma Cave. [see Vernon Cave].

High School Seniors on Senior Trip to Lake,
Circa. 1950s. Photographer Unknown.

Lake Benton -

While Bagnell Dam was being built, a controversy arose in the Missouri Legislature over what to call the new lake that would be formed by the dam. Several names were proposed. The name proposed by Benton County's Republican representative -- James A. Logan -- was "Lake Benton."

For the story of this controversy, see "Naming Lake of the Ozarks."

Lake Fork Heights *(Camdenton, Camden County)* -

Lake Fork Heights was established about six miles north of Camdenton on the west side of Hwy. 5 around 1946. The owner's name has not been determined but he was apparently from Chicago. The business advertised having stone cottages with private baths, cooking facilities and gas heat. A cafe was on the grounds and entertainment included dancing.

Lake Fork Heights may have experienced a period of closure or simply wasn't advertised in Lake of the Ozarks Association or Chamber of Commerce literature from about 1953 to 1960 when it was sold to El & Kay Nance who renamed it El Kay Motel [see El Kay Motel].

Lake McClurg -

While Bagnell Dam was being built, one of the names proposed for the lake to be created was "Lake McClurg" to honor former Gov. Joseph W. McClurg. This name was proposed by Camden County's representative, J. W. Vincent. For the story of this controversy early in the Lake's history, see "Naming Lake of the Ozarks."

Lake of the Ozarks Improvement & Protective Association -

When Bagnell Dam was complete in 1931, roadside and lakeshore businesses began to develop throughout the region and the new business community quickly recognized that the Lake needed to be advertised and promoted. The first large promotional effort came in February 1932 during the Better Homes and Building Exposition of the Real Estate Board of Kansas City. The Exposition was held Feb. 1-6, 1932, in the Convention Hall at Kansas City.

For this event, the Lake's business community pooled their resources and created an impressive diorama of Lake of the Ozarks. The 250-foot-long exhibit, which also included exhibits by various towns and organizations in the Lake region, drew large crowds. Lake of the Ozarks business people manned the exhibit and handed out large amounts of literature. Ward C. Gifford, president of the Kansas City Real Estate Board and vice-chairman of the brokers division of the National Association of Real Estate Boards, was instrumental in getting the Lake of the Ozarks exhibit included in the Exposition. He was also instrumental in organizing the region's first Lake area business association.

"The Lake of the Ozarks Improvement and Protective Association, formed for the development and welfare of the entire Lake region, was organized in Kansas City last week [around Feb. 7, 1932] as a result of the big co-operative display made by Lake of the Ozarks interests at the Better Homes Show in Convention Hall," said a news article on Feb. 17, 1932. [This new association was the predecessor of the Lake of the Ozarks Association that eventually became the Lake of the Ozarks Convention & Visitors Bureau.]

Ward Gifford became the first president and managing director of the new Lake of the Ozarks Improvement and Protective Association. Other officers and board members included Dr. W. L. Allee of Eldon, president of the Missouri State Medical Society; R. B. Petts of Warsaw; Hugh Stephens of Jefferson City, president of the Chamber of Commerce; Nathan Young of Kansas City, of the Star Boat and Motor Co.; Louis I. Baker of Versailles, president of the Chamber of Commerce and editor of the *Versailles Statesman*; Moreland Brown of Bagnell, president of the Arrowhead Beach Club; G. E. Crosby of Eldon, assistant to the president of the Union Electric Light & Power Company; J. H. Frederich of Cole Camp, president of Lakeview Heights Development Co.; L. A. Kelly of Zebra, president of Pla-Port; H. L. Traber of Kansas City, executive general agent of the Missouri Pacific Railroad; and Frank W. Tuttle of Kansas City, president of Tuttle, Ayers and Woodward Engineering Co.

Within a few weeks Gifford gave a more detailed explanation of the new association's purpose: to promote a friendly spirit among all concerned in the development of Missouri's big Lake; to protect fish and game and assist in the planting of fish; to preserve wildlife; to co-operate with the State Board of Health, game and fish wardens and highway patrolmen; and to extend an arm of protection around the entire Lake region. At the time, no one realized what Gifford had in mind by crafting the phrase "to extend an arm of protection around the entire Lake region." They would soon find out.

Among the first challenges the association faced was getting farm-to-market Lake roads created so that the Lake's shoreline was accessible throughout the region and finding a way to finance the roads in cooperation with county road commissioners. Plans for a paved, scenic road encircling the Lake of the Ozarks were devised in cooperation with the State Highway Commission and G. E. Crosby of Union Electric; and getting Lake of the Ozarks bridged along Hwy. 5 over the Osage and

Niangua arms so that north- and south-bound traffic would not have to depend on a motor ferry between Versailles and Camdenton.

In 1933, plans for three state parks and a series of parkways to be located near the Lake and connected with highways to St. Louis and Kansas City, were prepared by Harland Bartholomew and Associates of St. Louis, assisted by Hare and Hare of Kansas City. The proposed parks were to be located at Glaize Creek [junction of the Grand Glaize and Osage at the Grand Glaize Bridge]; at the junction of the Niangua and Little Niangua rivers; and at the great bend in the Lake near Proctor [Coffman Bend at the 55-mile mark].

The three parks would place 18,000 acres in public ownership at a cost of $1,000,000. The scenic drive encircling the Lake would extend from Bagnell Dam to Warsaw, cover 117 miles and have 30 miles of subsidiary roadway. It was projected to cost $1, 350,000, while connecting roads to Kansas City and St. Louis would add $4,097,000 to the price.

As these plans were made public, some people began to get nervous over not only the projected cost but the fact that the three proposed parks were in three choice locations and private development would be shut out of those areas. Then, as the weeks and months passed, it was proposed that "in addition to the three state park areas, [that] all of the two shores of the Lake from below the bluffs at Damsel to the proposed "Proctor State Park" and up the Niangua to the proposed "Niangua State Park," be acquired as state park land for a sufficient distance back from the waterline to preserve existing views and to prevent access to the Lake other than would be justifiable in any state park area such as for boat launchings [and] bathing beaches..."

Gifford became an outstanding spokesperson for these proposals. In addition, he took on another controversial trio of topics -- sanitation, the regulation of docks and the building of summer homes and cottages. "Plans are underway," Gifford said in September 1932, "for setting up subdivision restrictions which will insure the higher type of development which will lend personal pride to the owners of home sites. Regulation of sanitary conditions already is under way and this will be followed through next year. Nothing should be permitted which will in any way menace the health of anyone in the Lake area whether he is a permanent resident or...merely on vacation."

Gifford was soon viewed as too conservative and environmentally active for the Association's leadership. Not that these issues weren't important, but many members wanted to see less emphasis on environmental protection and more effort and money spent on advertising and promotion. Dissatisfaction with his leadership culminated by the beginning of 1934 with his resignation. A good face was put on the matter, however, by the Association and the media, less such squabbling reflect unfavorably on the region.

"Ward C. Gifford...esteemed president of the Lake of the Ozarks Improvement and Protective Association, has resigned his leadership," said a local paper on Feb. 8, 1934. One can read between the lines when Gifford said: "My enthusiasm for the Lake of the Ozarks, and my belief in the growth and prosperity of the area are not altered in any respect and I expect to continue to be actively interested in the region and its work." The news release stated that "during his administration, the Around-the-Lake road system [sic], park planning, work for sanitation, prevention of stream pollution, the Lake Ozark Trail, which is known as the innerbelt road...are a part of the things that have been promoted."

Late in February 1934, the Association was reorganized and the executive offices pulled out of Kansas City, where Gifford had them located, and brought to the Lake area. The words "improvement" and "protective" were dropped from the name and the number of directors was increased from 12 to 18. Thereafter, for more than 50 years, the organization was known simply as the Lake of the Ozarks Association and it focused almost exclusively on tourist advertising and promotion.

Lake Ozark *(Miller County)* -

The construction of Bagnell Dam necessitated the construction of a new 11-mile segment of Hwy. 54. This included the present Bus. Hwy. 54 that passes through Lake Ozark as a two-lane highway, and Hwy. 54 that passes through Osage Beach, but originally as just a two-lane highway.

As construction of the dam neared completion, businesses that had been in Bagnell and the temporary construction settlements of *Conner's Camp Ground, Victor City, Spring Camp* and *Damsite* -- located on the river road between Bagnell and Union Electric Village, -- began to relocate along the new section of Hwy. 54 beyond the west end of the dam. Through the summer and fall of 1931 and the winter, spring and summer of 1932, the roadside west of the dam witnessed a building boom as the future town of Lake Ozark began to take shape. Privately-owned cafes, hotels, filling stations, fishing camps and resorts, souvenir shops and grocery stores sprang up along the north side of what would eventually be known as the Bagnell Dam Strip. The south side of the highway, for the most part, remained undeveloped because of the steep drop-off that discouraged investment and building. The Great Depression was on and money was in short supply for private undertakings in construction that might be costly.

Lake Ozark, MO, Bagnell Dam Strip, *Circa. 1940. Photographer Unknown.*

The Union Electric Land & Development Co., a subsidiary of Union Electric Light & Power Co., incorporated its own commercial area at both ends of the dam and named it Lakeside. At the west end of the dam, the large parking lot that extended for about 150 yards westward was within the boundaries of Lakeside. To discourage encroachment upon the lot, the Land & Development Co. erected a fence to mark the boundary between Lakeside and Lake Ozark. This brought howls of protest from entrepreneurs who wanted to put up tents or snack shops on or close to the parking lot. Protests also arose from other business owners who maintained that the fencing not only looked ugly but was a hindrance to tourists who wanted to visit the dam. Their point made, the Land & Development Co. removed the fence after a short time.

Lakeside was also in a construction boom as the development company erected a luxury hotel called Holiday House on the bluff above Bagnell Dam, a restaurant and dance pavilion called Lakeside Casino Restaurant at the west end of the dam, and a facility officially called the Union Electric Bathing Pavilion and Exursion Boat Dock [but commonly called the U. E. Boat Dock] at the west end of the dam between the dam and the restaurant. They also added an excursion boat service.

At this point in time Lake Ozark had not been officially named. Tourists, of course, saw no distinction between the two developing, somewhat competing municipalities, although it was not the intent of the Unon Electric Land & Development Co. to compete with the privately-owned businesses of Lake Ozark. The development company's intent was to encourage tourism at a time when the Great Depression was making economic growth and development difficult. The people of Lake Ozark did recognize the fact that the tourist facilities built by the development company attracted people to the area and that it benefited everyone.

During 1931 and much of 1932, the people of Lake Ozark got their mail through the Eldon or Zebra [predecessor to Osage Beach] post offices because their was no post office in Lake Ozark. There was a clamor for a post office as well as electrical service. The businesses found themselves sitting next to a huge new dam that was generating electricity and shooting it half-way across the state to St. Louis and the lead belt of southeast Missouri, while they, right next to the dam, had to rely upon generators to produce electricity for their individual businesses.

Lake Ozark formed the New Bagnell Improvement Association for the express purpose of lobbying Union Electric for electrical service. Many of the nearby towns of Miller and Camden counties were also eager for electrical service from Bagnell Dam. It seemed unfair that Lakeside had electricity and no one else did.

Responding to this pressure, the Lakeside Light & Power Company obtained a permit from the Public Service Commission to construct electric lines from Bagnell to the Grand Glaize Bridge. By January 1933, the people of Lake Ozark, at least, had their electricity. Naming the town, however, was a different matter and involved a tug of war between competing interests.

In February 1932, the *Eldon Advertiser* reported that "although no permit has as yet been received from the government for a community post office, the post office department has promised that one will be issued as soon as a name can be decided upon.

Although three names, Lako, Lakeside and Lake Ozark have been suggested, the majority of residents and the post office inspector favor the name Lake Ozark." But two other names were also in the running -- New Bagnell and South Bagnell.

"A new school building is among the latest projects of a new community which is growing up at the west end of Bagnell Dam and was discussed at a recent meeting of the New Bagnell Improvement Association, an organization of residents interested in the formation of a new town there," a local newspaper reported. Two months later the newspaper headline said "South Bagnell Is New Town's Name. Committee To Seek Incorporation Charter Named By Improvement Association."

Not everybody in the Association's membership favored the name New Bagnell. "South Bagnell will be the name of the new community about the south end of the Bagnell Dam, if the South Bagnell Improvement Association succeeds in securing an incorporation charter as planned... The association voted to change its name from New Bagnell Improvement Association. The name was selected as distinguishable from that of the old town, Bagnell."

The name South Bagnell was still being used in July 1932. By this time the association was calling itself the South Bagnell Chamber of Commerce. Not only could they not decided on what to name the town, they couldn't even decide on what to call their organization!

As the tug-of-war continued over what to name the new town, the U. S. Postal Service issued their permit. "Although the permit gives the post office the name Lake Ozark, it is expected it will soon be changed to South Bagnell," said the newspaper.

There were 16 candidates for the office of postmaster, partially because of the factions that had developed over the naming, and partially because the Depression was on and good, solid, year 'round jobs in the Lake area were scarce. Frank V. Andrews was the favorite among the residents. The government chose Frank Andrews, who strongly favored Lake Ozark for the name of the new town. The U. S. postal authorities agreed with him.

Finally, by Aug. 1, 1932, the suspense was over. "A new town has sprung up on the southwest end of Bagnell Dam," said the *Lake of the Ozarks News*. "The name chosen by Uncle Sam is Lake Ozark. Frank Andrews, local pioneer, has received the appointment as postmaster. The new building for the [post] office is being erected by John Clark, contractor of Ulman, Mo."

Lake Ozark Strip, *Circa. 1930s. Photographer Unknown.*

For a few months, while the new sandstone-veneered post office building was being erected a few doors west of the White House Hotel, the post office operated out of temporary quarters in the west end of the hotel. The new town had a new name born of controversy but the town's idenity would remain murky for decades to come because its business community would promote the town through its Bagnell Dam Chamber of Commerce, not a Lake Ozark Chamber of Commerce as most communites would have done. As the years would pass, controversy, for the residents of Lake Ozark, would practically become a way of life.

Lakeside *(Miller County)* -

An early description of Lakeside located it on the bluff above Bagnell Dam and described it as "a village built and maintained by the Union Electric Light and Power Company, owner of Bagnell Dam. Rows of white frame cottages are occupied by company employees and their families [also called Union Electric Village]. The Holiday House is a two-story gray frame...hotel operated by the company. From Lookout Point, a railed parking space at the edge of the bluff, is a sweeping view of Bagnell Dam and the shining, many-armed Lake of the Ozarks. Within a small glass-enclosed structure on a corner of the point is a model of a section of the dam. The model demonstrates the operation of the hydroelectric plant and the floodgates."

The boundaries of Lakeside also included a portion of land at the west end of the dam where the Union Electric Land & Development Co. originally built the Lakeside Casino Restaurant and their boat dock facilities. The land once occupied by these structures is today leased to individuals who operate private businesses at the west end of the dam. Willmore Lodge and Oak Lodge at the northeast end of the dam are within the boundaries of Lakeside. The boundaries of Lakeside are indicated on most maps of the area sold today.

A relatively new observation deck area with information plaques now occupies the spot near where Holiday House once stood. Another area with educational plaques can be found below the dam near the powerhouse. Two of the original waterwheels used in the dam's electrical generating equipment were recently replaced and are now on display, one near the new Observation Deck on the bluff, and the other at the west end of the dam. [see Lake Ozark]

Lakeside Casino Restaurant *(Lake Ozark, Miller County)* -

A building housing the Lakeside Casino Restaurant once stood where the ticket office is today for Casino Pier Cruises just west of Bagnell Dam on the north side of Bus. Hwy. 54.

In today's culture, the word "casino" is generally used to denote a place of gambling but it also means a building used for entertainment and dancing or summerhouse. Not only was gambling illegal in Missouri at the time the Lakeside Casino Restaurant was built, Prohibition was still in effect and alcoholic beverages were also illegal. The word "casino" in the name of the restaurant denoted a place of entertainment, dancing and food.

The Lakeside Casino Restaurant opened for business in August 1932. An early account of the restaurant described it as "a two-story structure. Here is located a restaurant serving meals and sandwiches at modest prices; also a soda fountain. On the lake side of the Casino almost at the water's edge is a pavilion that has a variety of uses. The main portion is roofed and screened. Those so desiring may be served here. An open promenade, equipped with comfortable benches, extends all the way around the outside. No spot commands a more delightful view of the Lake by day or night. The floor is covered with a specially prepared canvas, excellent for dancing. Music is available through two loud speakers served by a concealed, automatic Victrola. Close to the Casino is a dock where privately-owned Lake craft can stop for fuel and other service.

Lakeside Casino Restaurant, *Lake Ozark, MO, Circa, 1940. Photo courtesy AmerenUE.*

In the early 1940s, when the Union Electric sold off the holdings of the Land & Development Co., the Lakeside Casino Restaurant passed into private ownership. It reopened in January 1942 under the ownership of Lawrence Fry of Lake Ozark. At the time, Lawrence Fry was also the owner of the White House Hotel and the postmaster of Lake Ozark. Before Fry's tenure of ownership, the Lakeside Casino Restaurant was first managed by Red Moore who was succeeded by Dean Ayers. Not long afterwards, Dean was killed in an automobile accident and his wife, Ruby Ayers, assumed management of the establishment. After Fry's acquisition, Mrs. Ayers moved to Webster Groves where she was employed by the St. Louis Gas Company.

In the early 1950s, when the Lake's first radio station, KRMS was established, it was, for a short time, located in the Casino building. It was also in the Casino that Lee Mace's Ozark Opry got its start. This building no longer exists.

Lakeview Heights *(Stover, Morgan County; Cole Camp and Warsaw, Benton County)* -

Lakeview Heights is located along the north side of the Lake at the mouth of Brushy Creek Cove at the 77-mile mark on the Osage Arm. The cove is distinguished by a spectacular bluff on the southeast corner at its mouth. This bluff, marked on maps as Rocky Cliff, towers a hundred feet high, arching out over its boulder-strewn footing, with its deeply undercut wall heavily streaked by mineral stain.

Lakeview Heights is scattered along the north entrance to Brushy Creek Cove as a residential area surmounting the crests of several hills that reach heights of 115-120 feet above the Lake.

The Brushy Creek area has a history dating back to the 1840s but Lakeview Heights was born in January 1930 when George H. Imbrie, I. N. Barry, G. E. Tobias, Robert D. Barry, and Arthur B. Tobias of Kansas City formed the Lakeview Heights Land Company. They had every intention of creating a discriminating community of property owners where all roads and paths would be "reserved for the use of the Lodge Site Owners and the company," and in their parlance "are not public highways." In essence, what some people today would characterize as a community for privileged people. Several such communities were proposed and to some extent, developed at the Lake during the early 1930s. All of them, without exception, lost their discriminating character after a period of time due largely to the Great Depression, which took a toll on their ability to sell property and support substantive development.

The Lakeview Heights Land Company bought 3,500 acres for park, recreation and development purposes, leased an additional 5,000 acres in the adjacent hills and along the Lake for exclusive hunting and fishing privileges. The company received their certificate of incorporation in January 1930 and dedicated their subdivision in November 1930. The Lakeview Heights Post Office was opened in 1932 and I. N. Barry opened a store and filling station along with 25 cabins that were available for rent, largely to prospective buyers and people who were building homes and their visiting friends and relatives. He also owned the property that today is known as Rex Ranch. A large clubhouse was constructed near the crest of a hill overlooking the mouth of Brushy Creek Cove, which company literature called a "lagoon," meaning a large body of water connected to a lake or river.

The main road into Lakeview Heights came down the spine of the ridge and circled the clubhouse. The clubhouse had a four-way fireplace in its center with an excellent dance floor. There was a 14-foot porch that circled the entire building.

The corporate papers for the land company suggest they had intentions of buildings hotels, halls, market houses, wharves, decks, dwellings of all kinds, and to establish steam, gasoline and other types of ferries. They planned a golf course, tennis court, riding academy, bathing beach, elaborate playgrounds for children, pergolas for the springs on the property, a bridle path, hiking trails, facilities for skating and dancing, an elaborate beach house, and moonlight steamboat excursions on the Lake.

"On the north shores of the new Lake of the Ozarks the Lakeview Heights Land Company has commenced the installation of what has the promise of being the greatest pleasure resort in this section of the United States -- Lakeview Heights. It is the ambition of the officers to make it so, and with the support now being received there seems to be no doubt their ambitions will be fully realized," said their promotional brochure.

As the years passed many dwellings sprang up in the development and some elaborate homes were built by wealthy, prominent Kansas City people. According to the *Cole Camp Area History 1839-1976*, for a time in the early years, Lakeview Heights was known as the "Million Dollar Development." The Depression, unfortunately, brought many of these plans to a screeching halt. "New families were not buying in the area. The Land Company sold its holdings, in fact those same holdings changed hands many times during the following years," says the Cole Camp history. "Businesses began to fold, feuds developed between residents, which helped to slow down further development. Many houses were empty, making it a lonely little town. There were further changes in the life style of people during World War II. At the close of the war, money was plentiful again...[and] new life emerged."

The Lakeview Heights Post Office closed in 1955 but Lakeview Heights continues to this day on the hills overlooking Brushy Creek Cove and Lake of the Ozarks.

Lazy Days Resort *(Linn Creek, Osage Beach, Camden County)* -

Lazy Days Resort was built in 1931-32 by V. Biggs who erected cabins on a peninsula of land at the 3-mile mark along the southwest side on the Grand Glaize Arm. The resort could be reached by road one mile off the highway on LkRd. 54-A25, later designated 54-62 and now called Lazy Days Road. The road runs down the spine of a ridge 160 feet above the Lake.

The Peninsula upon which the resort was located stretches 3,400 feet with narrow Lake coves on both sides. Brushy Hollow Cove, the largest and longest, lies on the southeast side of the peninsula and all of the land to the southeast is state park property. The unnamed cove on the northwest side is fronted almost entirely by private land. The Lazy Days Resort resort property originally consisted of 22 acres and was at the narrowest part of the peninsula where it is 400 feet wide. A small piece of land at the tip of the peninsula is state park property. The resort cabins faced northwest where there was 1500 feet of shoreline in a saddle between two high points of the ridge. Boat docking facilities were on the other cove facing the state park.

Lazy Days Resort, *Linn Creek, MO, Circa. 1930s. Photographer Unknown.*

Biggs began with six cabins clad with logs that had been split in half lengthwise. The cabins were wired with electricity and had running water and were fully furnished. He first charged $1.00 per person per day or $6.00 per week, but by 1935 had raised his weekly rates to $10.00. He built other buildings, one to house a general store next to which stood a tall, visible gas gravity pump.

Early ads for Lazy Days Resort played to fishermen with "a swell place to bring your wife and kids, quiet, exclusive." And "a swell place for lazy people." The resort didn't have a "floating" swimming pool; instead, he called it a "built-in-the-lake" swimming pool. Advertising said the resort was "surrounded by water," which it certainly was. And there were "sleeping porches." As the years passed, ads suggest that ownership may have changed several times. By the early 1950s, the resort had 17 cottages, a recreation hall and advertising said there were "no mosquitos," which was true, of course, because of Union Electric's mosquito boats that periodically sprayed all 1,300 miles of Lake shoreline to keep mosquitos from breeding.

By the early 1960s, the owners were Mr. & Mrs. Bob Hilton. By the late 1960s, the ownership had changed to Paul McGuire. The resort's prosperity is reflected in the size and quality of its ads. In the 1970s, the resort was placing half-page and full-page ads in the Lake of the Ozarks Association guidebook and the ads were packed with color photos. By 1971, the weekly price was $63.00 for a cottage. By 1979, the future of the resort was reflected with the building of a "condominium unit." Today, the resort no longer exists and the property is given over entirely to the buildings that comprise Lazy Days Condos.

Lick Branch Cove *(Rocky Mount, Morgan County)* -

Lick Branch Cove is the most extensive cove along the north shore of the Lake between the dam and the 6-mile mark. It is at the 5-mile mark.

In pre-Lake days, Stephen Houser Shoals was on the Osage River at the mouth of Lick Branch and Stephen's Island was one mile downstream. At the mouth of the branch along the west side, near where Chateau Du Lac is located on the Lake's shoreline today, was a small settlement called Wayham. It consisted of a general store, post office and a couple of farm dwellings.

Where LkRd. Y-13, [Red Arrow Road] ends at the head of Lick Branch Branch Cove, the road used to descend into the hollow and follow the valley to the Wayham Post Office, which opened in 1907. The road then followed the River west one-half mile, forded the Osage when the water was low, crossed the valley and climbed out of the bottomland near Kay's Point to connect with Linn Creek Road on Horseshoe Bend. A ferry operated at the Osage River crossing for a few years before Bagnell Dam was built. When the basin was being cleared for the coming of the Lake, the Wayham store and post office buildings were moved to higher ground. The post office closed in 1936.

Lick Branch Cove, about two miles long, is 1,000 feet wide at its mouth and maintains much of its width throughout its length. In some places it is up to 1,500 feet wide. The water is 50 to 70 feet deep for the first mile and then 10 to 30 feet deep for the second mile. The cove begins by running north and then gently curves to the northeast.

Numerous camps and resorts have been associated with this cove and on the Osage Arm near the mouth of Lick Branch Cove. The resorts have always been identified with Rocky Mount. The first camps on the cove were Cooper's Camp, Echo Valley Camp and Lillibridge Camp, all in the late 1930s. Most of these camps had stone cottages. In the 1950s and 60s, resorts associated with this area by name included Camp Wah-Kon-Dah, Trammell's Redwoods Resort, Wagon Wheel Resort, Millard's Lucky Point Resort, Lake Village Resort, Ham's Kottage Kamp, Freidrich Resort, Lake Breeze Resort and Tweedie's Cottages. Win-Rock Marina came along in the 1970s. None of these exist today.

Linn Creek *(Camden County)* -

Linn Creek is approximately two miles east of Camdenton along Hwy. 54 and has a population of about 300. It is a lively, growing community with a fairly new post office building and a busy industrial park. The town currently has the Lake area's only water park. Its largest employer in the downtown section is the nation's largest manufacturer of model railroad accessories. A campground is located at the head of Linn Creek Cove. The town is also the home of the Camden County Museum maintained by the Camden County Historical Society in the historic old Linn Creek School building.

The site of modern day Linn Creek was originally known as Easterville after the Easter family farm that once occupied the location before the Lake was created. Many of town's first residents were people who relocated there when Old Linn Creek was demolished, and many of them actually had their homes moved up the valley to this site. As a consequence, there are many houses in Linn Creek today that originally stood in Old Linn Creek.

Linn Creek School, *Camden County Museum. Photo by H. D. Weaver, 2004.*

The late Lucille Keller Harpham, who authored a book on the history of Camden County, said that when Union Electric began to buy out the homeowners of Old Linn Creek, the people already living at Easterville, changed the town's name to Linn Creek to encourage the people to settle there instead of at Camdenton. She said that the name of the Easterville post office was officially changed "somewhat to the chargrin of Camdenton residents who were still receiving mail by rural carrier."

For a few years following the creation of Lake of the Ozarks, Linn Creek was called New Linn Creek. For while, the Linn Creek Chamber of Commerce promoted the town as "The Miracle City." One of the chamber's promotional pieces carried the following text: "This little city, oft called 'Miracle City,' whose corporate limits extend to within a few feet of the shoreline of the Big Lake, is an ideal place for the tourist, sportsman or home seeker... Electric lights, drug store, three hotels, three general stores, four cafes, Odd Fellows hall, furniture store, two barber shops... To tourists, sportsmen and home seekers, the latch string is out."

Lowell's Niangua Bridge Boat Dock *(Camdenton, Camden County)* -

Elmer C. Lowell built Lowell's Niangua Bridge Boat Dock at the west end of the Hwy. 54 Niangua Bridge around 1940. It was close to the bridge on the downstream side. Lowell had previously been associated with Niangua Bridge Camp located at the east end of the bridge on the south side.

After Lowell built his business at the west end, Watson, his former partner at the east end of the bridge, began calling his place Watson's Niangua Bridge Camp so that people wouldn't confuse the two camps.

Lowell billed himself as a "pioneer in fine boating and fishing service." He was a distributor for Johnson Sea Horse Motors and provided sales and service at his camp.

Since there was limited parking on his property for vehicles, his customers would park along the highway. On weekends there could be dozens of cars parked up and down both sides of the highway near Lowell's place. In 1949, one news story said "Highway 54 was jammed with cars, all headed this way and bristling with fishing gear." Lowell had an explanation for it: "The fisherman's grapevine is the fastest known means of communication," he said.

Lowell's Niangua Bridge Boat Dock, *Camdenton, MO, Circa. 1940s. Photographer Unknown.*

Lowell and his guides and their devoted fishing fans were generally to be found at Ha Ha Tonka Cove or "Tonky Cove," as they called it. It was just one and a-half miles upstream on the Niangua from Lowell' docks. Old timers said it was sometimes like a "three-ring circus" on the cove when it became jammed with fishermen on weekends -- reminiscent of what it is like at Bennett Springs on the opening day of trout season each year. Bennett Springs, incidentially, is the spring that gives birth to the Niangua River but is many miles upstream from Ha Ha Tonka.

At Tonky Cove, "there would be dozens of boats lined up at anchor, all loaded with anglers, their fishing poles almost tip to tip. These were bait fishermen, offering minnows to their quarry. In a wider circle of anchored boats, casters were doing their stuff. And around the outskirts, a dozen other boats slowly circled, their motors purring at trolling speed." In the early years, black bass were popular among the fishermen but eventually lost their charm to white bass. By 1946, white bass made up 47.5 percent of the total catch on Lake stringers and many of the bass were taken on the Niangua Arm.

Lowell's facilities consisted of a long white building parallel with the hillside and Lake. Retaining walls formed terraces down to the Lake not far below. Boat dock and floating boardwalks formed a large well with a housed-in area along two sides. Lowell's boats were inside the well. He eventually turned the whole affair so that the entry was open to the channel.

Lowell sold his business in 1951 and new owners renamed it the "Camdenton Boat Dock," but were in business for only two seasons. Sadly, after that, Lowell's buildings sat vacant and abandoned for half a century, although the boat docks were removed a few years after the closing. With the coming of a new century, new developers quarried away the hillside that had pinned Lowell so close to the water and put up condominiums.

***Ha Ha Tonka Cove,** Camdenton, MO. Photo by H. D. Weaver, 2003.*

Malibu Beach Resort *(Osage Beach, Camden County)* -

About 1933, Carl A. Koopman built Malibu Beach Resort on a peninsula at the 2-mile mark on the Grand Glaize Arm at the end of LkRd. 54-A19, later designated 54-49 and now called Malibu Road.

Koopman began with 12 brick and stone cabins. According to the late Phil Tryon, who once owned the resort, the beams inside the cabins came from a bridge that crossed the Osage River before Bagnell Dam was built. Koopman had the beams hand hewn to the size needed for his cabins. The doors of the cabins were heavy, solid and ornate. All the cabins were large, handsome buildings. They were furnished and had kitchenettes.

LkRd. 54-49 runs down the spine of a peninsula, descending to Lake level at the point. The cabins were along this road but on the hillside facing the Lake. The road curved around to the left at the bottom of the hill and followed the shoreline for a short distance and then led back uphill to the entrance road. The peninsula also had an interesting feature at its point -- a narrow neck of land barely wide enough for a road that led out to an elongated island where the beach and some of the boat docks were located.

Malibu Beach Resort & Cottage, *Osage Beach, MO, Circa. 1950s. Photographer Unknown.*

Koopman charged guests $1.00 per day per cabin in the early 1930s. The resort had a guest capacity of 50, and advertised having a concrete boat launching ramp.

In 1935, Koopman came up with a catchy slogan for his resort ad, which said "A Real Resort for Real

People," a phrase that would be used in the resort's ads for several decades. The mystery is, what did he mean by "real resort," and who are "real people?"

By 1937, Koopman's ads were also telling people that the resort was on a 10-acre tract of land on a peninsula that extended out into the Lake with water on three sides, which meant there was always a cool breeze. By 1940, he was adding the words "formerly of St. Louis," probably thinking that because he was from St. Louis, it would attract St. Louis people to his resort.

In the late 1940s, Koopman built a lodge that was air-conditioned and had all electric kitchens in its units. The honeymoon suite was in the lodge penthouse. One of the cabins was also set aside for honeymooners, and both the cabin and the bridal suite in the lodge had private entrances.

By 1962, the peninsula had become the location of the Malibu Beach Yacht Basin. A person could rent a Drift-R-Cruz fiberglass houseboat for $50 to $70 per day. Advertising said these boats were "your cabin, motor and all in one package." They were fully equipped for up to six people, could drift at one mile per hour or cruise at a speed of 15 miles per hour for persons wanting to ski. The boats were said to be "the world's most diversified houseboats."

In 1965, the resort was sold to Phil and Darvene Tryon who would operate the business into the 1980s. About 1974, a condominium was built on the property and promoted under the name Malibu Shores Inc. The Moorings Yacht Club now stands on the point of the peninsula and Malibu Beach Resort no longer exists.

McClurg, Joseph Washington *(Old Linn Creek, Camden County)* -

Joseph McClurg was unquestionably Camden County's most distinguished citizen of the nineteenth century. Born Feb. 22, 1818, in Ohio, the son of Joseph and Mary [Brotherton] McClurg, he attended and graduated from Ohio schools. He taught school in Mississippi from 1835-36 and then returned to St. Louis where he became a deputy sheriff but the city did not suit him. He left St. Louis to attend law school in Texas and passed the bar. Shortly afterward he returned to Missouri to wed Mary Johnson in 1841 after which he tried his hand at lead mining in the Ozarks. He tried his luck gold mining during the California gold rush but returned to Missouri in 1851 to join his brother-in-law, John Jones, and other relatives who had opened a store in Camden County along the Osage River near the mouths of the Niangua River and Linn Creek. Their company was called McClurg, Murphy and Jones. McClurg was later influential in the founding of Old Linn Creek and in seeing that it became the county seat of Camden County.

During the Civil War, McClurg organized the Osage Regiment of Missouri Volunteers and the Hickory County Battalion. Southern sympathizers burned his store. His wife died in 1861. In 1862, he was elected to the first of three congressional terms and in 1868, was elected Governor of Missouri. He distinguished himself as governor, was responsible for reducing Missouri's debt, helped establish the Rolla School of Mines and the Agriculture School at the University of Missouri.

In 1871, out of office, Joseph McClurg returned to Linn Creek and engaged in various enterprises including lead mining, iron smelting and the building of steamboats that were put into service on the Osage River. McClurg had many misfortunes in business and debts eventually forced him to sell his Camden County lands including his mansion. His last government position was as government land-officer in Springfield, Missouri. His final days were spent at his daughter's home in Lebanon, Missouri, where he died Dec. 2, 1900.

Mel Adkins Airplane Landing Facility *(Gravois Mills, Morgan County)* -

This landing strip was built in the late 1930s by Mel Adkins, the owner of Adkins Resort, on the uplands northwest of the head of Mill Creek Cove. This cove is at the 5-mile mark on the Gravois Arm.

The airplane runway ran due north and south and was 2,210 feet long by 160 feet wide. It had a turf surface and was at an elevation of 810 feet. There was no communication or phone available and no landing lights. The only service was tie-down although Mel Adkins had a hanger at the south end of the landing strip on the west side for his own private use. Meals and lodging were available at the resort and the resort road left the landing strip at the south end on the east side. [see Adkin's Camp]

Mill Creek Bridge *(Brumley, Miller County)* -

Mill Creek is a tributary of Grandglaize Creek, which feeds into the Grand Glaize Arm of the Lake. Mill Creek hollow is wide and has a length of more than five miles. The town of Brumley is located in the hollow along Hwy. 42 at the junction of Hwy 42 and Route C about 2.5 miles west of Grandglaize Creek.

Two historic suspension bridges, which are close together, are located at the Mill Creek - Grandglaize confluence. The larger of the two bridges -- the Glaize Bridge -- spans Grandglaize Creek, while the smaller bridge spans Mill Creek. The bridges are at right angles to one another and 1,000 feet apart by roadway.

Both of these bridges were designed and built in 1931 [see Glaize Bridge] by Joseph A. Dice, the legendary swinging bridge builder of Warsaw, Missouri.

Mill Creek Bridge, *Brumley, MO. Photo by H. D. Weaver, 2004.*

Mill Creek Bridge is a steel cable suspension bridge with a total length of 135 feet and a span length of 96 feet. The roadway is 11.1 feet wide. Numerous modifications have been made to the bridge by the Missouri Highway and Transportation Department to reinforce and upgrade its structure since it was originally built. The original cost was $3,000. Dice used 20,000 pounds of steel, 40 miles of wire and 3,000 feet of lumber in the original construction.

The substructure currently consists of spill-through tower pedestals with cables anchored in concrete deadmen. The towers are steel I-beams with single strand straight cables and there are guardrails. The deck is corrugated steel over steel stringers.

Driving across this sturdy little suspension bridge is a different kind of experience to that of driving across most suspension bridges and even its adjacent Glaize Bridge. The corrugated steel decking of the Mill Creek Bridge gives a tooth-jarring vibration and sets up a startling wave of sound as a vehicle passes over it.

Mining Port *(Morgan County)* -

"The subject of mining," said geologist C. F. Marbut nearly 100 years ago, "is a very attractive one to the people of Morgan County... Lead, zinc, coal, iron, barite and clay occur in Morgan County and all have been mined to a greater or lesser extent." But records of actual mining in the county give no information on how much or what kind of mining occurred in the county before 1858. It is presumed, however, that the former settlement of Mining Port, at the confluence of Gravois Creek and the Osage River, received its name because it served as a shipping point for minerals mined in the county in the 1820s and 30s.

The former site of Mining Port is now inundated by 70 feet of water. It was along the banks of Gravois Creek and the Osage River at the 6-mile mark on the Osage Arm. It was just southwest of Meditation Point on an alluvial terrace where settlement began about 1819. Prior to this, Zebulon Pike camped near this location in the summer of 1806 and later the Harmony Mission Trace passed across the property, forded Gravois Creek, then turned north to follow the creek and pass through the site that would later become the settlement of Gladstone at the mouth of today's Gladstone Cove. Most of the early settlers of Morgan County came to the county by way of Gravois Creek and the Harmony Mission Trace.

By 1837, Mining Port was a sizable village but that year the Osage and Gravois flooded, virtually washing the town away. Some of the settlers rebuilt but most moved upstream and became the first people to settle where the village of Riffletown [and later Gladstone] came to be. There had been a memorable flood in 1823 but it was the flood of 1844 that finally convinced the survivors of the 1837 flood that Mining Port was too vulnerable to flooding to remain a townsite.

After 1844, Mining Port was no more. The land was later farmed by Joe M. Howard who owned the land on both sides of the creek at the mouth of the Gravois, beginning in the 1880s. One can only wonder what those early residents of Mining Port would have thought if someone had predicted that just 100 years in the future, the old town site would be permanently inundated by 70 feet of water and that the whole of their beloved Gravois Creek valley would be a vast lake of deep water.

Mountain Terrace Court *(Lake Ozark, Miller County)* -

In 1949, Arnold and Winna Welch built Mountain Terrace Court along Hwy. 54 in Lake Ozark one mile west of the dam. The Court was on an embankment on the west side of the highway a short distance southwest of Flynn Road and northeast of Hidden Acres Road.

Mountain Terrace Court opened for the 1950 season. As the 1950s progressed, the Welch's neighbors would come to include Oak Hill Court on the north side of the Welch property, and Dog 'n Suds Drive-In and the Missouri Aquarium on the south side. Directly across Hwy. 54 would be Rock Wood Court with Moore's Motel on the north side of Rock Wood and Deer Motel on the south side of Rock Wood.

The cottages of Mountain Terrace Court were not true giraffe rock houses so characteristic of Ozark dwellings in the 1930s and 40s because they did not have raised and painted mortar, but they did reflect the utility and natural materials of the Ozarks. More cottages would be added as the years passed and some would be frame.

Out front of the Court was a sign that said the cottages were cooled by "Vornado Air-Conditioning." By 1959, the Court had a filtered swimming pool and a new poolside cabana. In 1964, they advertised the "largest heated, filtered pool in the Lake area." The swimming pool had a 9 x 14 foot fiberglass sliding board, sun lounges, beach umbrellas and piped music. Ads indicate that by this time the Court had 21 units.

Mountain Terrace Court, *Lake Ozark, MO, 1958. Photographer Unknown.*

In 1968, the Welch's son, Harold, and his wife, Jo, joined the operation. Arnold died in 1973 and Harold and Jo continued operating Mountain Terrace Court until 1976 when they sold to Fred and Lena Dech. This couple operated the business for one season and then sold to Richard and Betty Wilhelmi from Atkins, Iowa. Their children, Jean, Jim and John also helped in the operation of the business. The Wilhelmis substituted "Resort Motel" for the word "Court" in the business name. They had Mountain Terrace Resort Motel for many years.

This resort motel no longer exists. Today, Christ King Lutheran Church sits where Mountain Terrace Court use to be. Another Welch son, Don, now owns and manages Quails Nest Motel in Osage Beach.

Musser's Ozark Tavern / Resort *(El Rancho Junction, Miller County)* -

In the 1930s, Hwys. 54 and 52 ran together from Eldon to the point where, three miles south of Edon, at the junction of Hwys 54-52, Hwy. 52 peeled off and headed east to Tuscumbia.

No sooner was Bagnell Dam complete than development began at this fork in the road, a fork that later became known as El Rancho Junction. Most of the property here belonged to William Cahill. In 1933, Gay's Tavern was built at the junction and in 1934, William Cahill built a gas station -- Cahill's Phillips 66 Filling Station -- called "The Model." It sat adjacent to Gay's Tavern. [Hwy. 54 underwent new construction in the 1970s. The businesses discussed here were on what is now an old abandoned strip of Hwy. 54 just east of the newer highway.]

On Aug. 13, 1936, a headline in the *Miller County Autogram* said: "Cahill Property To Be Converted Into Large Tourist Camp, Musser Tavern Company Starts Work On $12,000 Development At 52-54 Intersection."

Clarence W. Musser, an Eldon resident for several years and an employee of the Rock Island Railroad Company, teamed up with Attorney L. N. Musser of Kansas City, and purchased Cahill's gas station and property for $8,000. Later, Musser would also purchase Gay's Tavern.

Clarence Musser hired Marshall Harrison, a contractor who had built an elaborate tourist camp at Excelsior Springs, Missouri, to build his tourist camp. What arose over the next two years was an elaborate layout of fine English-style brick buildings and various recreational facilities. Musser named the business Musser's Ozark Tavern and would use the word "tavern" for several years before replacing it with the word "resort." The original two-story brick building was large, containing a cafe and coffee shop, cocktail room, dining room, amusement room, and the Crystal Ballroom with dimensions of 34 x 60 feet where live orchestra's and big bands performed. For a time even a radio station broadcast special events from Musser's place.

Musser's Ozark Tavern Resort opened to the public on Thanksgiving Day 1936. He soon added a 15-room hotel, a filling station next to the main building and eight steam-heated, air-conditioned brick rental cottages in the triangle of the junction facing both highways. He built a modern bath house with washrooms for men and women, a golf driving range, a double tennis court, and had plans for two swimming pools. "One pool will be 120 feet long and 80 feet wide, while the other will be 40 feet long and 20 feet wide," said a news story. The large swimming pool, when completed, had a lighted waterfall at one end.

The groups that performed at Musser's Ozark Tavern were largely from Kansas City and some were noted black jazz bands. In the 1930s and 40s, Eldon was a "sundown town" where blacks were not welcome, particularly after dark. But Clarence Musser had grown up on

Musser's Ozark Resort, *Eldon, MO, Circa. 1940s. Photo courtesy of Jim Lawrence.*

the rough side of life in Kansas City. He didn't take kindly to being told who he could and could not do business with or associate with. He was rumored to have had ties with Big Tom and the House of Pendergast in Kansas City.

Musser was short of stature, somewhat hot headed and often armed. He paid no attention to local racial attiudes. Musser didn't recognize the color of a person's skin. He was only interested in the color of a person's money or a person's talent. He put the blacks up at his resort and drew huge crowds of people who appreciated good music and food and liked to dance and party.

"Musser's Tavern is now the popular place to spend an enjoyable evening. An excellent colored orchestra coupled with what many have pronounced 'the smoothest floor near Eldon' have continued to draw bigger crowds each night," said the *Lake of the Ozarks News* on Dec. 15, 1936. "The orchestra plays until one o'clock each evening and with some encouragement has played much longer.

"Friendly hospitality and a grand time await all who enter the door. Ted Moore, formerly of the Casino, is the manager and Mr. & Mrs. E. J. John are host and hostess."

During the last half of the 1930s, Musser's Tavern gave the Lakeside Casino Restaurant and the White House Hotel, which were the hot spots on the Bagnell Dam Strip, stiff competition. Musser also tended to pirate good employees from other businesses on The Strip.

The quality of Musser's establishment and the entertainment that Musser was able to get from Kansas City drew the attention of politicians, both state and local, and their supporters. The year 1938 was a banner year for political shindigs at Musser's and kicking things off was the Miller County Republician Committee who sponsored a "Washington's Birthday Banquet" at Musser's Tavern on Feb. 22, 1938.

"The banquet is being sponsored by the Miller County Republican Commitee, and is one of several similar meetings to be held throughout the State of Missouri and other states," said the *Miller County Autogram*. "Mrs. Geo. B. Simmons, a speaker of national importance, has been engaged as the principal speaker of the evening. Mrs. Simmons is a Missouri woman whose fame has spread throughout the nation, as a forceful and interesting speaker on the issues now confronting the American people... Chas. R. Hawkins of Brumley, is Chairman of the Republican committee."

An estimated 300 people attended the event. But that was small potatos compared to the crowd that showed up in July 1938 when the friends of Judge James V. (Josh) Billings staged a big rally at Musser's. [Billings was a Pendergast-backed candidate for Supreme Court Judge, thus adding fuel to local rumors that Clarence Musser was a Pendergast "flunky."]

"Judge Billings will bc the honored guest and the principal speakers will be Hon. Howard Hannah, secretary of the Young Democratic Club of Missouri, and Judge J. M. Boyd, former Chief Counsel for the Missouri Public Service Commission.

"There will be delegates from every county of the State, and those in charge of the demonstration are expecting the largest crowd ever to assemble in Miller County.

"James W. Miller, of Eldon, a well-known Rock Island engineer, will speak in behalf of the people of Miller County.

"Don Gill's orchestra will furnish the music for the free dance which will follow the speaking...and it will be broadcast over radio station KFRU, Columbia, from 7:30 to 8:30."

The crowd was estimated at 2,500, which was certainly beyond the holding capacity of the Crystal Ballroom at Musser's Ozark Tavern.

"A platform and sound system were provided for the event on the east side of the highway, opposite the main building, and the crowd congregated on the green and overflowed the highway and adjacent grounds."

One of the principal speakers at the event "condemned Gov. Lloyd Stark for his stand against Pendergastism, declaring that Pendergast was largely responsible for Stark's election."

Musser's Ozark Tavern Resort prospered until January 1941 when a disastrous fire occurred.

"The main building at Musser's Resort...one of the best known nightclubs in the Lake of the Ozarks region, was destroyed by fire early Thursday morning," said the *Eldon Advertiser.* "The loss, estimated at about $55,000, was only partially covered by insurance. The Crystal Ballroom, dining room, amusement room, cafe, kitchen, liquor store, filling station and beverage storeroom were destroyed... C. W. Musser, manager of the resort, discovered the blaze. He awoke in a smoke-filled room and made his way to the main auditorium awakening the six employees who lived there. The Eldon Fire Department was summoned but flames, whipped by a stiff breeze, soon spread to all parts of the building. The electric wires connecting the water pumps, were severed by the flames, greatly handicapping the fire fighters. The fire department finally abandoned the main building and directed its efforts to saving the hotel, cottages and other...buildings."

Musser promptly rebuilt but on a smaller scale and reopened in 1943. Then in March 1945, trouble struck again when Musser was involved in an altercation with William E. Buckhart in Eldon. The two men exchanged gunfire and Buckhart was killed.

Musser was charged with second degree murder but on a change of venue to Jefferson City, he was acquitted. During the trial period, Musser sold the resort and all of its associated properties to Mr. & Mrs. Jefferson W. Mitchell. Mitchell was a veteran in the business of building and operating oil refineries. He had been superintendent of the Phillips Refinery in Kansas City, Kansas, from 1928 to 1940 when he went to Bartlesville, Oklahoma, where he was assistant manager of the refinery department of the Phillips Company. He was elevated to manager of that department in 1943 and resigned in 1945 when he and his wife purchased Musser's Ozark Resort.

It should be noted that the Phillips Oil Company has a financial investment in the property at El Rancho Junction. Phillips Oil Company products have been sold on the property for nearly 70 years.

The Mitchells had the business for one year and then sold to Jim Hannaford, Jim Lawrence and Francis Biselx who renamed it El Rancho of the Ozarks. [see El Rancho of the Ozarks]

Naming Lake of the Ozarks -

"Much can be learned about men and places from their names," said Robert L. Ramsay in *Our Storehouse of Missouri Place Names* [University of Missouri Press, 1973]. "A man's name reveals his family and his ancestry, often also his nationality and racial background... Just so may the place names of the State disclose...a host of hidden facts about its origins and traditions..."

Ramsay's book was based on earlier work done between 1928 and 1950. It was a pioneer study of Missouri place names. His references to the naming of Lake of the Ozarks, however, leave something to be desired because they are incomplete, misleading and inaccurate. They lead a reader to believe that the name of the Lake should be *Lake Benton* instead of Lake of the Ozarks, ignoring the controversy surrounding the naming of the Lake and other names proposed for it.

In a list of prominent Missouri leaders who have left place names behind them, Ramsay listed Lake Benton under the heading of Thomas Hart Benton. He then added "now usually known as Lake of the Ozarks." On another page he said "...and the latest of all, by act of the State Legislature in 1931, of Lake Benton for the largest artificial body of water in the world [sic] even though the forgetful public persists in calling it Lake of the Ozarks."

Thomas H. Benton.
Photo from Missouri, The Center State 1821-1915, Volume Two, S. J. Clark Pub. Co. 1915.

Further along in his book, Ramsay again chides the public for using the name Lake of the Ozarks, seemingly in defiance of the State Legislature, by saying "Lake Benton, name assigned by act of the State Legislature in 1931, but superceded in popular usage by the name Lake of the Ozarks." Ramsay ignores other names proposed for the Lake and bills submitted to the Legislature. He even disregards the fact that the 1931 bill he alludes to was vetoed by the govenor and all subsequent bills related to the same issue failed to pass.

While Ramsay labored to impress upon readers that Lake of the Ozarks is misnamed, he did not say how Bagnell

Dam acquired its name although he did give the origin of the name for the small village of Bagnell downstream from the dam. That town, he said, was named for William Bagnell in 1882.

Is Lake Benton really the proper name of Lake of the Ozarks? Were any other names proposed in the General Assembly? Who was this Thomas Hart Benton for whom the Lake was supposedly named? Is "Bagnell Dam" really the proper name for the dam? Was there any controversy over the Lake's name more than 70 years ago? How did it really come to be Lake of the Ozarks?

A variety of names for the proposed Lake to be created by a dam across the Osage River upstream from Bagnell can be found in newspaper stories through the 1920s. During what turned out to be a rather long and drawn-out effort by the company that initially started the project in 1925, newspaper editors were hungry for a name they could use for the future Lake in news stories, features and editorial comment.

It was often referred to as the "*Big Lake on the Osage*," "*Lake Osage*," or simply "*Big Lake*." The Missouri Hydro-Electric Power Company of Kansas City, who initiated the project in 1925, generated considerable newspaper publicity between 1925 and 1928 in their futile efforts to get the project under way and get the dam built. Even heavier news coverage was generated after Union Electric took over the project and completed the dam between August 1929 and June 1931. If one were to measure the total number of newspaper column inches devoted to the subject between 1925 and 1931, it would probably stretch for miles.

James A. Logan, *Benton County Rep. Photo from State of Missouri Book: The Story of its Industries & Resources, Lewis Printing Co., 1932.*

Just as soon as Union Electric took over the project, Freshman legislator, James A. Logan, the Republican representative from Benton County, stepped forward to propose that the future lake be named *Lake Benton.* Logan was from Warsaw and hoped to get a jump on anyone from Camden, Miller or Morgan counties who might want to see the future Lake named after one of their favorite sons. Logan wanted to honor Thomas Hart Benton, after whom Benton County was named.

Thomas Hart Benton [1782-1858] was elected to the U. S. Senate from Missouri in 1820 and quickly became the state's most prominent and powerful political leader of that period. There are more than 30 place names in Missouri honoring Thomas Hart Benton and Benton County is one of them.

In 1929, Logan introduced H. B. 930 titled "An Act to Designate the Name of the Lake to be formed in Miller, Morgan, Camden and Benton counties, Missouri, by the construction of the hydroelectric dam on the Osage River." The bill was read and 750 copies of the bill were printed. It was read a second time on April 25, 1929, and referred to committee, which came back with a "do pass" recommendation. The vote in the House was unanimous that the name of the Lake be "hereby legally designated Lake Benton in honor of Missouri's greatest U. S. Senator, Thomas H. Benton."

Gov. Henry S. Caulfield. *Photo from State of Missouri Book, The Story of the Industries & Resources, Lewis Printing Co., 1932.*

Unfortunately, Logan had stepped on some political egos with his bill, even in his own party, by referring to Benton as "Missouri's *greatest* U. S. Senator." The bill passed but when it landed on the desk of Republican Governor Henry S. Caulfield, the governor promptly vetoed it. In returning the bill to the House, Caulfield had the following to say: "I have the honor to transmit herewith *without my approval* [italics by the author], H. B. 930... I have no objection to the avowed purpose of this bill, that is the designating as Lake Benton of a lake to be formed...on the Osage River. Although I would personally prefer postponing the naming of the lake until it shall be constructed and then perhaps giving it a sylvan or an Indian name or perhaps the name of the engineer who will build the dam, but I would not veto the bill on that account. I do object to that portion of the bill which unnecessarily designates Thomas H. Benton as 'Missouri's *greatest* U. S. Senator.' I would not object if he were designated as Missouri's *great* Senator... Neither do I assert he is not Missouri's greatest Senator. I do not however believe it is proper for the legislature to unnecessarily and without any hearing select one of our former Senators and proclaim him the greatest. Such a course invites controversy and unnecessarily wounds feelings and arouses the prejudices of those of our citizens who revere and love Missouri's other great Senators. When the legislature convenes again, the construction of the lake may at least be begun and if the legislature still deems it proper to designate the lake as Lake Benton, I will be glad to join with them provided the objectionable portions of the bill is omitted."

No effort was made to override the governor's veto and so the bill died for the time being.

In 1931, Representative Logan reintroduced his bill with the same text as in 1929. But by this time J. W. Vincent, the fiery, outspoken editor of Camden County's famed newspaper -- *The Reveille* -- was a member of the House of Representatives. Vincent wanted to name the soon-to-be body of water, *Lake McClurg*, to honor Camden County's most distinguished pioneer citizen -- former governor Joseph W. McClurg. Vincent immediately introduced H. B. 235, which was worded exactly the same as Logan's bill, except for the proposed name. Thus two counties in the designated lake area were suddenly at loggerheads over the name of the new lake, had the State

J. W. Vincent, *Camden County Rep. Photo Courtesy of Camden County Historical*

Gov. Joseph W. McClurg. *Photo Courtesy of Camden County Historical Society.*

legislature between them, and were ready to duke it out on the floor of the House.

Logan's original bill to name the reservoir Lake Benton had sailed through the House in 1929, but in 1931, both it and Vincent's bill came out of committee with a "do not pass."

During the fracas, Representative William Elmer of Dent County, in a vein of humor and in an effort to calm everyone, suggested they call it *Lake Benton-McClurg of the Ozarks.*

Apparently nobody in the Legislature had bothered to ask the Union Electric Light & Power Company officials what they thought of the matter. Union Electric not only owned the dam but all the land that would be inundated and thereby, through right of ownership, had the authority to give the new lake whatever name they might choose.

William P. Elmer, *Dent County Rep. Photo from* <u>*State of Missouri Book: The Story of Industries & Resources*</u>*, Lewis Printing Co., 1932.*

With the issue seemingly dead in Jefferson City, Union Electric acted. It was their land, their dam, and their lake, and they considered it their privilege to name both.

On March 12, 1931, the *Miller County Autogram* of Tuscumbia, summed it up: "It has been a stupendous job to build Osage Dam near Bagnell and now that the laborious part of the job is about completed, the matter of giving the big lake...a name seems to be worrying a lot of people... Then the Union Electric...officially declared the name of the lake to be *Lake of the Ozarks*, which seemed to meet the approval of people in this section. The company also officially named the dam *Osage Dam* and the town site at the dam, *Lakeside*... To the casual observer, it would appear that...Union Electric...would have a right to name its own offspring and the name Lake of the Ozarks would meet the approval of most everyone and thus get the matter out of politics."

It took several years for the name Lake of the Ozarks to become the accepted name. News stories, even as late as 1933, still referred to as the Big Lake.

To the Federal Power Commission, it was *Project No. 459.* To Union Electric, it began as the *Osage River Development Project.* In an article in the Unon Electric Magazine in 1929, it was called the *Union Electric Dam at Bagnell.* Then in October 1930, the company magazine called it *Bagnell Dam on the Osage River.* In May 1931, the magazine called it *Osage Dam and Lake of the Ozarks*, but in November 1931, the magazine again called it Bagnell Dam. By popular acceptance and persistence of usage, the name *Bagnell Dam* has become the accepted name for the dam. Through a merger, Union Electric became AmerenUE of St. Louis in recent years, but to AmerenUE, it is Bagnell Dam, with the powerhouse officially called the *Osage Power Plant.*

Navajo Beach Resort *(Gravois Mills, Morgan County)* -

In the early 1930s, Mr. & Mrs. Alva Tate built Navajo Beach Resort at the head of Red Hollow Cove, which is along the west side of the Gravois Arm at the 7.3-mile mark. Today, Kelly's Port sits at the mouth of this cove on the north side. By road, the site of the old Navajo Beach Resort can be reached by LkRd. 5-14, which forks into Twin Bays Road and Red Hollow Road.

The resort's accommodations were scattered along the shoreline of the cove's north side. There were rock and log cabins for guests as well as a store and cafe on the grounds. The resort was open all year and advertised modern and semi-modern housekeeping cabins as well as a safe beach for children. Crappie beds were established nearby.

About 1938, the Tate's built a new business at the northeast end of Bagnell Dam called Grand View Camp, which was a much smaller operation and less work as well as being in a more highly visible location with a high traffic count. Navajo Beach Resort was sold to C. B. Irwin.

In the 1940s, Irwin sold to Alfred and Leeta Huffman who would own and manage the resort during the remainder of its existence. Alfred had retired from the military and chose to operate a resort to keep himself busy and as a source of retirement income. His ads added the catchy phrase "hard surfaced road from your door to our door," words that resonated with many who vacationed at the Lake because in the early years very few Lake roads were paved.

Navajo Beach closed at the end of 1974 after more than 25 years of management by the Huffmans.

Navy Plane Lands On Lake, 1942 -

During World War II a U. S. Navy patrol plane was forced to land briefly on Lake of the Ozarks and it created some excitement in Lake Ozark

"A large U.S. Navy coastal patrol plane flew about the Lake of the Ozarks, Sunday [Feb. 12, 1942], and settled down on the water near Duck Head Point. Quite a crowd was attracted to the roar of the motors and by the time the plane had taxied into the cove behind Lake Ozark they had gathered on the lake shore.

"Members of the crew tied the plane with ropes to three trees. Some of the crew wore heavy fur coveralls and rubber overshoes, while others had on waterproof suits that were fur lined. They left Chicago about 8 o'clock Sunday morning and arrived at the lake about 11:30 a.m., being forced down by bad weather. Ice had formed on the wings of the plane. They were on their way in about an hour.

George Cunningham was in a boat helping them. After listening to the noise being made by a flock of wild ducks, he said: 'I'll bet that's the biggest duck they ever saw on this lake.' That broke up the party and most everyone went home."

Niangua Arm of the Lake -

Bagnell Dam backs up the waters of the Niangua River for a distance of about 16 miles. Without argument, they are some of the Lake's most scenic and historic miles.

The Niangua, also called the Big Niangua, joins the Osage River just above the 31-mile mark on the Osage Arm. Today it is an exceptionally wide confluence with the north and south shores being almost one mile apart, but in the old days the river banks at the confluence were less than 500 feet apart, with a broad and fertile floodplain where farmers raised some of Camden County's best crops. Those farmlands are now beneath 50 to 70 feet of water.

Along the south shore of the Lake at the mouth of the Niangua is Lovers' Leap Bluff, a place of legend, topping out at 140 feet above the water. Beneath the Lake at the confluence are the sites where Aaron Crain was licensed in 1841 to operate a ferry across the Niangua; where Joseph W. McClurg built his home and business in the 1850s; where a toll bridge was built across the Osage in 1911, and where some of the remains of that bridge are probably still lying in the river bed beneath the Lake.

Less than two miles upstream is the new Hwy. 5 Niangua Bridge and beyond the bridge, as the river turns south, are hills to the east that rise 250 feet above the Lake. It is along here that the sites of the old Arnhold Mill, Arnhold Onyx Cave, Arnhold Natural Bridge, Chimney Rock, Chimney Rock Cave and Stone Face lie inundated.

Impressive, geologically intriguing bluff scenery begins at about the 9-mile mark where condos surmount Oak Bluff on the west side of the Lake and Ladinsky Bend is on the east side. The bend forces the Lake to make a sweeping curve between mile marks 9 and 11. The bend has a narrow neck and a broad point.

A sharp-eyed boater here at the 9-mile mark will see that the layers of dolomite and limestone exposed along the Lake's shore to the left going upstream, are not level -- they dip sharply into the Lake, betraying a fold or fault-related structural feature. That fracture, hidden in Thunder Mountain to the north, across from Ladinsky Bend, is the underground gap along which some people believe that Bridal Cave was formed.

A keen-eyed search of the Thunder Mountain shoreline before reaching the Bridal Cave boat dock will reveal a chain-link fence on a bluff prominence. This is along Bridal Cave's Thunder Mountain Nature Trail and close to the entrance of Neongwah Bear Cave. Permission from Bridal Cave is needed to enter the Bear Cave.

Thunder Mountain and Bridal Cave Entrance building, *Camdenton, MO. Photo by H. D. Weaver, 2003.*

The southeast side of Ladinsky Bend forms Bull Run Bluff, another remarkable cliff along the Niangua. This rugged, broken, terraced bluff borders the Lake for three-quarters of a mile, making a sweeping curve to the left going upstream. This particular area along the Niangua was described 150 years ago by G. C. Swallow, Missouri's first State Geologist in the following way: "The bluffs usually rise from the bottom in a perpendicular wall to a height of 100 feet, and then in a gentle slope by terraces to the top of the formation. The rise in each of the terraces varies from one to three feet, according to the thickness of the stratum which forms it. Each presents a surface from five to ten feet wide, covered with a luxuriant growth of grass, shrubs and vines. The bluffs thus formed rise by gentle slopes into rounded knobs, surrounded by the terraces above mentioned. The whole reminds one of the vine-clad hills of the Eastern world; while the rich soil, the natural terraces, and the salubrious climate, all adapted to the growth of the grape, invite vine-growers to occupy the beautiful and picturesque valleys of the Niangua and Osage."

A woodcut illustration depicting Bull Run Bluff and its adjacent hills can be found in *The First and Second Annual Reports of the Geological Survey of Missouri* by G. C. Swallow on page 131. Keep in mind that 10 to 30 feet at the foot of Bull Run Bluff is now inundated.

The entrance to Bunch Cave can be seen along the west shoreline at the 12.5-mile mark just before reaching the Hwy. 54 Niangua Bridge. The large, arched opening is surrounded by development and it is surprising that the cave entrance and the cave beyond have managed to survive this long in such a highly developed area.

Beyond the condominium developments that have stolen some of the natural integrity and Ozark beauty of this section of the Niangua Arm on both sides of the Hwy. 54 Niangua Bridge, there is still more outstanding bluff beauty between the 14-mile mark and Ha Ha Tonka Cove. Here the towering limestone and dolomite bluffline reflects a whiteness out upon the Lake.

Nothing anywhere at the Lake compares to the astounding beauty and wonders to be seen at the head of Ha Ha Tonka Cove, which is surrounded by all of the wonders of Ha Ha Tonka State Park.

Ha Ha Tonka Cove was once occupied by Lake Ha Ha Tonka because an old nineteenth century dam lies beneath the water near the mouth of Ha Ha Tonka Cove. The water in the Cove, while now partially backwater from Lake of the Ozarks, is also water from the Ha Ha Tonka Spring branch. At the head of the branch Ha Ha Tonka Spring discharges 48 million gallons of cold water every day. The cove, called "Tonky Cove" by early day fishermen, has always been a fisherman's paradise.

A mile-and-a-half upstream on the Niangua from the mouth of Ha Ha Tonka Cove is still one more natural surprise just beyond the 16-mile mark -- a cave with its entrance on the water -- Onyx Cave. Here, a person can actually boat back into a very mysterious realm of the underworld amid the cooing of pigeons that claim the twilight heights, and where the irregular and cavity-riddled walls of the cave are streaked with white mineral stain tinted in places with the green of moss and algae, and where spiders and small critters have spun webs to give the cavern a spooky atmosphere.

Beyond Onyx Cave the Niangua becomes a river again. If one is in a small craft suitable for shallow water, the river can be traveled upstream for a good distance. It is a pleasant journey of quiet, woodland beauty, where the waters are tranquil, the fishing memorable and wildlife plentiful. In the fall of the year when the leaves change tint, the Niangua is surrounded by a riot of color.

Niangua Bridge Camp & Boat Dock *(Camdenton, Camden County)* -

Niangua Bridge Camp & Boat Dock was once at the east end of the Hwy. 54 Niangua Bridge west of Camdenton. It was on the south side of the highway close to the bridge. The camp was built in 1931 by Fernando Hanks. On Jan. 17, 1932, the camp was the scene of the first baptism in the Lake [see Baptism in the Lake].

The camp was operated by Lowell and Watson in 1938 but by 1940 Elmer Lowell had taken his interests across the bridge to the west end on the downstream side where he built Lowell's Niangua Bridge Boat Dock [see Lowell's Niangua Bridge Boat Dock].

Watson continued the operation of his camp and advertised it as Watson's Niangua Bridge Camp to distinguish his place from Lowell's.

Hank's camp offered complete fishing services, heated cabins, a cafe and a filling station. His cabins were both rock and frame structures, some with screened-in porches but there were no indoor bathrooms at first. Each cabin had its own outhouse. The boat dock was a floating boardwalk running straight out into the Lake and boats were tied up along the sides. They were a mixture of wooden Ozark long-john boats and more conventional skiffs or rowboats with pointed bows. Motors were available for rent. At the end of the boardwalk was a square dock surrounded by a railing with a rectangular center-opening for fishing.

By the mid 1940s, the camp had new owners -- Red & Stell Wells -- who, in 1951, changed the name of the camp to Tonka Villa Resort. The resort continued in operation until the 1990s when the property was purchased by the Missouri Department of Transportation so the resort could be demolished to make way for the construction of a new Hwy. 54 Niangua Bridge.

Niangua River -

The Niangua River rises well beyond the Lake of the Ozarks region, originating in Webster County before entering Camden County 15 miles or so upstream from the headwaters of the Niangua Arm of the Lake. Between the head of the Niangua Arm and the Camden County line is Lake Niangua impounded by Tunnel Dam where a hydropower facility generates electricity. Tunnel Dam was built at about the same time as Bagnell Dam but is not owned by AmerenUE. Unlike Lake of the Ozarks, Lake Niangua is small, with a surface area of only 300 acres.

The Niangua River drains a basin of about 1,040 square miles in extent and upper reaches of the river is a loosing stream, meaning that the water is lost to karst drainage underground. The Niangua is noted for its numerous caves and cold springs. It is a popular fishing and floating stream and its meandering miles are rich in history surrounding old mill sites, scenic bluffs and early settlements.

Oak Grove Beach Resort *(Hurricane Deck, Sunrise Beach, Camden County)* -

Oak Grove Beach was established in 1932 by M. P. Shull about 1,200 feet from the head of Welcher Hollow Cove at the 36-mile mark on the Osage Arm. The mouth of the cove is about one mile upstream from the Hurricane Deck Bridge. The cove is about 5,000 feet long with water 30 feet deep until near the location of the old Oak Grove Beach Resort where it lessens to 10 feet. Here, the cove is about 500 feet wide. The resort was on the southeast side of the cove accessible from LkRd. 5-21, later designated 5-43 and now called Utica Drive.

An early description of the resort said: "To fishermen, hunters and those who love the great outdoors, tucked away in the mountains, just a short drive off the highway, you find this camp -- for both fisherman and family, for here in a cove you will find the beach safe for the children to swim, and row a boat, and as for fishing -- well, it's one of the best -- and the guides know where they are 'biting' best. The cabins are clean, cool and comfortable and there is plenty of shade. This camp is open all year round and you who like to hunt for turkey, rabbit, quail and squirrel, please remember this place."

After several years, Shull built a lodge to compliment his semi-modern housekeeping cabins, and put in a grocery store and bait shop. A guest could eat meals in the lodge dining room.

As the 1930s gave way to the 1940s, Shull sold to E. W. Dixon who advertised it as Dixon's Oak Grove Beach. Dixon's tenure of ownership was short. He sold to Bill Weimar who continued the operation under the name Oak Grove Beach. His advertising slogan was "the friendly resort."

About 1945, Oak Grove Beach had a neighbor upstream on the cove -- Briney's Cove Yacht Club and then, by 1964, Briney's Cove Yacht Club & Resort. By 1965, Briney's had closed. Lucky Strike Resort, which was near the mouth of this cove, survived to 1969 before closing, bringing the resort era on Welcher's Hollow cove to an end.

Osage Beach Post Office *(Osage Beach, Camden County)* -

The Osage Beach Post Office has occupied several buildings along Hwy. 54. It began as the Zebra Post Office in 1886. The Zebra Post Office was discontinued when the Osage Beach Post Office was established in 1935.

The Zebra Post Office was originally near the end of LkRd. 54-30, now called Redbud Road. The 12- by 20-foot building was moved to a site along the new stretch of Hwy. 54 near the west end of the Grand Glaize Bridge in 1930. This building stood near the entrance to Redbud Road. The building was demolished when the post office was renamed.

In 1935, the new Osage Beach Post Office opened along the south side of Hwy. 54 in a small, white frame building facing the entrance to LkRd. 54-10, later designated 54-24 and now called Osage Beach Road.

About 1960, the post office moved across the highway to the north side to occupy the former Folded Hills Dining Room building, which was remodeled and given a red brick veneer. Not many years later, the post office moved again, this time to the southeast corner of Hwy. 54 at the junction of LkRd. 54-29 or Passover Road [now also called Old Post Office Road]. Here, the post office occupied a tan-colored brick building.

The Osage Beach Post Office moved from this location in the 1990s to a much larger and more modern post office building along Hwy. 54 west of the Grand Glaize Bridge at the northwest corner of Normandy Road.

Only one of the former post office buildings remains in use -- the one at the corner of Passover Road. The original post office building is gone and Beabouts Bait & Tackle currently occupies its location. More recently, the building the post office had occupied on the other side of the highway at the corner of Osage Beach road has also been demolished. Until 2005, that building had been occupied by Arnold's Country Corner.

Osage Beach Tavern / Hotel *(Osage Beach, Camden County)* -

In 1931-32, B. Ray Franklin of Jefferson City built Franklin's Osage Beach Tavern on LkRd. 54-10, later designated 54-24 and now called Osage Beach Road. There were no other resorts on this peninsula at the time and the resort was located about halfway between the head of the unnamed cove that it faced and the mouth of the cove, which is at the 18-mile mark on the Osage Arm. The business was on the north side of the peninsula. Later, Kirkwood Lodge would be built adjacent to the Osage Beach Tavern.

In August 1932, the Osage Beach Tavern was described by the *Lake of the Ozarks News*: "Upon entering the spacious lobby, you find to your left a real fireplace handsome in its design of native rock with a 27-foot foundation. The mantle rock is one piece seven inches thick and over 12 feet long. The hearth and mantle rock by diligent search was secured at Hahatonka by the builder, Mr. S. Kelsay... To your right is a specially designed showcase that has in it accessories for the fishermen... The lovely dining room is also spacious and overlooks the cove, you might say at your very feet and commands a fine view of Franklin's boat dock and the Lake. The kitchen is a marvel of cleanliness, and persided over by a woman chef who is not discounted by any of the large city hotels. There are 23 rooms with shower baths and they are equipped with Simmons beds and springs. Mr. Franklin has spared no expense in the Tavern's furnishings for the pleasure and delight of the guests. Electricity is from a huge diesel engine installed by W. A. Bybee, Etterville, Missouri, agent for the Fairbanks-Morse Company. The rates at the Tavern are exceptionally low.

"The Tavern is equipped with marine railway for inside and outside storage and at the Franklin dock you will find boats from Joplin, Kansas City, Jefferson City, St. Louis and Columbia and from several nearby towns. Here guests will find for their use the humble rowboat at $1.50 per day up to the powerful cruiser of the mighty Chris Craft, $5.00 per day for a full capacity load...

"Mr. Franklin is a resident of Jefferson City and is well known in both newspaper circles and the outdoor loving public. His son, Jimmy, formerly a linotype operator at Botts Printing and Engraving Company of Jefferson City, is the pilot and master of the Franklin dock...

"The Tavern was built at an expense of $40,000. Mr. Franklin has yet to add several unfinished necessities such as two large porches overlooking the Lake and a 50 x 12 front porch to the entrance..."

The front of the building suggests the hotel might have only two floors but there are, in fact, four levels because it is on a slope leading down to the Lake. The building's front and sides are veneered in cobblestone, which was in vogue at the time. Cobblestones, also known as fieldstones or "Ozark diamonds," could be from fist size to volley ball size, irregular in shape and of almost any kind of rock, though typically in the Lake region dolomite, limestone or chert [flint]. They were generally gathered from stony fields in the Ozarks. Many of the cobblestones used in the Lake Ozark and Osage Beach area in the 1930s and 40s came from Miller County around Iberia.

Once the Tavern was open for buisness, the front windows had large striped awnings over them. The central doorway had an even larger awning. A rectangular porch without a roof gave access to the front door and the portals were flanked by two lighthouse-like cones sitting on the posts and both cones were topped by white,

Osage Beach Tavern Hotel, *Osage Beach, MO, Circa. 1940s. Photo by L. L. Cook, Milwaukee.*

disc-shaped round glass globes on which the name of the resort was painted. Presumably, these were lighted internally at night. A cobblestone-veneered garage sat to the right when you faced the hotel.

On the Lake side, the building is wood-veneered. The second floor has a deck that runs the full width of the building and is supported by pillars. The ground floor on the Lake side has entry doors large enough for a good-sized boat to be brought into the building.

After opening, the Tavern advertised having a guest capacity of 50 people. The dining room served excellent meals and a chicken dinner in 1940 cost 50 cents.

The world "Tavern" was replaced with the word "Hotel" in the late 1930s.

B. Ray Franklin died in the mid 1930s and his wife continued the operation until selling it in 1946 to the Bruners from St. Louis. Descendents of the Bruner family still own and occupy the building.

The Bruners promoted their beach, one of the first to be built at a resort in Osage Beach. By 1960, the hotel had been closed and it has been used as a private residence ever since.

Osage Iron Works / Smelter *(Climax Springs, Hurricane Deck, Camden County)* -

About one mile up Bollinger Creek Cove at the 44-mile mark on the Osage Arm, stands an ancient-looking structure rising 18 feet above the waterline. Lake water laps at three sides of the pyramid-like monolith, which is fashioned out of enormous blocks of dolomite limestone. At the waterline it has mysterious v-shaped notches, one in the middle of each side, and it stands largely in the water although a slope of hillside waste soil and rock now attaches it to the land.

Recreational boaters who come upon this oddity for the first time are often puzzled, guessing wildly at its origin, for there is nothing posted to inform them of how it came to be. It is visibly old and in its surroundings of lake homes and boat docks it looks strangely out of place. But if the boaters continue to frequent this area they eventually learn that it is an old iron furnace built more than 130 years ago for smelting iron ore. It is the only significant pre-Lake man-made structure that was left in the basin when the basin was cleared between 1929 and 1931 for the coming lake.

Iron Smelter Furnace 1929, *Laurie, MO. Photo Courtesy AmerenUE.*

Why was it left when the timber was cut, farm homes razed and the county seat town of Old Linn Creek leveled? Even the dead were disturbed, their cemeteries moved from the basin. To the pioneer families of the Osage River valley, it seemed as if the Union Electric Light & Power Company, who was building the dam, considered nothing sacred. Yet this monument to a short-lived mining venture survived to become a reminder of forgotten dreams!

In 1840, before Camden County was organized, Stephen and William H. Bollinger homesteaded here, bequeathing their name to the creek and future Lake cove. They had much timber to clear because it was a densely wooded area. The only good farmland was in the Osage River bottomlands and its major tributaries. The Osage was navigable, on average, nine months out of the year, but only for boats of light draft, which made it a difficult river for steamboats to use. The local people also relied upon timber harvesting and mining to make a living. Lead and iron ore were abundant minerals in the hills about them.

"The summer of 1870 brought much excitement to Camden County as rumor of a new business venture was discussed in the various general stores," said Neta Pope in her history of the Osage Iron Works Company. "Two capitalists, a Dr. A. Condee and a Mr. Alex J. Campbell, were going to start a mining operation...that promised to be the biggest industry in the Osage Valley."

In 1872, the two men organized their company, known as the Osage Iron Works. Their superintendent was an experienced iron man from Ohio and they brought a stonemason from Ireland to build the furnace. The furnace was only part of a much larger complex of structures. They invested nearly $100,000 in land, buildings and labor [which in today's currency would be close to $1,000,000]. By the time pig iron production began in April 1873, the company was nearly broke. They "expended their capital in erecting the works, and, not having sufficient capital to operate them, were compelled to suspend business after having run only a little over a year," said an 1889 account.

The furnace, the only part of the Osage Iron Works operation that remains, cost $35,000 to build, which would be more than $250,000 in today's currency. Limestone was quarried a short distance away and the huge blocks of stone were laid without mortar.

At the base, the furnace covered more than 200 square feet and rose to a height of about 30 feet. A furnace stack added to its height... It had a capacity of 10 tons of iron for every 24 hours and once started, ran continuously day and night. Iron ore, coke, and in this instance charcoal and limestone, were fed through the top of the furnace into the hollow interior. Hot blast [pre-

Iron Smelter Furnace, *Laurie, MO. Photo by H. D. Weaver, 2002.*

heated air] was delivered at the bottom through the notched sides. This burned the coke and generated gases and heat required to reduce the iron from its oxide minerals in the ore, and to melt limestone and unwanted materials in the ore to form slag. Molten slag and iron were removed through the bottom. Temperatures in the furnace reached 3000 degrees Fahrenheit. The first shipment of pig iron produced by the furnace went to St. Louis and was adapted to car wheel manufacture.

A settlement known as Irontown grew up at the site with its own post office, which opened in 1872. The town had a population of more than 250 people [see Irontown].

Low water on the Osage River prevented shipment of subsequent production and the nationwide financial panic of 1873 brought the financially-weakened company to its knees. The operation died forever. The miners turned to tie hacking. By 1900, the timber supply was exhausted and in 1904, the last business in town closed its doors. By 1931, when the Lake was formed, nothing was left at the site but the furnace, now a historic curiosity for boaters.

Our Lady of the Lake Catholic Chapel *(Lake Ozark, Miller County)* -

The architectural landmarks of the early decades at Lake of the Ozarks are vanishing so fast today that soon, none will be left. Our Lady of the Lake Catholic Chapel, a landmark along Hwy. 54 in Lake Ozark, met its fate 40 years ago and its loss is still lamented by many of the people who remember it, whether Catholic or not.

The Chapel sat on a knoll overlooking the 15-mile mark of the Lake. Not only is the church building gone, so is the small hill upon which it sat. Both once stood where Monarch Plaza has been for a number of years -- along Bus. Hwy. 54 about one-quarter mile southeast of LkRd. 54-15 and Our Lady of the Lake Catholic Church.

From the 1890s to the 1930s, Eldon was considered a "mission town" attended to by a Catholic priest from a distance of 42 miles. To remedy the situation, Rev. Edwin V. O'Hara, Bishop of the Kansas City, Diocese, appointed a resident pastor to the Sacred Heart Parish in Eldon.

In September 1939, Fr. William J. Conrad, pastor of the Sacred Heart, was given instructions from the Diocese to "build a Chapel at the Lake on Highway 54 somewhere within five to seven miles of the dam" and to have it ready for the summer of 1940.

The deadline was somewhat ambitious since the money needed to build a chapel at the Lake was nowhere in sight. So a plea for donations was made to the Lake's business community and in a short time, a surprising amount of money was raised, some of it coming from people who were not even Catholic. The list of business men and women who gave reads like a Who's Who of that day and time.

From Lake Ozark major donors were: "*Arrowhead Beach Club* (Moreland Brown); *Arrowhead Lodge* (Arthur Kelly); *Atteberry Cafe* (Magnus Atteberry); *Atteberry Grocery* (Ward Atteberry); *Ballenger Cabins & Shop* (Harry Ballenger); *Conrad Cabin Court; Cop-*

Our Lady of the Lake Catholic Chapel, *Lake Ozark, MO, Circa. 1943. Photo by L. L. Cook, Milwaukee.*

per Kettle Cafe & Dog House; Cunningham Novelty (C. J. Cunningham); *Cunningham Barber Shop* (George Cunningham); *Dixcel Service Station* (Ross Clayton); *Fish Haven* (Fred L. Smith); *Tal Gorer Refreshment Stand*; *Chas. Fleetwood Dock & Cabins; Gore Boat Yard Co.* (G. W. Gore); *Knifebird Indian Shop* (Paul Oechlc); *Lakeside Casino* (L. M. Fry); *Lake Ozark Ice & Storage* (E. R. Smith); *Osage Garage* (B. R. Teague); *V. Red Moore Novelties; Overfelt Grocery Store; Stanton's Novelty Co.; Sutton Refrigeration & Electrician* (L. F. Sutton); *Thomas Cabins & Cafe* (Frank Thomas); *Holiday House* (Union Electric); *White House Hotel* (L. M. Fry); and *Young's Cafe & Barbecue*."

From Eldon major donors were: "*Buehler's Drug Store* (Carl Buehler); *Eldon Bakery* (C. A. Humm); *Gensert's Texaco Station; Eldon Hardware & Lumber Co.; Eldon Cheese Co.; Clem Iven; Lehr's Cafe* (W. E. Lehr); *Maples Hotel* (Mrs. Myrtle Witt); *Ozark Central Telephone Co.*; and *Ozark Tackle & Supply* (Matt Dolby)."

From Osagc Beach major donors were: "*Baker's Grand View Lodge; Barber's Grand Glaize Camp; Berry's Lodge* (Leslie Berry); *Bridge View Resort* (C. B. Clark); *Brockman Camp & Grocery* (C. E. Brockman); *Buena Vista Hotel* (E. Tuttle); *Cossey's Camp* (Fred Cossey); *Cannady Grocery Store & Cafe*; *Franklin's Hotel; Frank's Resort* (Frank Frudeger); *Frack's Acre* (Harry Frack); *Golden Sunset Cafe & Cabins; Harrico Cabin Camp* (K. R. Harris); *Hawkeye Cabins & Service* (Harry Greer); *Hildebrand's Resort; Hazelcrest Resort* (Bill & Hazel Evans); *Hyme's Kottage Kamp; Jack Frost Camp* (C. E. Porter); *Johann Service Station & Camp; Kepner's Cottage Camp & Service Station* (Emmit Tettly); *Lazy Days Resort* (V. M. Biggs); *Little Bohemian Resort* (Joe Treybal); *Malibu Beach Resort* (Carl Koopman); *Oakdell Inn* (H. H. Loeffler); *Pla-Port Resort* (A. L. Kelly); *Pooler's Store* (J.

W. Pooler); *Powell's Supreme View; Stoecker's Modern Cottages; L. E. Warren; Williams Grocery* (J. T. Williams); *Wilson's Hill* (Edgar Wilson); *Wiseman's Service Station; Woodbine Cafe; Ware's Cabin Camp* (Ella Ware); and *Wood's Lake Cove Lodge.*"

From Camdenton major donors were: "*Blair Hotel* (John Blair); *Camden County Bank* (Joe V. Foster); *Dr. E. G. Claiborn; Conard Drug Store; Dunn's Bottling Works; Ha Ha Tonka Castle; J. K. Estes; Hopi Camp* (C. F. Hansen); *Lowell's Boat Dock* (Elmer Lowell); *Morgan's Service Station* (Ralph L. Morgan); *E. B. O'Brien Lumber Co.; Red Bird Camp* (J. A. Voss); *The Reveille Newspaper* (G. T. Richards); *Sinclair Gas* (L. W. Morgan); *Singing Hills Resort* (B. D. Knox); *Standard Oil Distributors* (J. W. Bunch); *Walter's Modern Camp; Claud White's Store; Willard Drugs;* and *White's Cash Market.*"

The list of donors provided above was prepared by Fr. William J. Conrad shortly after the church was built. Construction of the church began Nov. 12, 1941. The architect was Marcel Baulicault of St. Louis; the contractor, Schell Construction Co. of Jefferson City; and the superintendent, Loyd Gampher of Eldon.

Dimensions of the building was 67 feet by 32 feet with an inside height of 17 feet from the floor of the Chapel to the peak of its gabled roof. The Chapel was given a rustic design, the exterior of dark, multicolored, uncut surface stones of flint, limestone, crystal and granite with rough, unplaned native oak. The interior walls were made of native cut sandstone in light colors and broken ashler pattern. Roof supports were heavy native oak timbers. The belfry was of the same materials and made on the grounds. The altar was of solid walnut timber cut and finished locally, assembled on the grounds and had a weight of 1800 pounds. The communion rail was also of native walnut 4-inches thick. Partitions and inside stairways were of finished native oak, tongued and grooved locally. The light fixtures and heavy hardware on the front doors and beam plates were designed and executed locally of wrought iron. The large front doors, including their wrought iron, were made and donated by Carl A. Koopman of Malibu Beach Resort. Glass in the fixtures was plain window glass, sandblasted. A parking area for 150 cars was provided.

The cross on top of the belfry was lit at night with blue neon and boaters on the Lake could see it for a distance of eight miles.

Cost figures for the church vary in accounts from $13,000 to $17,266.45. It is said that over a period of several years that Fr. William Conrad actually spent about $25,000 in building and improvements, which was a considerable sum of money in the early 1940s.

The dedication and laying of the cornerstone occurred on May 30, 1942. Bishop Edwin V. O'Hara, DD of Kansas City, officiated at the ceremony. Fr. Conrad celebrated Mass in the new Chapel for the first time on Sunday, May 3, 1942. In May of 1943, Fr. Conrad was transferred to Kansas City and thereafter, the priest from Eldon's Sacred Heart Church served as pastor for the Chapel.

The number of Catholics in the Lake area was limited at the beginning but tourists were many and the church saw large crowds. By 1962, it had reached the point where it was necessary to hold Mass from 6 a.m. to Noon every Sunday simultaneously upstairs and downstairs by two priests to accommodate the people.

A new Catholic church was built just north of the Chapel in the mid 1960s and the little Chapel and its property were sold to a group of 13 investors. The Chapel was later demolished by developers, much to the dismay of a group of parishioners who had formed a committee to try to save the building. It was bulldozed down overnight before any formal protest could be launched.

Ozark Caverns *(Camdenton, Linn Creek, Camden County)* -

Lake of the Ozarks State Park Public Beach No. 1 is located on the upper reaches of the Grand Glaize Arm off Hwy. 42 at the end of Hwy. 134. The Lake is broad and shallow here, with a maximum depth of 10 feet when the Lake is full. Due south across the Lake from the campground is Coakley Hollow Cove 1,200 feet long and 400 feet wide. It is within the state park and the banks are wooded and undeveloped.

Anyone taking a swim in Coakley Hollow Cove during the hot summer months may discover that just a few feet below the surface of the warm Lake water, is a layer of very cold water. This is the combined flow of water that discharges from Coakley Hollow Spring and Ozark Caverns. Even though the spring and cave are three-quarters of a mile up the hollow from the cove, their water discharges from the underground at a chilly temperature of 56 degrees all year and it is still cold when it reaches the Lake, where it sinks into the waters of the cove. The hollow through which the spring branch flows is full of natural and cultural history, some of which

Entrance of Ozark Caverns, *Linn Creek, MO, Circa. 1952. Photographer Unknown.*

can be enjoyed by visiting the Ozark Caverns Interpretative Center and natural area. [see Coakley Hollow Coves]

Another way to reach Coakley Hollow and Ozark Caverns is to take Route A off Hwy. 54, which is 1.5 miles north of Linn Creek, or about 7.5 miles south of the Grand Glaize Bridge. On A Road it is about seven miles to the Ozark Caverns turnoff at Freedom [County Road A-33 or McCubbins Drive].

While the location seems remote, it was not so remote to the people who settled this territory in the early 1800s. The Ozark Caverns area was officially opened to settlement in 1820. Settlement in the locale came from two directions -- by way of Auglaize Creek to the south in the 1830s, and from the northeast by way of Tuscumbia and Brumley areas as early as the middle 1820s. The uplands along the southeast side of Coakley Hollow were part of the Salsman homestead. In 1854, William Salsman and Scott Strong built a gristmill and sawmill three miles downstream from Coakley Hollow near what later became known as the Popplewell Place. The road on the ridge carried traffic between Freedom and Salsman's mills. A spur of this road passed very near the cave, up and over the cave hill, and on to the settlement of Passover.

The first known exploration of the cave occurred in the mid 1850s. Names and dates from this period can be found in the cave, the oldest being on the flow-stone cascade known as the Name Wall. In the 1970s, the oldest of these dates were still faintly visible beneath the layers of calcite that have grown over them since they were written.

Sometime in the 1880s, an Irishman by the name of Coakley built a dam to impound the flow of water from the spring and cave and then built a gristmill and sawmill. The dam was located about 1,000 feet down the valley from the cave entrance.

The operation of the mills brought many people to the valley and it soon became a popular place for picnics and socials. But getting to the cave itself was tricky because of a bog that existed in front of the cave entrance. It was fed by springs along the hillside. Cattle, horses and even people, it was said, could get mired down in the mud. The cave had to be approached from the hillside. It was during this period of time that that the cave became known as Coakley Cave.

In 1888 there was a lead strike not far from the cave but no mining operations resulted. A series of shallow assay holes dug along the hillside proved it was just a small pocket of "float lead."

About the year 1900, Coakley moved his milling operation to a location nearer to Linn Creek and the Coakley site was abandoned. It is said that the mill burned some years later. The dam is still present, although it was later breached to drain the lake behind it.

In 1948, Bridal Cave north of Camdenton was opened to the public. Shortly thereafter the developers of Bridal Cave purchased Coakley Cave to develop it even though the cave was in a location that was not likely to make it a popular tourist cave or a profitable operation. It was simply too far off the beaten track.

According to the late Ralph Ohlson, a former owner of the cave, it was developed by the Bridal Cave Development Corp. simply to keep it from becoming competition because after Bridal Cave was opened to the public, rumors circulated that other local interests were considering the development of Coakley Cave.

Development of the cave began in 1951 and it was opened to the public in 1952 as Coakley Cave. Two years later, the name was changed to Ozark Caverns, a name that the owners felt had greater consumer appeal. Its development was carried out by Jim Banner, B. F. Krehbiel and R. L. Wilkerson. Arthur "Slim" and Eva Logan were hired to manage the cave.

Initially, there was very little advertising but a couple of directional signs were put up along Hwy. 54 between Route A and Camdenton. Visitors to Bridal Cave were told about Coakley Cave and urged to go visit it, so most of the visitors were referrals. Visitors would find a small camping trailer to the left of the big cave entrance, which the Logans called home, and a small wooden ticket building to the right of the cave entrance. A concrete fish pond fed by the cave stream was to the left of the entrance overhang. About 50 feet inside the cave was a balustrade made of oak slabs and a doorway. Eva sold tickets and Slim guided. The cave was electrically lighted.

In 1955, a building was constructed in front of the cave entrance to house in the cave, provide a gift shop and ticket counter, and living quarters on the second floor for summer cave guides.

In 1956, the cave was sold to Ralph H. & Mary P. Ohlson. They owned the cave until it was sold to the Missouri Department of Natural Resources in 1978 to become part of the natural history program at Lake of the Ozarks State Park. After acquiring the cave, the department removed all electrical lighting from the cave so that lantern tours could be given, and restored the original natural wet meadow in front of the cave that had functioned as a bog before 1951. This bog had been filled with gravel and sediments removed from the cave during its commercial development in 1951.

Ozark Caverns has a commercial trail that follows a winding underground stream course for over 1,000 feet. The cave has lavish exhibits of secondary cave formations including a great abundance of flowstone, stalactites, stalagmites and columns as well as fascinating solution features. It is noted for having thousands of delicate helictites, rare spathites, and a rare display of giant shower-head stalactites with large crystal catch-basins. This display is called the Angel's Shower. The cave is also a habitat for endangered grey bats and has a diverse eco-system that includes blind cave salamanders.

Ozark Inn / Cafe *(Lake Ozark, Miller County)* -

One of the first gas stations to be built along the Bagnell Dam Strip in Lake Ozark was the Diamond Filling Station, which sat on the south side of The Strip adjacent to The Bagnell Dam Gift Shop on its east side. This would be on the east side of today's business called Frick & Frack. Just to the west, on the north side of

Bus. Hwy. 54, is Beach Road and almost directly across from the old Diamond Filling Station location today, is the road to Lodge of the Ozarks.

The filling station was in operation for only a short time before the location was leased by Mr. & Mrs. Bruce J. Duffy of Kansas City.

On April 4, 1932, the *Lake of the Ozarks News* reported that the Duffys "will soon have in readiness an outstanding Inn and cabin resort thoroughly modern in every respect. Besides a dining room and counters, there will be a dance annex where dancing will be free. The resort will be known as Bruce's Ozark Inn and will cater to the very best element. Hot and cold showers, best attention and service, a barbecue pit will be installed and improvements made in general." The newspaper quoted Mr. Duffy saying: "I have come down here to be one of you and do my bit in serving the tourist that will visit the lake. I will have the interest of the lake always at heart and you can rest assured I mean it." Bruce Duffy had experience in catering clubs and hotels in Kansas City.

Duffy built 22 small frame cabins that stood in two rows at a 45-degree angle from Hwy. 54. The cabins formed a wide "V" in orientation with the highway. In the center of this V was the building housing the dining room and dance annex. Out front, somewhat removed from the dining room building, was a small canopy beneath which were two, visible gas, gravity pumps that dispensed Standard Oil gasoline.

The dining room and annex was soon being advertised as the Ozark Inn Cafe. Upon entering, a customer found a row of stools along the counter on the left and a row of tables to the right. At the far end was a Victrola with a model ship on top and to its right stood a life-size cardboard cutout of a lady advertising beer. Mounted on the wall behind the serving counter was a stuffed eagle. The curtains on the windows were flowery and the tiled floor had a pattern of large circles that appeared to have wings.

By 1935, Duffy had sold, and the business was called Thomas Ozark Inn. The Inn's guest capacity was 60 and a cabin was available for 75 cents per person per day. Their advertising slogans were "One Stop Service" and "Ice Water by the Thousand Gallons."

Ads that appeared for a time after 1936, had an unusual phrase which said "Coldest in Winter, Coolest in Summer." One can only guess at what the meaning of the words "coldest in winter" were intended to convey. One might consider it a typo except that the ads were continued for more than one season and such a printers mistake would surely have been caught rather quickly.

By the early 1950s, several cabins had apparently been taken out of service as they advertised having only 18 units. In 1954, the business changed ownership and was renamed Van's Motel, the word "motel" having been introduced to the traveling public nationwide in the 1950s. By this time, the telephone company no longer listed accommodations under the headings of "cabins," "cottages," or "camp," but were almost exclusively putting such businesses under either "resorts" or "motels," which also encouraged roadside businesses to make such changes to the names of their establishments.

By 1957, the business was advertising only 14 available cottages, as if the place were shrinking. Perhaps some cabins were removed to make room for recreational facilities like the new heated, filtered swimming pool that had been added, as well as the gift shop and a miniature golf course.

In the early 1960s, the business sold again and became Boot's Motel, which managed to continue in business until about 1970. The buildings were thereafter removed when thc property was sold for the erection of Fun City USA, a small theme park with a variety of carnival-type rides. Some of the more permanent buildings erected on this tract of land during Fun City's short occupancy, are still present and in use today by other types of businesses.

Ozark Tavern Hotel *(Camdenton, Camden County)* -

In January 1932, when the new town of Camdenton was experiencing its initial building boom, Boyd H. Harwood and son, Boyd W. Jr., of Kansas City, bought property on the north side of the Camdenton Square for a hotel. It was one of a number of lots still vacant. They hired J. H. Hultgren to fill and grade the lot and construct the building.

"The hotel, to be known as the Ozark Tavern, will be a two-story brick with 12 guest rooms," said the local newspaper. "It will be constructed so that two or more stories can be added and a west wing built on if needed. In the lobby and dining room of the hotel, a rustic effect will be carried out and the...building will be modern.

The winter of 1932 brought a cold wave that temporarily interrupted construction work but they were still able to project an opening date of April 1, 1932.

Ozark Tavern Hotel, *Camdenton, MO, Circa. 1930s. Photographer Unknown.*

Their first summer on the square was encouraging. By fall, the Harwoods began doubling the size of their building, adding a second building that gave them 15 additional rooms. The first construction had cost $15,000 and this second surge of building set them back another $15,000.

"Mr. Harwood says that he is favorably impressed by the development of Camdenton and it can be said of him that he is expressing his confidence in the town's future in a very material manner," said the local paper in September 1932. "Citizens of Camdenton have often pointed with pride to the Ozark Tavern, one of Camdenton's outstanding enterprises and it has caused much favorable comment by the traveling public. A hotel such as the Ozark Tavern is a valuable drawing card for any community."

Architecturally, the two brick-veneered Tudor-style buildings were among the most handsome and imposing buildings on the Camdenton Square, taking up more than half of the space available for building along the square's diagonal north side. By 1934, the buildings were complete. The Ozark Tavern Hotel and Cafe occupied the east building while other merchants occupied the west building. Between these two, was a one-story connecting building, looking squeezed but functional. It housed a small gift shop.

The hotel was under the management of B. W. Harwood, Jr. By this time the town of Camdenton had four restaurants, two churches, two doctors, one dentist, a theater, a bank, bakery, four food markets, two drug stores, service stations and garages, and approximately thirty fishing and vacation camps within a radius of five miles.

By 1938, the name of the establishment had changed from Ozark Tavern Hotel to Harwood Hotel. In the 1940s, Harwood Hotel was approved by Duncan Hines for its excellence in service. The Hardwood's placed the phrase "Approved by Duncan Hines" on the hotel building.

The 1950s brought new operators -- the Fordyces' -- who renamed it Harwood Motor Lodge. In 1959, their advertising said: "See Missouri's largest collection of antique plates and the most interesting gift shop in the Ozarks."

The Fordyces erected a billboard-sized sign in the lot east of the two buildings -- between their hotel and Lake Plaza Hotel, which was on the corner adjacent to Hwy. 54 and Harwood's closest competitor.

Harwood Motor Lodge survived to the mid 1960s. While the name no longer graces the Camdenton Square, the two Harwood buildings survive. The east building, which housed the hotel, still presents the same architectural face to the junction of Hwys. 5 & 54, but the west building has undergone some exterior remodeling. The small building that once connected these two buildings and housed the gift shop, no longer exists.

Palisades *(Linn Creek, Camden County)* -

One meaning for the word "palisade" is "a line of bold cliffs." Although the word could easily be applied to other cliffs that border the Osage, only one particular line has traditionally been known as "The Palisades" since the days of steamboat pilots. They are located between the 27- and 28-mile marks on the Osage Arm bordering the Lake's east side. The unbroken wall of rock begins at the mouth of Shoop Hollow Cove less than one mile up-Lake from Tan-Tar-A Island, and continues in a gentle curve for a mile-and-a-quarter to play out at the mouth of Racetrack Hollow.

Topping out between 120 and 200 feet above the water, the wall has a high talus slope covered by heavy vegetation so that only the upper half of this majestic cliff-line is exposed. To this day no development breaks the natural beauty of its shoreline or the rim except near its southern end where a boat dock sits beneath a break in the cliff. Currently, houses on the rim can be found only near its southern tip.

In the summer, the Palisades talus slope is a blanket of various shades of green intermingled with blooming vines that burst with color. The upper lip of the bluff is irregular and craggy with picturesque rock features and ancient cedar trees with gnarled and twisted trunks and limbs.

The Palisades, *27-Mile Mark, Osage Arm. Photo by H. D. Weaver, 2005.*

At one place can be seen an enormous block of dolomite that has fallen from the face of the bluff to land at the base of the talus slope, its lower edge at the water line. High up one can see the place where this huge boulder lost its hold. The fracture lines are sheer, sharp and fresh enough to indicate that this behemoth has fallen in historic times. The Lake had nothing to do with its dislodging. It sheered along two vertical fractures or joints, one parallel with the bluff, the other at a 90-degree angle. Water invading the joints probably caused the dislodging through the freeze and thaw process. The evidence here is enough to prove that cliff faces can be unpredictable and present potential hazards at any time of the year.

Pioneering Spirit -

European and American settlers who arrived here in the 1820s and 1830s found the region heavily wooded. There were no roads other than Indian trails, yet these restless immigrants were filled with the "pioneering spirit" and rose to the challenge of subduing the wilderness.

In the early 1930s, the people who arrived at the newly formed Lake of the Ozarks also found a region heavily wooded. No lake roads provided access to the Lake's shores and no electrical service was immediately available. But they were filled with the "pioneering spirit" and rose to the challenge of creating a recreational playground out of the undeveloped resource.

The editor of the *Lake of the Ozarks News* recognized this and said in January 1932: "Pioneering is not dead. Of course the days of coonskin caps, leather breeches and flint locks are over but there are other fields requiring [the] skills, daring and vision of those other days. The Lake of the Ozarks today offers outlet for the pioneer spirit... There are dozens of things to be done around the lakeshore requiring vision of the pioneer.

Those of us living here today are reaping the benefits of the pioneering spirit of our predecessors."

Pla-Port Resort *(Osage Beach, Camden County)* -

Where the Grand Glaize and the Osage meet at what is today the 19-mile mark on the Osage Arm, the village of Zebra once thrived. It was a busy port of call for steamboats. There was the "lower part" of town along the banks of the Osage below the steep nose of Zebra ridge at the southeast corner of the confluence, and the "upper part" of town scattered along the single gravel road that ran up the steep nose of Zebra ridge and then down the spine of the ridge toward the uplands to the east. Dwellings and a few business establishments were along the ridge road. The high point at the nose of the ridge, where the hill-road leveled out, was called Observation Heights. Today, the road leading to this spot is double LkRd. 54-30, one fork called Lighthouse Road and the other Redbud Road.

During the construction of Bagnell Dam the people of Zebra moved their businesses, homes, and the Zebra Post Office building to the new stretch of Hwy. 54

Pla-Port Lighthouse, *Osage Beach, MO, 1935. Photographer Unknown.*

that ran from Bagnell Dam to the new Grand Glaize Bridge. This would be where Shoney's Restaurant is located today at the corner of LkRd. 54-30.

The people of Zebra left behind several empty houses, including an old concrete house that crowned Observation Heights. In 1931, after the Lake had formed, L. A. Kelly, a man of vision and ambition, recognized the scenic value of Observation Heights and proceeded to buy up the land along the ridge where Zebra had once been.

Kelly envisioned a working lighthouse crowning the ridge with park-like grounds surrounding the structure, and native stone cottages for fishermen and vacationers [vacationists in 1930s terminology]. He hired Thomas "Tommy" H. Forrester, a local architect, to design and landscape the resort with an eye to "Spanish beauty," and instructed him to use as much native material as possible such as rocks, logs and wood. Kelly thought at first to name his resort Pla-Point but changed his mind and decided on Pla-Port. He told Forrester: "Sometime, perhaps in the near future, I will build a lighthouse over the point. I feel it will not only be of use to boaters but an added attraction for Pla-Port."

In the spring of 1932, Forrester set to work with a crew of 35 men. As the rustic cottages were completed, they were given romantic names. The cottages were also numbered and included:

No. 1, the ***Waltonian***, the largest stone cottage. It was big enough for large families and had three double beds with room for a roll-a-way bed. The cottage had a living room, glassed-in porch, kitchen, fireplace, and sat beneath large oak trees. It faced the Grand Glaize on the south side of the peninsula.

No. 2, the ***Ozark Lodge***, was half log and half wood siding. It was family size with large windows, a living room overlooking the Lake, two bedrooms, an additional studio couch [a couch that can be made into a full-sized bed by sliding out the spring frame fitted beneath it], kitchen, dinette and bath. It faced the Grand Glaize.

No. 3, ***The Osage***, a modern stone cottage with fireplace, living room with studio couch, bedroom, complete bath, and a kitchenette. It faced the Grand Glaize.

No. 4, the ***Grandview***, and No. 5, the ***Whipporwill*** were wood-sided and had large windows overlooking the Lake. Each had two bedrooms, kitchen, sitting room with studio couch, and a complete bath. There was space for additional cots. These cottages faced the Grand Glaize.

No. 6, the ***Redbud***, and No. 7, the ***Hawthorne***, were duplicate stone cottages. They were 200 feet from the playground. Each had one bedroom, living room and studio couch, kitchen, dinette and bath with tub. These two cottages were on the north side of the peninsula, facing the Osage Arm.

No. 9, the ***Shamrock***, a wood-sided cottage, was right on the point with large windows overlooking the Osage Arm and had a view that stretched for miles. It was insulated for winter and summer use, had two bedrooms, one living room, kitchen, dinette and complete bath.

Why there was no No. 8 is a mystery.

Before these cottages were even completed, Kelly and his son, Orville, decided they simply had to have the lighthouse and Forrester found himself in a rush to meet their deadline -- Decoration Day 1933.

The peak of the lighthouse was 130 feet above the water's edge. The lighthouse sat more toward the south side of the point than the north side, with the slope of the south side giving way to rugged rock outcrops and low bluffs bordering the Grand Glaize Arm.

The lighthouse had three floors of apartments with three bedrooms in each and a living room with studio couch. The bathrooms had showers. There was a kitchen in each apartment and each apartment could accommodate seven or eight people.

The third floor apartments had two bedrooms, a kitchen, bath with tub, and a shaded balcony. These apartments became a favorite of honeymoon couples. "The rock walls, which rise to the third story, present a gallery of rock formations of many colors and are native to the Ozarks," said the *Lake of the Ozarks News*.

The top of the lighthouse had a rotating green and white light in an enclosure. It could be seen on the Lake at night for a distance of 14 miles.

In addition to the lighthouse and cottages, there was a recreational clubhouse next to the office, boat docks along the Grand Glaize Arm and elsewhere a rustic log coffee shop and dining room with a seating capacity of 62 and ample room for dancing. The beach was along the Osage Arm.

The Pla-Port Lighthouse was unique, somewhat medieval in appearance and during its lifetime, advertized as the only operating inland lighthouse in the United States. Even in the daytime the tower could be seen far out upon the Lake and acted as a guidepost and compass for boaters. In fact, in more recent years the hill upon which it was built has been called Compass Point.

But time marches on and by 1960, the Pla-Port Lighthouse as well as the cottages, had been demolished by new owners, with new structures put up in their place. Each new owner who has had the privilege of developing this historic site for the past 35 years has demolished much and sometimes all of his predecessors buildings. Businesses that succeeded Pla-Port on this property include Mai-Tai, a resort with a Polynesian flavor; Osage House, with a massive horseshoe-shaped main building; Breckenridge Resort and Compass Point Resort. Lands End Condominiums now occupy Observation Heights.

But the charm of old Zebra and the spirits of the Pla-Port Lighthouse still linger here where the steamboats used to land when Zebra was a port of call on the Osage; where Lake boaters hailed the guiding light, photographers couldn't get enough pictures, and lovers came to consummate their vows. The old postcards of the Pla-Port Lighthouse are now among the favorites of collectors who cherish not only lighthouses but the vanishing landmarks of the early days of Lake of the Ozarks.

Poolers Modern Cottages, Store & Bus Stop *(Osage Beach, Camden County)* -

Pooler's Apartment Cottages were built by J. W. Pooler along Hwy. 54 in Osage Beach in 1931. The business was located about one-quarter mile northeast of Osage Beach Road where Village Marina Boat Sales is located today across the highway from the Wal-Mart Super Center. This would be about halfway between Bluff Drive and Jo Jo Lane.

Pooler's Modern Cottages, Store & Bus Stop, *Osage Beach, MO, Circa. 1930s. Photographer Unknown.*

The Poolers began with four cabins, one of which was a duplex. They had both native stone and frame cabins with wood siding. Toward the west end of the camp along the highway was a small building with a water tank on top, which may have been a well house and storage building. Just beyond it was a building that housed the Pooler Store with two gravity-fed visible gas pumps out front. The business sold Standard Oil gasoline.

Pooler's was one of the first grocery stores in Osage Beach, although at that time the town was called Zebra. According to Victoria Hubble's history of Osage Beach -- *Town of Two Rivers* -- Pooler's Store served as a temporary post office when residents of the town initiated a movement to change the town's name from Zebra to Osage Beach. This would have been in the 1934-35 period. After the change was made, the new post office building was located just down the road on the opposite side of the highway at the junction of LkRd. 54-24 or Osage Beach Road. The new post office sat where Beabout's Bait & Tackle is today.

Pooler's Store was also a Missouri Pacific Bus Stop.

About 1940, the business was sold to Fred Cossey who renamed it Fred Cossey's Modern Camp. He continued to improve the camp, adding cottages, a trailer campground and a large fishing barge along the Lake shore in what later became known as Kirkwood Lodge Cove. In 1942, his ads said: "Fish on the Big Fishing Barge where you can catch them."

Fred Cossey operated the camp through the 1940s and 50s and sold it about 1960. The new owners renamed it Cleland's Cottages. The camp closed at the end of the 1967 tourist season.

Powell's Supreme View Cottages / Court *(Osage Beach, Camden County)* -

Initially called Supreme View Camp, this Osage Beach business was established along Hwy. 54 in 1932. It was located on the south side of the highway across from the junction of Bluff Drive and the northeast entrance road to the Wal-Mart Super Center. The camp entrance was where The Pasta House sits today and the camp's cottages sat on a knoll that has since been bulldozed away to create the Wal-Mart parking lot.

The camp's advertising slogan was "DeLuxe Cottages for Exacting Folk." By 1935, the name of the camp had become Powell's Supreme View Cottage Court.

The business consisted of a group of large, well furnished stone and log cottages. Each cottage had a fireplace. "Our cottages are home-like and tastefully furnished," said the ads. The rocks used in cottage construction were colorful, often large, and reflected the great variety to shapes, color and types of rock found in the Lake region. A close inspection of the rock walls also revealed complete cave formations as well as fragments of stalactites, stalagmites and other cave deposits. They came from local caves.

Along the highway frontage was a stone retaining wall that also featured cave formations. Where steps led up from the highway shoulder onto the property were two large stalactites that had been taken from a local cave that was later commercialized, according to the late Ralph Ohlson, former owner and operator of Ozark Caverns. The stalactites were turned upside down and mounted as corner posts where the steps broke the retaining wall.

Close to this entry was a small rock building that served as an office during the busy summer months, and where guests registered. Since the Court's cottages were well back on the knoll among the trees and not easily seen from the highway, the office building along the highway made it easier to attract guests.

Powell's Supreme View was built on a high point overlooking the Osage Arm. From the windows of the cottages a person cold look for miles across the hilltops and forest crown, hence the Court's name. The two inverted stalactites mounted along the roadside are to be seen in one of the postcards sold to guests, a card that promoted the scenic view.

Powell's Surpreme View Cottage Court was in operation until about 1979. It sat vacant for a number of years before the property was bought, the buildings demolished and new development occurred. During this period of time, the two stalactite posts along the retaining wall vanished.

Prairie Hollow Cave *(Roach, Camden County)* -

Two folktales surround this cave, which is located in a bluff at the waterline in Prairie Hollow Cove at the 5-mile mark on the Little Niangua Arm. One is that from time to time a waterfall can be heard in a remote part of the cave. The other is that

Prairie Hollow Cave Entrance, *Prairie Hollow Cove, Little Niangua Arm. Photo by H. D. Weaver, 2003.*

the cave completely penetrates Gulliver Ridge and that a second entrance to the cave is along the Little Niangua River on the other side of Gulliver Ridge. Experienced cave explorers have not been able able to find that second entrance and have not been able to make passage through the ridge, but then such stories are legion about caves in the Ozarks and often untrue.

The sound of a waterfall, while not entirely true, does have a basis in fact because the waterfall sound is produced in a small passage of the cave where there are several small dome chambers with echo qualities. The cave is a habitat for a colony of endangered bats. At times, when the bats are flying through the small passage, they circle around in the small dome rooms before flying either into or out of the cave. En masse, the flight of the colony through these chambers produces the thundering sound of the waterfall, which can be heard some distance through the cave.

Because of the bat colony, exploration of the cave is unwise. The bats are a protected species and about 350 feet into the cave is a room where bat guano covers just about everything. The floor here ponds and has become a guano lagoon. The lagoon's overflow pollutes the cave's small stream, which cavers call "Guano Creek." The disagreeable smell of the room is almost overwhelming because of poor air circulation.

The entrance to Prairier Hollow Cave is a triangular opening 30 feet wide and 12 feet high. During normal Lake reservoir levels, water floods the entrance to a depth of four or five feet. The Lake backs into the cave for some distance and when the water level drops below the cave entrance, fish are often trapped in lingering pools in the cave. If the Lake remains low for any length of time, the fish die in the cave, adding another disagreeable odor. Dropping water levels can also leave great amounts of driftwood debris inside the cave for up to 50 feet.

Prairie Hollow Cave has a length of about 800 feet. The first 300 feet has a ceiling height of 12 feet. The passage is narrow, meandering, with ledges projecting from the walls and the stream passage and floor areas repeatedly disappear into deep meander cuts of the wall that generally cannot be entered to make exploration easier.

The cave does have some nice formations but most of them are small and found in the areas splattered with bat guano. Garrett's Column, the largest secondary formation in the cave, has a length of four feet. The name recognizes the cave's secondary name, which is Garrett Cave.

Purvis Beach Resort *(Sunrise Beach, Camden County)* -

Purvis Beach Resort was born from the ashes of the little village of Purvis, which once sat close to the Osage River at what is today the 39-mile mark on the Osage Arm. The old village site out from the mouth of Brush Creek Cove, is now beneath 50 feet of water. The water over Old Purvis is actually 10 feet deeper than the water over Old Linn Creek. The village of Purvis was little more than a post office, a few stores, a steamboat landing and a few dwellings.

The village had its inception when a post office was moved southwest from near Gladstone to the Purvis site, a distance of about eight miles on the Gladstone-

Purvis Beach Resort, Café, Hotel & Post Office, *Sunrise Beach, MO, 1933. Photo by Schuster Studio.*

Linn Creek Road. The move actually shifted the post office from Morgan County to Camden County. The year was 1888 and the postmaster was Jack Purvis.

Among the residents of Purvis was Nora McDonough in whose home the post office was located a few years later. About 1905, the office was moved to a building owned by Peter J. and Pricilla McDonough. The assistant postmaster was Charley Purvis.

For reasons unknown, in 1910 the post office was moved from the McDonough building across the road to a store owned by Wiley McGinnis. Within a few years the McDonoughs bought McGinnis out and once again Peter J. McDonough became postmaster. He had the position until 1923 when Ivy and Ora Purvis bought the store and Ora became postmistress.

Shortly thereafter, word reached the village that a great dam was going to be built near Bagnell. When representatives of the Missouri Hydro-Electric Power Company showed up in 1926 and began securing options for the purchase of the basin land, Ivy and Ora saw opportunity where so many of their neighbors saw no future for themselves in Camden County.

When, a few years later, Union Electric took over the dam project and began awarding contracts for clearing the basin, Ivy Purvis secured the contract for the basin from Cartwright Springs [sic] at what is today the 45-mile mark on the Osage Arm, and Proctor at the 55-mile mark. He hired as many as 80 men to help with the work and the men came from many far flung places because the Great Depression was on and jobs were scarce. The work was difficult because this stretch of the Osage River valley is noted for its bluffs and precipitous slopes. But the contract was lucrative for the Purvis family and they invested in upland acreage above the 660-

foot elevation at the mouth of Brush Creek Hollow where the Purvis general store and post office had been relocated.

With the basin cleared and the water rising, Ivy and Ora began building their resort and by the end of 1931, had seven frame cabins and two log cabins. By 1932, Purvis Beach Resort had 12 cabins to compliment the store, cafe, post office and their home.

In the early 1930s, there was no rural electricity in the area, so Ivy invested in a Delco plant, which was installed in 1934.

The resort grew along the shoreline, cottages were added and so was another large, one-story rectangular building, which, in the 1930s and 40s served as a recreational center and gathering place. By the mid 1940s, the resort had 18 furnished cottages. The cafe was noted for its chicken and ham dinners and they advertised as "one of the oldest camps on the lake, no hills."

The Purvis Post Office functioned until 1945 when Ora Purvis gave it up due to ill health. The post office was discontinued and the mail transferred to another local post office.

With the advent of the 1950s, a new slogan came along: "Home of the Giant Crappie." And so did a new owner and operator, their son, John Purvis.

In the 1930s, the only neighboring business was White Way Beach Resort. Later came Uncle Jim's Resort, Mickeyland Resort, Hickory Point Resort, Delaney Boat Yard and Longacres Beach, which later became Cowan's 5-Acre Resort and then Grewell's 5-Acre Resort.

In 1976, John Purvis sold the resort to A. & B. Potts who added a travel trailer campground but kept Purvis Beach Resort as the resort's primary name. This resort is on LkRd. 5-29, which is now called Purvis Beach Road.

***Purvis Beach Resort Recreation Center**, Circa. 1930s, Sunrise Beach, MO.*

Racetrack Hollow & Cove *(Osage Beach, Camden County)* -

Racetrack Hollow Cove is the south arm of a double cove at the 28-mile mark on the Osage Arm. The history of this cove will be in Volumn Two.

Ranch House Grill *(Osage Beach, Camden County)* -

Ranch House Grill was an Osage Beach business along Hwy. 54 about one block west of Bluff Drive in the 1940s. It was previously the Red Feather Cafe & Camp. [see Red Feather Cafe & Camp]

Red Feather Cafe & Camp *(Osage Beach, Camden County)* -

The Red Feather Cafe was an Osage Beach restaurant in the latter half of the 1930s. It stood along the north side of Hwy. 54 about one block west of Bluff Drive and across from today's Wal-Mart Super Center about where the Phone Station and Ozark Realty are currently located. This would have been between Bluff Drive and Jo Jo Lane.

The cafe opened in 1935 or 1936. It was a log building sitting parallel with the highway. In appearance, it was reminescent of two log houses, attached end-to-end with the left half having a series of square windows that were connected while the right half had three sections of three connected windows. The business opened with only one of these buildings but added the addition a year or so later. The larger dining room was in the right half. The cafe sign over the doorway was long, narrow, and had the word "Beer" at one end and "Cafe" at the other. Between the two words a red feather was painted on the sign.

The interior of the cafe was finished in knotty pine and the decor was very rustic, the kind that would appeal to fishermen and hunters. In the left half of the building, which led to the kitchen, there was a serving counter and it was where patrons paid their bill. A small room with tables was to the rear and had served as the initial dining room. To the right was the doorway into the larger dining room. A deer's head and steer horns were mounted over the doorway. In the dining room, a moose head was mounted on the wall. A wagon wheel chandelier hung from the center of the dining room.

Red Feather Café, *Osage Beach, MO, 1937. Photographer Unknown.*

The Red Feather Cafe specialized in country ham and smoked barbecue meats. Their ads promoted plate lunches, chicken fried in butter, fish thoroughly cooked, and a cafe supervised by a host. There were also rental cabins on the property.

The Red Feather Cafe & Camp ceased operation under this name about 1940 or 1941. The cafe continued in business for several years as Jo Jo's Ranch House Grill, which specialized in steak and chicken dinners, grilled hamburgers and fries and had take-out service.

Apparently this building was vacated a few years later and the people who operated the business moved to another building about a quarter-of-a-mile west and opened up Jo Jo's Restaurant, which used to be where the 54 Diner is today just west of Bob Evan's Restaurant.

Riverview *(Stover, Morgan County)* -

Riverview is located at the 70-mile mark on the Osage Arm. It is on the north side at the mouth of Possum Trot Hollow Cove and Big Buffalo Cove in the extreme southwest corner of Morgan County where the counties of Benton, Camden and Morgan join. On old maps, the town's name appears as both one word and two.

A settlement named Riverview was established here before the post office was opened in 1877 with John H. Hunter as postmaster. Most of the land within the settlement area was owned by members of the Hunter family. Hunter's steamboat landing was at the mouth of Big Buffalo Creek. A quarter-of-a-mile east along the river stood a warehouse and a steam flour mill and sawmill on J. H. Hunter property. The J. H. Hunter residence and several other dwellings, including the home of J. S. Hunter and the Riverview School, sat about one-quarter mile north of the landing on the ridge along the road in Section 31 at an elevation of 860 feet.

Riverview had two distinctions in its early days -- it was a shipping point on the Osage River, and a ferry site for traffic between Zora, Boylers Mill, Todd, Loderma and Stover to the north, and Lively, Sagrada, Spring Valley and Climax Springs to the south.

The town's post office was discontinued in 1906 and mail was transferred to the nearby village of Zora at the upper reaches of today's Big Buffalo Cove.

When a suspension bridge was erected across the Osage River in 1908 about one mile upstream from Riverview, it is believed that the ferry ceased operation. The bridge, while convenient, was more than just a frequent source of discord between the officials of Benton and Camden counties over its maintenance and its name. The people of Sagrada, on the south side of the river, in what later became known as Big Bend Acres, called it the Sagrada Bridge. The people of Riverview called it the Riverview Bridge.

When Lake of the Ozarks was formed and the suspension bridge dismantled, a ferry operation resumed between Riverview and the point of Big Bend, but was called the Sagrada Ferry. Since the ferry was reinstated at the instigation of Chet Edmonds, the developer of Big Bend Acres, it is odd that it wasn't called the Big Bend Acres Ferry.

The ferry was operated by Keith Critton and Tip Flippin. The boat was said to have been able to carry eight cars and was rated at 84 tons, which seems to be a very high rate for being able to carry only eight vehicles. Ferries rated at even less than 50 tons could usually handle 15 to 20 vehicles. [see Big Bend Acres; also Sagrada; Sagrada Bridge]

Besides John H. Hunter, the community of Riverview also had another distinguished citizen in the latter part of the nineteenth century -- Judge John H. Alfter.

The Judge owned more than 640 acres just east of Riverview. His home overlooked the Osage River and his land was noted for having several high points, one of which was named Mount Alfter in his honor. His residence was located near the great bluff in the southeast corner of his property. The Judge was visited in pre-Lake days by the editor of a Versailles newspaper who later said:

"One of the chief attractions at Riverview is Mount Alfter, affording a commanding panoramic view of the Osage valley, an extensive stretch of scenic charm and landscape beauty. It was while on a visit to Judge Alfter's Riverview home -- I accompanied the Judge to a high cliff overlooking the romantic Osage.

Riverview (Sagrada) Bridge, *Stover, MO, 1928. Photographer Unknown.*

Deeply impressed with the commanding and majestic eminence, the suggestion it be named 'Mount Alfter' in honor of the Judge, was plainly, with due modesty, acceptable to that highly esteemed citizen. And through the columns of the *Versailles Gazette*, the writer ever and often referred to the bluffs as 'Mount Alfter.' And that's how the big bluff came by so appropriate a name -- a name in keeping with its grandeur and sublime beauty."

Early resorts at Riverview included Riverview Heights Camp, Carpenter Developments, Clear Water Beach and Shady Point Camp in the 1930s. Twin Beach Resort came along later. Across the Lake from Riverview was Paradise Hidden Acres Resort owned and operated by Leo Paradise in the Big Bend area.

Roaring Oaks Camp / Resort *(Laurie, Morgan County)* -

Roaring Oaks Camp was established at the 7.5-mile mark on the Osage Arm about 1938. It was owned and operated by Jane Cox. She advertised having modern and semi-modern cabins equipped for light housekeeping, boats, motors, and a swimming beach. Her neighbors by 1942 included Platt Boat & Dry Dock, Wonder Bay Resort and Stover's Shady Rest Resort.

The resort ceased operation under the name Roaring Oaks about 1952 and is thought to have been renamed Pelican Point Resort by new owners. Pelican Point Resort was in operation from 1952 to about 1974. Pelican Point is now an established landmark on most Lake maps. The point is accessible by Route O out of Laurie.

Rock Hill Camp *(Osage Beach, Camden County)* -

Rock Hill Camp was established by H. W. Nichols at the west end of the Grand Glaize Bridge about 1932. He had six cabins and charged $2.00 and up per person per day. He offered boats, bait and guides. He sold the business in 1934 and it became Bond's Grand Glaize Camp.

Rock Hill Camp was one of a cluster of camps that were established along the south side of the highway at the west end of the bridge in the early 1930s. The sequence of these businesses is not easy to trace and can be more than a little confusing. The following succession may or may not be entirely correct in every instance.

Going west after leaving the west end of the Grand Glaize Bridge, the businesses in 1932 along the south side would have been, in order: Barber's Grand Glaize Camp, Shady Slope Camp, Rock Hill Camp, Otten's Lakeview Camp and Kepner's Cottage Camp. This would have brought you to LkRd. 54-B16, later designated 54-47 and now called Winn Road or Kapilana Road, the latter because Kapilana Beach Resort was once at its end.

As the years passed, Barber's Grand Glaize Camp [1932-1939] became Hymes Kottage Kamp # 1 [1939-1948] and then Sherwood Resort, which is still in operation. Shady Slope Camp [1932-1975] became Lake Chateau Best Western, which is still in operation.

Rock Hill Camp, Osage Beach, MO, Circa. 1930s. Photographer Unknown.

Rock Hill Camp [1932-1934] became Bond's Grand Glaize Resort [1935-1958], which became the Grand Glaize Resort [1959-1965] and Sherwood Restaurant in 1966. Today, Glaize Bridge Liquors is located where Sherwood Restaurant used to be.

Otten's Lakeview Camp [1932-1951] became Devall's Lakeview Camp, which also acquired Neely's Cafe [previously called Turrin's Cafe and then Jeffries Ozark Cafe] and changed it to Lakeview Cafe, which stood about where the entrance to Hawks Nest Road is today.

Kepner's Cottage Camp, at the corner of LkRd. 54-B16, was also a Shell filling station.

In the 1940s, Churchill's Bridgeport was established at the west end of the Grand Glaize Bridge where Bridgeport Boat Rentals is today.

Rockway Cabin Court / Motor Court *(Osage Beach, Camden County)* -

Rockway Cabin Court was opened for business in the early 1940s along Hwy. 54 in the heart of Osage Beach about two blocks north of LkRd. 54-24, now called Osage Beach Road. The business was on the south side of the highway where Rockway Center sits today, and was adjacent to Lake Lumber Co. [this company and its buildings no longer exist], which was on its west side. The Pickett Line Inn was on the east side. The Pickett Line Inn occupied a building that was originally part of Frack's Acre [this building no longer exists].

Rockway Cabin Court was owned and operated by Mr. & Mrs. C. E. Hayes. The slogan for Rockway was "In the heart of the Recreational Area," which it certainly was. A swimming pool was added in 1959 when the business was sold to Don & Lee Hutchinson who replaced the words "Cabin Court" with "Motor Court." The Court had several rock cottages and a motel segment.

By the 1960s, their neighbor to the east was Evelyn's Rathskeller, occupying the former Pickett Line Inn site.

In the 1970s, Rockway Motor Court was sold to John and Mary Ann Willuhn. By this time the Court had 22 motel rooms but was still using a couple of the rock cottages.

About the year 2000, most of the Rockway Motor Court buildings were razed to make way for the Rockway Center Mall, however, one original Rockway Cabin Court rock building and a motel unit are still standing and in use between Rockway Center and the Conoco Station property.

Rocky Mount *(Miller County; Morgan County)* -

Rocky Mount is on Y Road southwest of Eldon but its current location is not its original location.

In 1839, a store and post office under the name Rocky Mount was established along a well traveled wagon road that followed the Harmony Mission Trace between the future site of Eldon and the valley of Gravois Creek. The store was about four miles northeast of Gravois Creek. This road left a road junction in the valley bottom near what is today the 3-mile mark on the Gravois Arm near the mouth of Gladstone Cove. The south arm of the "T" went to the site of Cape Galena on the banks of the Osage, and the north arm of the "T" went to Gravi Mills [later spelled Gravois Mills], which was on the banks of Gravois Creek further upstream in a region of springs and mills.

Riffletown, later known as Gladstone, would become the settlement at this T-junction. The northeast wagon road to Rocky Mount would later become Y Road and that portion climbing out of the Gravois Creek valley would become LkRd. Y-19. The hilly region through which LkRd. Y-19 passes was called "the Osage River breaks" and the land where Rocky Mount originally grew up at the edge of the plateau was called "the Prairie."

By the early 1900s, the original Rocky Mount had a general store, two blacksmith shops, a drugstore, a Baptist church, a school and several homes. The post office was housed in the general store. The nearest railroad was the Bagnell Branch Railroad three miles due west on the Rocky-Mount-Aurora Springs Road. The population of Rocky Mount was about 50 and the locale was known as a coal mining area. The richest coal site was the Stover Coal Bank three miles northwest.

In 1919, the Rocky Mount Post Office was closed and the office moved down Y Road and reopened in Morgan County. Today, the post office is located three miles south of the junction of Y and W on Y Road. Interestingly, this location has an eating place, a general store and a filling station, and the post office is housed in the store. So, in a sense, very little has changed for Rocky Mount in more than 160 years, at least for its post office. There are, however, a variety of businesses scattered along Y Road for a distance of several miles to the north that identify with Rocky Mount, so the community is larger than it appears.

Former resorts that identified with Rocky Mount and which have been located on the Lake around the 5- to 6-mile mark on the Osage Arm, and between the 1- and 3-mile mark on the Gravois Arm have included Millard's Lucky Point Resort, Pla-Mor Beach Resort, Ham's Kottage Kamp and Lake Breeze Resort.

Sagrada *(Climax Springs, Camden County)* -

Sagrada was a small settlement once in the northwest corner of Camden County. It was 3.5 miles due west of the point of Brown Bend, which is at the 63-mile mark on the Osage Arm. It was 1.5 miles due east of the Benton County line on Route FF.

A post office was established at Sagrada in 1886. It closed in 1933 after the community became isolated due to the removal of the Sagrada Bridge over the Osage during the clearing of the basin for Lake of the Ozarks. The road carried traffic from Stover, which was serviced by the Chicago, Rock Island Pacific Railroad, to Climax Springs and other points south. Although no business establishments in this vanished town site remain, local place names survive and it lives on in the folklore of the Sagrada Bridge.

Sagrada Bridge *(Climax Springs, Camden County; Riverview, Morgan County)* -

The Sagrada Bridge, also called Riverview Bridge, was built across the Osage River in late 1907 and early 1908 by Benton County surveyor Kidwell at what is today the 71.2-mile mark on the Lake. The bridge cost about $8,000, half of which was raised by subscription from the merchants of Stover, Riverview and Sagrada.

This suspension bridge had a span of 540 feet between its wooden, 30- to 32-foot high towers. It had main cables of 600 each no. 10 steel galvanized wire. The east end of the bridge, which was on the Camden County side, exited onto the bench of a bluff that was about 50 feet above the bed of the Osage River. At its west end, the bridge tower stood on the floodplain.

The road that passed over the Sagrada Bridge came up the Osage River valley from Riverview, hugging the west side of the valley. It then turned due east about where there is a cove on the west side of the Lake today, and crossed the floodplain headed straight for the bridge. After crossing the bridge, the road followed the bench of the bluff to the right for about a hundred yards before climbing to the hilltop and continuing on to Sagrada. The bridge was often a source of conflict [see Riverview].

In late March 1931, contractors clearing the basin for Union Electric, first attempted to burn the Sagrada Bridge but this did not work since the bridge burned only in spots. They then cut the cables and let it fall into the river. "Destroying the bridge," said the *Miller County Autogram*, "cut off much of Stover's business as a

Sagrada Bridge Ruins, *(see Riverview Bridge photo), Stover, MO. Photo by H. D. Weaver, 2004.*

considerable freight and some flour, feed, bread and other food stuffs were supplied to that territory [Big Bend] south of the river by way of the mail truck. This truck was discontinued February 28 [1931]."

A few ruins of the east end foundation of the bridge still exist on the bluff bench and consist of two low walls of badly weathered concrete exhibiting creek gravel aggregate in which timbers for the bridge were anchored. Remnants of old wooden post butts can still be seen in several holes.

In late 1931, with the Lake full and no means across the water, a ferry was reinstated and called the Sagrada Ferry. This was done by Chet E. Edmonds, the developer of Big Bend Acres, to provide access to his land and for the use of investors in Big Bend Acres property.

"Plans are now underway to attempt to have a bridge placed across the Lake of the Ozarks at Sagrada on the south of Stover..." said the *Lake of the Ozarks News* Sept. 15, 1936. "Mr. C. M. Edmonds, proprietor of Big Bend Acres, a large development on the south side of the Lake directly south of Stover, is behind the movement and is sparing no time or effort to see that this sector of the Lake is opened up. Mr. Edmonds has been at work on the plan for some time and now is asking the county courts of Camden and Morgan counties for permission to build the approaches to the bridge. He expects to finance the project with WPA funds."

Edmonds noted that people at the east end of the Lake, through cooperative efforts and the great number of new businesses springing up near the dam, were able to secure good roads and keep them maintained. "But as to the developments on the far reaches of the Lake, most of the roads have to be built and financed by the individual resort owner which entails a great amount of expense. The Lake of the Ozarks is some 100 miles [sic] long and for the most part is undeveloped because of lack of roads and proper crossing facilities. With a bridge at this point another fine sector of the Lake will be opened and there can be no question that fishing and other recreational facilities would be as great there as at any other sector of the Lake.

"At present time resorts on the south side of the Lake have not been built in the same proportions as they have near the dam and Versailles because they have not had the inducement of good roads and bridges. There is no reason to think that if this bridge is constructed and roads are built connecting it with highways on both sides that resorts will not be developed and that a good trade will be enjoyed there too.

"Possibly no other one thing has held up the developing of the Lake of the Ozarks as has the lack of good roads and bridges..."

To this day there is no bridge across the Lake at the Riverview -- Sagrada location. In fact, there is no bridge across the Osage Arm anywhere between the Hwy. 65 Bridge at Warsaw and the Hwy. 5 Hurricane Deck bridge north of Camdenton, a distance, by water, of some 54 miles. For more than 70 years this lack of a bridge has discouraged significant development on both sides of this 54-mile stretch of the Lake.

Salt Road *(Camden County)* -

Generally referred to as the "Old Salt Road," this historic road had its inception more than 100 years ago. Joseph W. McClurg [see Joseph W. McClurg] opened a store in Hazelwood, Missouri, near the town of Seymour in Webster County. This was before McClurg established his famous wholesale house in Linn Creek on the Osage, which supplied all of southwest Missouri with goods before the Civil War. While in Hazelwood, the future governor of Missouri cut a wagon road from his store in Jackson Port on the White River.

The first boatload of salt ever bought by one merchant in the Ozark country was hauled from the river in Hazelwood over this road. Up to the breaking out of the Civil War, this wagon road down the southern slope of the Ozark Mountains was known as McClurg's Old Salt Road. Next to powder and lead, salt was the most important article of commerce among the pioneers of the Ozarks. It was used all year round to preserve the wild meat killed from day to day by the hunters and to tame livestock that grazed on the rich pastures of the new land.

The Old Salt Road that Camden County people know about extended from Salt Shoal [now inundated] on the Osage River, in a southwestern direction, passing 3.5 miles east of Old Linn Creek, to Springfield and points south in Arkansas. A boat load of salt detained at the shoals by low water, gave the shoals its name. In the same portion of the county is Salt Hollow and Salt Ridge along which the road extended. Immense quantities of freight were afterward discharged at the Salt Shoal and hauled out to the southwest along the Old Salt Road, which afforded a better approach to the river than the road to Linn Creek.

Some maps currently in circulation showing Osage Beach mislabel Salt Hollow Cove at the 21-mile mark on the Osage as Miller Hollow Cove. This is a three-arm cove. Salt Hollow Cove is the east arm, while Ben Anderson Hollow is the arm farthest to the west. Miller Hollow Cove is between the two. Nichols Road on the east side, and Three Seasons Road on the west side, and their tributary roads embrace Salt Hollow & Cove.

At the mouth of Salt Hollow before the Lake was formed, was Chiles Island along the north side of the Osage River. The island was three-quarters of a mile long and 1,000 feet wide at its widest point. It tapered in at both ends and at the upstream end was Salt Shoal No. 1, and at the downstream end was Salt Shoal No. 2. These features are now beneath 68 feet of water.

The Old Salt Road ran up Salt Hollow as it climbed out of the river valley. It ran through the Dogwood Hills Golf Course property before turning south in the vicinity of Damsel. Hwy. 54 from Damsel to near Linn Creek generally follows the Old Salt Road, which is no longer labeled on most maps.

Shady Slope Camp / Resort *(Osage Beach, Camden County)* -

In 1931-32, Dan D. Dudley built Shady Slope Camp near the west end of the Grand Glaize Bridge in Osage Beach. It was along the south side of Hwy. 54 one-quarter mile west of the bridge. Coming up hill at this point, the highway was entrenched, placing the camp on a heavily wooded knoll sandwiched between the highway and the first deep Lake cove south of the Grand Glaize Bridge. What could be seen from the highway was the Dudley home, a large house veneered with sandstone interspersed with large chunks of unfinished rock. The camp office, which was also a well-stocked grocery store, was in the lower, walk-out level of the house and entered through a doorway next to the garage door, which was under the house. People on the highway could also see a tower built over the well house and a water tank on top of the tower.

Dudley began with eight cabins, both frame and log. The cabins were dispersed in among the trees behind and largely to the south of the residence-office. Guests could leave either by the driveway up to the office, or by another road that paralleled the highway and rejoined the highway at the west end of the property. A small log cabin stood near this exit.

Staying busy during the latter half of the 1930s, Dudley kept building additional cabins and adding features for his guests. His advertising slogan was "Home for the Fisherman."

Around 1940, the camp was sold and for a brief time was advertised as "Fry's Shady Slope." By about 1945, it was again under new ownership, this time that of Charley W. Stetter who changed the resort's advertising slogan to "The Lake Resort with City Utilities." He also employed the phrase "The Best for Less" in some of

Shady Slope Camp / Resort Cabin, *Osage Beach, MO, Circa. 1950s. Photographer Unknown.*

his ads. By this time the resort had 16 cottages advertised as "ultra-modern cottages" although not all of them must have been housekeeping cottages since he also said "several refrigerators," implying that not all of the cottages had kitchenettes with refrigerators.

The resort changed owners again about 1953 and the new owner, A. D. Cox, kept the same slogan. Cox apparently added a launderette for the convenience of his guests. And by 1962, he had built new motel units, added air-conditioning, screened porches, a covered boat dock with private wells for guest boats, and a filtered swimming pool.

Early on, Shady Slope Resort was advertised as a stop for the Missouri Pacific Bus Service. By 1962, the wording had been changed to "Missouri Transit Lines Bus Service."

In 1972, the resort was sold to Charles and Dee Franklin who changed the slogan to "An Ideal Family Resort." The Franklins advertised an "Electric Lift to Waterfront."

The resort was sold again about 1975, new development occurred on the property and in 1976, it reopened as Lake Chateau Resort Inn and is still in operation.

Though changes have been made, the original Dudley house, with its fine rock exterior, is still standing, and one of the small log cabins, nicely painted and well preserved, can still be found at the west exit to the property. Together, these two structures create historic links to the resort's beginning.

Shawnee Bend *(Camden County)* -

The Osage River created four great bends between today's Lake Ozark and Camdenton. Going south they are, in order -- Horseshoe Bend, Shawnee Bend, Turkey Bend and Linn Creek Bend. In this distance, the river and now Lake, travels 38 miles. Horseshoe Bend lies within the "U" formed by the Lake between the dam and the 16-mile mark. It forms the "U" of Shawnee Bend between the 11- and 24-mile marks. It forms the "U" of Turkey Bend between the 21- and 27-mile marks. And it forms the "U" of Linn Creek Bend between the 24- and 37-mile marks.

All of these bends were named well before the Lake was ever dreamed of, names bestowed upon them by the local people and the steamboat pilots who had to navigate a troublesome river around the bends, a river with seemingly endless meanders and shoals.

Horseshoe Bend and Shawnee Bend were considered the crown jewels of the Lake area by the Lake's creators. By 1928, almost all of the land within these two great bends was under the ownership of the Kansas City Joint Stock Land Bank, a company allied with the Missouri Hydro-Electric Power Company through the persons of Walter Cravens and Ralph Street. After Union Electric acquired the project, this choice acreage was placed in the hands of the Union Electric Land & Development Company, a subsidiary of Union Electric.

Horseshoe Bend, the massive peninsula closest to Bagnell Dam, saw at least the creation of a scenic drive into its peninsula area [see Horseshoe Bend Road]. But the Development Company was dissolved in the early 1940s and therefore did not have an opportunity to consider any development on Shawnee Bend. And later,

Carroll Bluff (Carrot Bluff) Shawnee Bend South Side. *Photo by H. D. Weaver, 2002.*

major development did not occur because there was no bridge connecting Shawnee Bend to the Lake's busy east side. Some limited development did occur along the bend's north shore between the 11- and 13-mile marks, but the vast east end of the peninsula remained an undeveloped woodland.

Before Lake of the Ozarks formed, the main road from Versailles to Zebra passed through Shawnee Bend. Portions of today's Route MM are part of that old road. After the Lake was formed, the east half of this road deteriorated and saw little use and no noticeable development between mile marks 13.5 and 21. The woodland at the bend was called the Shawnee Bend Shooting Preserve.

By the 1970s, much of the undeveloped land was under the private ownership of L. O. Nichols and Lodge of the Four Seasons. Development began to creep eastward along the coves of the north shore beginning in the late 1970s, and along the southeast corner of the Preserve area where the pre-Lake road originally dropped into the floodplain as it headed for Zebra. Development has been vastly accelerated since the opening of the Community Bridge in 1998. Developers have characterized it as the Lake's "newest frontier" for development and opportunity. The wooded shoreline is rapidly being deforested for the construction of large housing projects and the interior is being opened up.

Shawnee Bend contains about 6,000 acres. The bend runs east by west parallel to Horseshoe Bend. It is roughly five and three-quarters of a mile from neck to point, and 2,300 feet wide at its narrowest point. Along the south shore is a nearly continuous bluff that most Lake maps currently in circulation misname Carrot Bluff. It was originally called Carroll Bluff. Though not exceptionally high, it is the most scenic natural area between the 22- and 24-mile mark on the Osage Arm.

The first two resorts to open along the north shore of Shawnee Bend were Lone Oak Point Resort and Lake View Beach Resort in 1931-32. These were at the 11-mile mark and just barely on the peninsula. Unfortunately, for the two resorts, their first season was marred by a high profile tragedy.

"*Bloodhounds Lead Hunt for Lost Child On Lake of the Ozarks Shores: All-Night Search Fails to Pick Up Trail of 2-Year Old Boy Who Disappeared From Family Picnic*," read bold headlines in a Kansas City newspaper on Sept. 19, 1932. The story, date-lined Shawnee Bend, went on to say:

"Bloodhounds led a determined group of Ozarkians through brush and timberlands...in the search for 2-year old George Anderson, who disappeared from his parents' view Sunday, while the family group was picnicking in this Lake of the Ozarks resort. Spurred on by the cries of his hysterical mother, the searchers followed ravines in the hope of finding a trace of the lost baby.

"Some of the searchers feared the boy may have ventured into the Lake waters skirting the resort and drowned...

"The child was missed just before sundown...when his parents, Mr. and Mrs. James Anderson of Versailles...prepared to return to their home. After shouting frantically in an effort to locate the missing baby, the father, as darkness set in, appealed by telephone to friends in Versailles to rush to the scene and aid him in the hunt.

"No party was ever organized more quickly in this lightly populated hill country. Within an hour thirty men, all equipped with lanterns and flashlights, had driven from Versailles... Immediately a systematic search was under way.

"The scene of the boy's disappearance is one of the wildest on the Lake. Heavy timber flanks the resort, and in some places it is so dense with underbrush and scrub oaks as to be almost impassable.

"Anderson's neighbors beat through the hills and hollows, now and then calling for George in the hope of awakening him if he had become exhausted and fallen asleep. But there was no response.

"As the sun rose over the Lake waters, the searchers were still empty handed. Several hours before, the father had telephoned Springfield, Mo for bloodhounds. The dogs arrived at 8 o'clock and the tired searchers resumed the hunt..."

This event was every resort owners nightmare and a tragic beginning for the resorts of Shawnee Bend. Unfortunately, it ended sadly. The child's body was later found floating in the Lake.

Sherwood Resort / Restaurant *(Osage Beach, Camden County)* -

Sherwood Resort is located along the south side of Hwy. 54 at the west end of the Grand Glaize Bridge. The resort began life about 1935 as Barber's Camp [see Barber's Camp].

About 1939, Barber's Camp was sold to Charles M. and Hazel D. Hymes who changed the name to Hymes Kottage Kamp # 1 [see Hyme Kottage Kamp].

In 1948, after the death of Charles Hymes, the camp was sold and new owners renamed it Sherwood Resort. In 1952, a lodge was added to the accommodations and the business advertised having an "adult and children's playground." It makes one wonder what the "adult playground" was like.

By the mid 1950s, ads stated that the resort was "adjacent to a floating swimming pool and excursion boats," which would have been part of Churchill's Bridgeport. The resort offered both "air-cooled" and "air-conditioned" units completely furnished and with or without kitchenettes.

By 1956, the resort was being promoted as Sherwood Resort & Motel. The business was under the ownership and management of Clara and George Haar and they now had a cafe and gift shop in the same building as the resort office. The building had a green sod roof, which was unusual for the area. Later, a building at the foot of the hill with highway frontage was acquired for the cafe and gift shop, which then became Sherwood Restaurant. The slogan for the restaurant was "Welcome to a bit of Denmark." The restaurant had an open beam ceiling with wagon wheel chandeliers. Large windows gave a nice view of the Lake. By the early 1960s, the restaurant building also had an attached liquor store and diners could order cocktails.

Advertising would suggest that the business had some ups and downs in the late 60s. At this time the motel featured ceramic baths, private wrought iron balconies, and a filtered swimming pool on the hill overlooking the Lake. An ad that appeared in the 1967 Lake of the Ozarks Association annual guidebook had unusual text. It said: "Of the two or three million ads in this book, take 90% of their combined claims and you have Sherwood and a vacation of a lifetime!"

A disasterous fire put the restaurant out of business in the 1970s but the resort continues in operation. Glaize Bridge Liquors now does business at the location of the former Sherwood Restaurant.

Show Caves -

A show cave is a cave that has been improved for public touring, advertised in some fashion as being open to the public, and for which an entry fee is charged. Improvements include the development of walking trails through the cave, the elimination of hazards, and provision for guides to protect the cave from vandalism and the public from harm. Guides also provide information that is both educational and entertaining. Some form of artificial lighting is provided.

Missouri show caves must meet strict guidelines for public safety and be regularly inspected by state mine and cave inspectors. The show caves of Missouri have an excellent safety record. Cave inspections, however, were not required before the 1950s. Each year more than 60,000 people tour the show caves at the Lake. The show caves of the Lake region follow in the order they were opened to the public.

Ancient Grotto - also known as *Klinger Cave* and *Vernon Cave*. This cave is near Eldon. It was shown between 1890 and 1910. The cave is on private property and no longer open to the public. [see Vernon Cave; also Klinger Cave]

Jacob's Cave - near Versailles, was opened to the public in 1932 and became the first Lake area cave to be developed after the creation of Lake of the Ozarks. This cave is privately-owned and still open to the public. [see Jacob's Cave]

Flander's Cave - near Eldon was opened to the public in 1933 and continued in operation until 1942. The cave is on private property but no longer open to the public. [see Flander's Cave]

Big Niangua Caverns - also known as *Bunch Cave*, is near Camdenton on the Niangua Arm. This cave was shown commercially by lantern in 1937 and 1938. It is on private property but no longer open to the public.

Bridal Cave - near Camdenton and on the shores of the Niangua Arm, was opened to the public in 1948. The cave is privately owned and still open to the public. [see Bridal Cave]

Mystic River Cave - also known as *Berry Cave* and *River Cave*, is in Ha Ha Tonka State Park. The cave was opened to the public in 1948 and shown intermittently on a private basis until 1969. In the 1970s, the Missouri Department of Natural Resources bought the Ha Ha Tonka properties and created Ha Ha Tonka State Park. Show cave guided tours of River Cave are not given but it can be visited as a wild cave by permit from park authorities. Since the cave protects a colony of endangered bats, access is available at only certain times of the year.

Stark Caverns / Fantasy World Caverns - near Eldon, was opened to the public in 1950 and was in continuous operation until recently. The cave is privately owned. [see Stark Caverns]

Ozark Caverns - near Linn Creek, was opened to the public in 1952 and privately operated until it was purchased by the state in 1978. The cave is in Lake of the Ozarks State Park and operated by the Missouri Department of Natural Resources. It is currently open to the public. [see Ozark Caverns]

Indian Burial Cave - near Osage Beach, was opened to the public in 1960 and in operation for about 30 years. This cave is on private property but no longer shown to the public. [see Indian Burial Cave]

Arrow Point Cave - near Brumley was opened to the public in 1967 and operated for less than six years. The cave is privately owned but no longer shown to the public. [see Arrow Point Cave]

Stark Caverns / Fantasy World *(Eldon, Miller County)* -

Very few caves have had as many names as this cave. It's most recent names -- *Stark Caverns*, *Enchanted Caverns* and *Fantasy World Caverns* -- have all been promoted since it was opened to the public 55 years ago. But even in its pre-commercial years, it had more than one name. It was also *Aurora Cave*, *Aurora Springs Cave*, *Aurora Caverns*, *Miller County Cave*, and the *Mammoth Cave of Miller County*. Old newspaper articles and postcards published between 1886 and 1950 document all of these names.

The road to Fantasy World Caverns is located about one mile southwest of the junction of Hwys. 54 & 52 south of Eldon. The cave can be found near the bottom of a steep hill at the end of Cave Road. The entrance, 55 feet wide and 8 to 14 feet high, is in an outcrop of rock at the head of a small valley.

One thousand to 2000 years ago, the cave was a burial site and frequent camping area for Late Woodland Indians. When it was first seen by European and American settlers isn't known but the presence of the cave became well known locally after the property was purchased around 1836 by William Bunker, a veteran of the War of 1812. He lived above the cave in a log cabin with his six children. Here his children grew up and he died in 1869. The property was later bought by Elisha V. Stark, whose name became permanently associated with the cave. It was generally spoken of as "Stark's Cave," which inspired the men who opened the cave to the public years later to name it Stark Caverns. Although the words "cave" and "caverns" are synonyms of one another, the public tends to regard a cavern as being larger than a cave, so the developers used the word caverns to give it greater consumer appeal.

The cave's late nineteenth century and early twentieth century history is intimately associated with the history of Aurora Springs [see Aurora Springs].

One of the very first news stories about the cave appeared Nov. 11, 1886, in the *Jefferson City Daily Tribune*. In the article, the cave was called "Miller County's Mammoth Cave." The story was quite fanciful and the cave's length, grandeur and size exaggerated, but the story reveals that at that time the cave still possessed much of its secondary beauty in the form of stalactites and stalagmites.

What is significant here is that between 1886 and 1950, a great many of these natural adornments were broken and removed from the cave by visitors, souvenir

Stark Caverns Entrance, *Circa. 1950s. Photographer Unknown.*

hunters and vandals. The scars of this damage are still visible in the cave. This sad fact was alluded to in 1932 when Flanders Cave, less than one mile southwest of Stark Caverns, was being opened to the public. "Flanders Cave," said the newspaper story, "is in its natural state within and the management will have the beautiful display of stalagmites and stalactites protected so that they cannot be broken off and carried away as has been done in Aurora Cave."

In Aurora Springs boom days, large parties of people would leave Aurora Springs following an old wagon road that led south two miles to the cave, and there spend a day picnicking and exploring the cave or attending a dance. One such trip was described in the *Versailles Leader* on June 22, 1900, and, while fun to read, also documents how the cave's beauty was treated. In part the article said:

"Perusing our course we arrived at 11:00 a.m. After a short rest, dinner was spread and the feast began... Dinner over, the always welcome Kodak was brought into requisition and a group picture of the party was taken. Then the cave, which was found to be the largest and most interesting we've ever seen. Room after room was visited and many specimens and souvenirs were obtained..."

Lengthy accounts of visits to the cave appear in early newspapers. In 1901 three local boys, one of whom -- E. H. Shepherd -- would grow up to become the publisher of the *Eldon Advertiser*, got lost in the cave when they lost their lights. The rescue generated considerable local publicity. The boys were unhurt. Shepherd never tired of retelling the tale of the rescue and published it several times in the *Eldon Advertiser*.

At different times between 1890 and 1920, dance floors were built in the cave's ballroom about 300 feet inside but the floors never lasted long due to the humidity of the cave and periodic flooding by the cave stream. The dance floor was used for both roller skating and square dancing, winter and summer. In the winter, cold air from the large entrance would often freeze ponded areas of the shallow cave stream back for 50 yards or more into the cave and local youths would ice skate inside the cave.

On May 11, 1950, Stark Caverns was opened to the public by Jim Banner and R. L. Wilkerson of Camdenton, who were involved in the development of Bridal Cave in 1948. Also participating in the development of Stark Caverns was F. L. Hammitt and Sons of Eldon. The following year, F. L. Hammitt purchased the interest of Banner and Wilkerson. Kenneth B. Sweet of Waynesville, was also instrumental in the cave's development. Later, the cave was sold to Harvey and Vivian Fry of Eldon.

In 1967, during Fry's ownership, Indian burials were discovered in the cave by two Eldon boys -- Glen Bashore and Kent Buehler -- who were summer guides at the cave. About 1971, the cave's ownership changed and it was briefly operated as Enchanted Caverns. In the mid 1970s, the cave again changed ownership when it was purchased by Glen Whitman and David Marose of Osage Beach and their associates. The cave underwent new interior and exterior development and was reopened in 1975 as Fantasy World Caverns. The cave is currently owned by Curtis Whitman, a son of the late Glen Whitman.

Sunrise Beach / Sunrise Inn *(Camden County, Morgan County)* -

Sunrise Beach is 16 miles north of Camdenton on Hwy. 5. The town began as a private development along the shoreline of the Lake at the 9-mile mark and it had a prestigious beginning in the spring of 1931. Not only was it one of the very first "new" towns to be established in the Lake area after the dam was finished, it was also the creation of Phil A. Bennett of Springfield, Missouri, a former Lieutenant Governor of the State. His associates were Harve Turner and W. A. Buell of Springfield, and Judge D. Gabriel and Ora Leatherman of Versailles.

The name Sunrise Beach was coined by these men and their Sunrise Beach Corporation. They bought 350 acres of land along the west side of the Lake off Hwy. 5. The purchase gave them 3.5 miles of shoreline that largely faced east. It is said that the name of the corporation was derived from the beautiful sunrises that can be seen from the shoreline.

Phil A. Bennett was Lieutenant Governor of Missouri in the mid 1920s. During this time in office he was a strong promoter of tourism in the Ozarks and, it is said, helped lay out the course of Hwy. 54 through what was to become the Lake of the Ozarks area. He was later instrumental in getting the new highway graded and paved with gravel. He envisioned Hwy. 54 as the principal transportation corridor for traffic between Springfield and Jefferson City.

The Sunrise Beach Corporation entered into an agreement with Mrs. Myrtle Witt of Eldon for the construction of a 20-room hotel and work began under the charge of G. S. Millen of Elliott Construction Company of Kansas City.

By the end of the summer of 1931, the corporation had completed their 490-foot deep well, installed a 20,000 gallon water tank, erected several rental cabins and a restaurant building 20 x 60 feet, and began planning for the installation of a light plant for electrical service.

Keith McCanse, the former commissioner of the old Missouri Game and Fish Department, was also on board. McCanse served as president of the Sunrise Beach Sales Department. McCanse, from St. Louis, was the author of a series of very successful Ozark tourist guidebooks published between 1928 and 1932. He had given up public office to throw in his lot with the Sunrise Beach development.

Promotion of the new development began in earnest in the fall and on Sept. 17, 1931, the Sunday edition of the *Kansas City Star* carried a large display ad that announced the sale of lots for $200 each. The ad also featured a map showing the location of the new Sunrise Beach resort area. In addition, the promoters chartered a special Missouri Pacific train out of Kansas City to Versailles on Sunday, Oct. 4, 1931. The ticket price included round trip fare on the train, bus transportation from Versailles to the Sunrise Beach area, a boat trip to Bagnell Dam, and a family style chicken dinner. The price of a ticket was $5.90 per person.

McCanse engaged Dr. William DeShetley, an internationally known industrial educator to disseminate information about Lake of the Ozarks and in particular, Sunrise Beach. Dr. DeShetley went on the lecture circuit throughout the Midwest and did much to awaken people to the recreational potential of the Lake of the Ozarks region.

By March 1, 1932, the ball was rolling. "Sunrise Beach...is to become a large recreational club, according to S. T. Mattinson, until recently of San Francisco, as the results of deals closed this week," said the *Lake of the Ozarks News*. "The club will be patterned after successful clubs conducted by Mr. Mattinson in California. It will be known as Edgewater Club and will be composed of people of accepted business and social standing in Missouri and other mid-western states.

"Our greatest effort will be to provide a place where people can play and enjoy themselves," said Mattinson.

"...Tennis, archery and croquet courts are to be provided... Bridle paths will be made for equestrians and trapshooting for the sportsmen with, of course, duck and bird hunting and fishing in season. Motor boat racing and yachting are to be major activities during the coming vacation season.

"The clubhouse is now in readiness as Sunset Inn will hereafter be known as Edgewater Club and Mrs. Witt will act as club hostess. Thus, the first members of the club are provided with the highest type of accommodations -- rooms with bath, steam heat and a fine dining room. A new clubroom of the rathskeller type has been built in the basement..."

The corporation's Board of Governors included the following: L. L. Adams, E. E. Norquist and Henry Depping of Kansas City; J. Henry Caruthers, Hiram Martin and Keith McCanse of St. Louis; Means Ray of Jefferson City; Chas. L. Woods of Rolla; Mercer Arnold of Joplin; George Olendorf of Springfield; Dale Hoffman of

Trenton; Carroll Wisdom of Bowling Green; Thos. P. Bedford of Fayette; Ray Hamlin of Hannibal; Col. Theodore Ziska of Boonville; Judge C. A. Barnes of Mexico; Phil Fowler of Kirksville; and John M. Atkinson of El Dorado Springs.

Sunrise Beach was definitely off to a grand beginning but disaster loomed. In September 1934, the Sunrise Inn burned to the ground.

"The fire broke out around 2:30 a.m., presumably in the room occupied by Mr. & Mrs. Wood of Kansas City, when a lighted cigarette was dropped on the bed linen. Mr. and Mrs. Wood and Lucky Scott, another guest...were forced to drop from a second story window to the ground when the flames entrapped them.

"The manager of the hotel, Raymond McKee, was severely burned, and two other employees were burned about the hands and face while fighting the flames. Fifteen guests were in the hotel when the fire started but all escaped uninjured...

"The hotel was constructed in 1931 and was owned by Mrs. Myrtle Witt, who formerly was in the hotel business in Linn Creek before Bagnell Dam was built... It was constructed at a cost of approximately $35,000.

"Located as it was some 75 feet above the water, a commanding view of the Lake could be had from either of its long verandas. The hotel was one of the most popular places on the Lake, especially among those who wanted to get close to nature and still have the modern conveniences.

"Although the hotel proper represents the greater part of the loss, the value of the furnishings, many of them antique pieces, can be conservatively estimated at several thousand dollars. The huge fireplace in the commodious lobby, due to its unique construction, was admired by hundreds of visitors... It, together with the stone foundation, was the only thing left standing after the destructive fire."

A few months later, Mrs. Witt purchased the James House at Eldon, then one of the oldest hostelries in the Lake of the Ozarks region.

Sunrise Beach had an auspicious beginning. It has done nothing but grow since it was established and is now the fastest growing area at the Lake's midpoint.

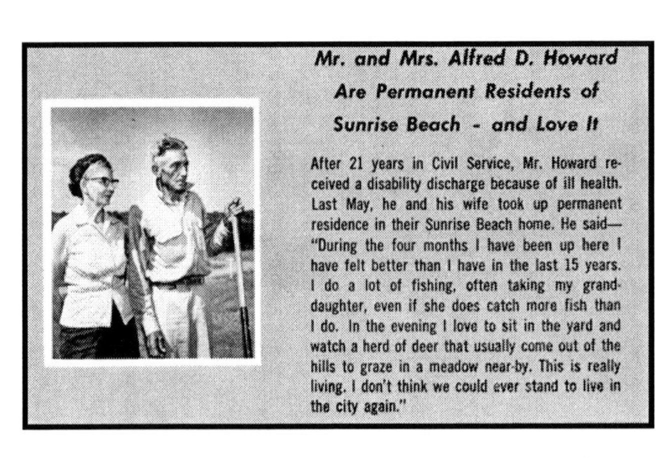

Sunrise Beach, MO, Testimonial Advertising Card, *Circa. 1930s. Photographer Unknown.*

Ti-Sun Terrace Resort *(Sunrise Beach, Camden County)* -

This resort was established in 1932 near the 9-mile mark on the Osage Arm off LkRd. 5-17, later designated 5-35, now called Beachwood Drive. It was near the big curve off Kansas City Way.

Ti-Sun Terrace Resort was built by Mr. & Mrs. Fred J. Theison. The Theisons began with seven cabins, added a bait and tackle shop, a grocery store and cafe. They had a guest capacity of 45.

Neighboring businesses in the 1930s included Thickstun Store up-Lake from them, and Sunrise Lodge, Jock Reeder's Resort and the Ellis Rod & Gun Club down-Lake along Kansas City Way.

During the 1940s, the resort was owned by Maynard W. Breden and his operating slogan was "It's Fun At Ti-Sun." He redecorated the cottages, advertised that the cafe served "home cooking," and among the recreational opportunties at the resort were swimming, boating, fishing, croquet, horseshoes and softball. Breden also made sure that guests knew that no liquor was allowed on the premises.

By the late 1940s, the resort was under the ownership and management of Mr. & Mrs. Sheldon Singleton. By 1950, the resort was vacant and sat vacant for awhile until apparently Sunrise Lodge, adjacent to it on the south, bought the property and added the cottages to their accommodations. Thereafter, the Lodge was promoted as Sunrise Lodge & Cottages.

Tonka Villa Resort *(Camdenton, Camden County)* -

This resort began as the Niangua Bridge Camp & Boat Dock in 1931. When it was sold in the mid 1940s to Red & Stell Wells, it was renamed Tonka Villa Resort.

The Wells advertised having "Beauty Rest Beds," safe air heaters in their cabins and cool, insulated units. They said their resort was "Inspected - Approved by Kelly's Luxury Courts." Their slogan was "Fish at the Home of the Silver Bass," a slogan used in their ads through the early 1950s.

In 1955, the resort was sold to Bette & Leonard Kelly who flood-lighted the boat dock for night fishing, made improvements such as adding air-conditioning to the Tonka Villa Restaurant close to the highway, and challenged people to take a ride on their new Yellow Jacket boat. The resort's slogan was changed to "Where Friends Meet."

By 1962, the resort had new owners -- Raymond & Madeleine Malloy. In 1973, the Malloys added a new filtered swimming pool.

In the late 1960s, Faylor's Lake Trailer Park was established adjacent to them on the south, which, several years later, became Water's Edge Camping. Still further south in the 70s and 80s came Cedar Green Resort and then Drift-In Resort.

In the late 1970s, the Malloy's sold the resort to Don & Deane Bowman and at the beginning of the twentyfirst century, Tonka Villa Resort gave way to the construction of a new Hwy. 54 Niangua Bridge. The resort no longer exists.

Trail's End Camp *(Gravois Mills, Morgan County)* -

In 1935, Trail's End Camp was opened at the 4-mile mark on the Gravois Arm at the end of Route P. It was operated in conjunction with Gateway Lodge & Cottages of Versailles. The resort was located on what is today called Gibson's Point and their advertising slogan was "A Beauty Spot on the Lake."

In 1936, the property was sold and the camp reopened in 1937 as Happy Days Resort, which would continue in operation at this location for nearly 30 years. [see Happy Days Resort]

Tuxhorn Resort *(Hurricane Deck, Camden County)* -

In 1931-32, the Ozark Land Company of Kansas City purchased a reported 800 acres at the head of Crabtree Cove along the cove's south side. This cove is located on Linn Creek Bend at the 26-mile mark on the Osage Arm. The cove lies along the bend's northeast side. By road it is accessible off Route F out of Hurricane Deck on either Cozy Cove Road or Oak Bend Road and Irish Drive.

Here, the Ozark Land Company, headed by B. M. Tuxhorn, began an extensive development resulting in the creation of three resort properties -- Tuxhorn Lodge, Airway Lodge and Chinquapin Cottages.

One of the first tasks to be accomplished was the construction of an airplane landing strip so that Tuxhorn and his associates could get to the property easily and quickly. A 2,500-foot landing strip was built on the plateau above the cove. While this was being done, the lodge and half a dozen cabins for Chinquapin Cottages were under construction. The landing strip was completed by the spring of 1931 and Damian Costa, secretary of the Ozark Land Company, later described the airport's inauguration:

"We began by inaugurating a new air port, now known as Tuxhorn Air Port, in honor of B. M. Tuxhorn of the Municipal Air Port, North Kansas City.

"He left Kansas City Sunday morning, May 29 [1931] at 7:30 a.m. and made a perfect landing at Chinquapin Springs at 9 a.m. He was accompanied by Damian Costa, secretary of our company... There was a great deal of excitement on the occasion of this landing, and many people of the nearby territory came rushing to the field and engaged Mr. Tuxhorn to take them over the Lake and the Bagnell Dam. From the air the Lake presents a magnificent view -- it was too wonderful for words. Mrs. Tomy Mara made two flights, it being her first time in a plane. The plane made a couple of trips to Versailles, in the way of errands, at one time bringing back a new tire for our automobile. Many flights with passengers were made on Monday, Decoration Day, some passengers being from Kansas City, and many from the Lake region. Mr. Tuxhorn will make flights from Chinquapin Springs to Bagnell Dam and surrounding Lake points every weekend.

"Mr. Tuxhorn was so happy over the successful opening of Tuxhorn Air Port, at Chinquapin Springs, that he purchased some ground there fronting the Lake, and is bringing over his big cabin cruiser -- intending to explore the Lake from the water as well as from the air."

As the Chinquapin Cottages development was coming along, work on Tuxhorn Lodge and Airway Lodge began. Five log cabins were built by early 1932, one of which was double, and the cabins were fully furnished and paneled with knotty pine. In addition, the Tuxhorn Lodge had five sleeping rooms and a dining room. Airway Lodge and Tuxhorn Lodge opened in the summer of 1932.

Airway Lodge and the Chinquapin Cottages development was visited by the editor of the *Lake of the Ozarks News* in 1932. He reported the following:

"It was something surprising to find so much had been done there and work progressing rapidly. One of the things that is needed on the Lake is accommodations for more vacationists so the thousands that want to spend their outings here can find places to stay. Aero Lodge is a large, attractive building that is to be used for serving meals and lunches and dancing, card playing or other general camp activities.

"There are four cottages completed and five under construction... Mr. W. T. Rogers, who is in charge, says they will build at least 20 cottages and probably more. Everything is to be completely modern. The electric plant is on the ground as is the water tank and both are to be installed immediately..."

An associate of Tuxhorn's, A. W. Nelson of Versailles, built a "Colorado-type" hotel and dance pavilion at the head of the cove that is fed by the discharge of Chinquapin Spring. In 1936, a news story about the Chinquapin development noted that the cottages were "approached by a long foot bridge, 500 feet long and 24 inches wide, and are on the Lake. It has been said the footbridge is the longest known and it would be a good spot to fish from when the Lake is at normal level."

Chinquapin Cottages and the resort's Runners Rest Lodge were operated by Mrs. Tomy Marey [sic] who was one of the truly unique personalities of that area and of the early years of the Lake. During the visit by the editor of the *Lake of the Ozarks News*, he met Marey and had the following to say about her:

"As we sat on the veranda overlooking the Lake, she very vividly recalled just how the territory had looked before it was under water. Mrs. Marey went with Union Electric surveyors to help determine just where the contour lines would be. Due to a previous survey of her own, she saved them much time and expense. She has developed an unusual hobby of collecting rocks and Indian relics. Most of her Indian collection was collected during the construction of the dam -- when the old graves were moved. To talk with Mrs. Marey is a study in history. She brings before your very eyes the scene of migration from the beautiful land of the lakebed and the sorrow of moving from friends, leaving relatives and homes their ancestors had made for them. It must have been a scene of wild confusion. Very few people stayed, the money from their lands bought new land and now all of it gone but the memory. The Lake has brought happiness, new life and prosperity to many. It's a great achievement in our civilized world but as with all great ventures -- some broken hearts are left behind -- hearts that money cannot mend."

As the years passed, properties changed hands and the resorts changed name. Airway Lodge became Harmony Cove Resort while Tuxhorn Lodge became Grace Lin Resort and then Wildwood Resort. Today there are no resorts in operation in this cove.

Twin Bays Camp *(Gravois Mills, Morgan County)* -

Twin Bays Camp was established in 1931-32 by L. O. Williams at the 8-mile mark on the west bank of the Gravois Arm. The camp was at the end of LkRd. 5-5, later designated 5-14, and now called Twin Bays Road.

In the early 1930s, Williams had the largest camp in existence on the upper Gravois Arm. By 1934, he had 25 two- and three-room cabins designed for light housekeeping and each cabin had a screened porch. The cabins could be rented for $1.00 - $3.00 per day or $6.00 - $17.50 per week. Any cabin rental entitled a person to the free use of a row boat but the more expensive cabins entitled the guest to a boat with a motor. The camp had a fully stocked bait and tackle shop as well as a grocery store and gas pumps.

The camp continued to grow as Williams added more cabins [for a total of 36], a cafe and dance hall. Excursion boats were available. There was daily mail service

Twin Bays Camp, *Gravois Mills, MO, Circa. 1930s. Photo by M. E. Atkinson*

right to the camp office and the camp's advertising slogan was "A Big Time All The Time."

The largest building on the property, which housed the camp office, cafe, grocery store and dance hall was an impressive two-story building with a cobblestone foundation, wrap-around screened windows and transitional roof design. The gas pumps sat perhaps a hundred feet out in front of this building. The boat docks and swimming beach were behind the main building and the ground leading down to the Lake shore was a gentle slope.

In the 1930s, the only neighbor to Twin Bays was Clearwater Resort on the up-Lake side. In the 1940s, it was joined down-Lake by Red Hollow Resort, Lane's Resort and Gatlin's Boat Yard.

Unfortunately, L. O. Williams died in the late 1930s and for nearly a decade the camp's management was under the administration of the L. O. Williams Estate. Then about 1947, it was sold to Oscar & Nellie Schwader who continued the camp under the same name. They increased the advertising, lighted the boat docks, and kept the resort open all year.

In 1957, Twin Bays Camp was sold to Elmer & Helen Butts, who ran the operation in partnership with Jay & Nina Fleener. By 1962, it was under the management of Jay & Nina Fleener with Jim & Dorothy Marr. And by 1970, Jay & Nina Fleener with Larry & Elsi Witman. During the operation by these couples, Twin Bays produced large, colorful ads with a wealth of information to appeal to fishermen and vacationers. They advertised having 37 units with 20-inch window fans. They had a heated, filtered swimming pool for guests who preferred not to swim in the Lake. There was a snack bar at the waters edge and a "drive-in theater within walking distance" of the resort.

This camp no longer exists but the naming of the road that once led to it -- Twin Bays Road -- honors the camp's nearly 50 years of welcoming fishermen and vacationers from far and wide to the shores of Lake of the Ozarks.

Two Waters Resort *(Gravois Mills, Morgan County)* -

In 1931-32, M. H. Towne built Two Waters Resort at the end of LkRd. 5-6, later designated 5-16 and now called Santa Fe Road. The resort was on the banks of Soap Creek Cove, which is at the 5-mile mark on the Gravois Arm.

At the beginning, the resort had eight cabins and a store with gas pumps. Where the resort was built is a narrow peninsula of land. Two Waters was on the side facing Soap Creek Cove. This location is said to have once been an Osage Indian campsite. A legend recorded by local historian Elizabeth Riffle Andrews, tells of an Indian chief whose wife was expecting a child. It happened at a time when Gravois Creek and Soap Creek were in flood. The morning the child was born, the new mother looked out of her teepee and saw the two mighty streams of water. "My son will be called Chief Mighty Two Waters," she is supposed to have said. The resort was named for this legend.

In the early 1940s, the resort either had some financial difficulties or worked in collaboration with Washburn's Point Resort because Two Waters was promoted only in ads placed by Washburn's Point.

In 1947, Two Waters Resort was sold to Ed & Marge Carrington and Clarence Boyer. They operated the resort together until 1951, when the Boyers bought Taylors Grocery on LkRd. 5-14, and renamed it Boyers Market.

Ed and Marge stayed with Two Waters Resort. In later years their advertising slogan was "Fishing Is Our One & Only Business." Their ads in the late 1960s were colorful and indicative of a very successful resort operation. As the 70s turned into the 80s, they were still operating the resort, but now, more than two decades later, the resort no longer exists.

1968 Gravois Arm Lake of the Ozarks Tourist Guidebook Ad, *Gravois Arm Association.*

1970 Gravois Arm Lake of the Ozarks Trouist Guidebook Ad, *Gravois Arm Association.*

Uncle Jim's Camp *(Sunrise Beach, Camden County)* -

In the period 1931 to 1937, there was a boom of resort development at the 39-mile mark on the Osage Arm. Development stretched from the mouth of Brush Creek Cove, where Purvis Beach was located, to the head of Porter Mill Cove. This area was reached by way of LkRd. 5-14, later designated 5-29 and now called Purvis Road after the first camp to open along this one mile stretch of coves and small inlets. The camps included Green & White Camp, Stults-Drummond Camp, Longacres Beach, Walt Reid's Camp, Uncle Jim's Camp and White Way Beach.

Uncle Jim's Camp was in operation by the summer of 1932 and was located near the mouth of Porter Mill Hollow Cove. V. J. Matthey was the proprietor and he advertised having cabins, boats and "a very clean camp for families and fishermen." Most of the cabins w[illegible] covered with oak bark planks that gave the cabins a very primitive look. F[illegible]abins, the bark planks went all the way to the roof and on others covered jus[illegible]er half of the frame.

This camp was sold about 1940 and is thought to have later become Mitchell's Resort, then Cowan's 5-Acres and eventually Silver Sand Resort by the 1970s. No resort exists here today.

Union Electric Land & Development Company -

This company was a subsidiary of Union Electric Light & Power Company of St. Louis and was formed during the construction of Bagnell Dam for the purpose of disposing of some 40,000 acres of surplus land along the shores of Lake of the Ozarks. It was property acquired during the purchase of basin lands. The company was also concerned with the development of land within Horseshoe Bend, Shawnee Bend and the incorporated area of Lakeside.

Toward these ends, the Development Company built a road into Horseshoe Bend to allow access to the bend's 5,400 wooded acres; built Holiday House and Cottages, a luxurious hotel on the bluff overlooking Bagnell Dam; built the Lakeside Casino Restaurant at the west end of the dam; and built the Union Electric Bathing Pavilion and Excursion Boat Dock business at the west end of the dam. This dock became commonly known as the U. E. Boat Dock. The Development also supplied the Excursion Boat Dock with several of the finest and most expensive excursion boats available in that day and time.

In the early 1940s, due to new federal government regulations regarding the operation of electric utilities, Union Electric had to dissolve the Land and Development Company. The properties previously mentioned were sold to private owners and the excess acreage was purchased by Cyrus Willmore, a St. Louis realtor who also purchased the company's Lodge that became known as Willmore Lodge.

Union Electric Light & Power Company -

The roots of the Union Electric Light & Power Company, who financed the construction of Bagnell Dam and collaborated with Stone & Webster Engineering in the dam's construction, reach back to the nineteenth century.

St. Louis entered the age of electricity in 1882 when the Brush Electric Association was organized and the first extensive street illuminations were erected in the city. In 1884, the city passed an ordinance that permitted almost anyone to go into the electric utility business and within a short time 22 companies materialized. The results was great duplication in effort and skyrocketing costs that inhibited growth of the industry. So, to correct this situation, a group of three companies were combined into the St. Louis Illuminating Company in 1889. This company was absorbed the following year by the Municipal Electric Lighting & Power Company, which later merged with the Edison Illuminating Company of St. Louis. More consolidations occurred that resulted in the formation of the Imperial Electric Light & Power Company and in 1902, this company became the Union Electric Light & Power Company.

Union Electric grew rapidly. By the 1920s, the company was serving a population of 1.5 million in Greater St. Louis, four adjoining Missouri counties, and in East St. Louis; Alton, Illinois; and in the vicinity of Keokuk, Iowa. The company was operating several steam plants in and around St. Louis and two hydroelectric projects. One of the hydroelectric projects was the great dam across the Mississippi River between Keokuk, Iowa, and Hamilton, Illinois. The Keokuk Dam was built by Stone & Webster Engineering Inc.

The Bagnell Dam project was originally initiated by the Missouri Hydro-Electric Power Company of Kansas City when the company applied for a Federal Power Commission permit in December 1923, to dam the Osage River. The company had many ups and downs between then and early 1927 when it became apparent that the company was not going to be able to complete the project.

In April 1927, an Option Agreement was signed between the Missouri Hydro-Electric Power Company and Stone & Webster Engineering, Inc. -- Dillon, Read & Company jointly -- whereby the latter were given the right, for at least one year [and under certain circumstances longer], of acquiring all of the property and assets of the Missouri Hydro-Electric Power Company attaching to the Osage River project. Stone & Webster began exercising various terms of the option agreement from May through August of 1927 when the Federal Power Commission received a letter from Stone & Webster that said "Dillon, Read & Co. and ourselves acquired an Option on this project and have since been developing plans for its construction and for the sale of the power therefrom..."

By August 1927, Stone & Webster had brought Union Electric Light & Power Company into the project and in December 1927, L. H. Egan, president of Union Electric, authorized the project. In December 1928, Stone & Webster entered into agreement with Union Electric whereby Stone & Webster sold all the property involved with the dam project to Union Electric. The negotiations also involved the stockholders of the Missouri-Illinois Railroad Co. and agreements with the St. Joseph Lead Co., and the Doe Run Lead Company, who would be purchasing power produced by the dam's hydroelectric plant.

The legal procedures that were necessary between the various parties involved in the effort to bring about the construction of Bagnell Dam are much too complex to be fully explained in this brief history. Suffice it to say that Union Electric became the owners of the project and Stone & Webster contracted to design and build Bagnell Dam, the dam's power station, and all tansmission lines.

Work on the dam began in August 1929 and the structure was complete by the spring of 1931. The water level in the reservoir reached the spillway crest elevation of 638.0 feet by May 20, 1931, forming Lake of the Ozarks. Since that date the dam has been regulated by the operation of the units and the spillway crest gates. Commercial operation of the power plant began in October 1931.

Union Electric announced a definitive merger agreement with Central Illinois Public Service Co., or Ameren CIPS, in August 1995. The merger was completed Dec. 31, 1997. A new holding company, Ameren Corporation, was formed as the parent of both Union Electric [now known as AmerenUE] and AmerenCIPS. This merger made it possible for the company to operate more efficiently than as two separate companies.

Upper Suspension Bridge *(Warsaw, Benton County)* -

There were once three suspension [swinging] bridges crossing the Osage River at Warsaw -- a lower suspension bridge near where Hwy. 65 crosses the Osage today on a bridge of modern vintage; a middle suspension bridge that no longer exists but if still in place would carry LkRd. 83-6 across the Osage; and the Upper Suspension Bridge, which still exists and formerly carried Hwy. 7. A bridge of modern vintage now carries Hwy. 7 and the old Upper Suspension Bridge has been preserved for its historic value. Until fairly recently, foot traffic was permitted on the old swinger, but currently the bridge is off limits to even foot traffic.

This suspension bridge sits in a historic location for it was near this spot that the first pontoon bridge was constructed across the Osage River in 1861 by Union General John C. Fremont so that troops and equipment could be moved across the river during the Civil War. In his rush to get the bridge built, Fremont dismantled half the town of Warsaw to get enough lumber.

The first suspension bridge at this location was a toll bridge completed in September 1904. The bridge was designed and constructed by Joseph A. Dice, a

Upper Swinging Bridge, *Warsaw, MO, 1962. Photographer Unknown.*

Warsaw area resident who, over the two following decades, would become renowned for his expertise in bridging rivers and creeks up and down the Osage River valley. It was not his first bridge, however, for he had several previous suspension bridges to his credit.

The first Upper Suspension Bridge had a span of 558 feet and wooden towers, one of which was 45 feet high. The cables were made up of 600 wires each and the bridge was built at a cost of $5,500.

On June 27, 1924, the Warsaw area was hit by cyclonic winds that broke telephone poles, uprooted trees and wrecked many buildings. Two bridges across the Osage were blown down -- the Peal Bend Bridge and the Upper Suspension Bridge.

"The bridges will almost have to be rebuilt in order to allow those living across the river to have access to the town," said the *Warsaw Times*. "...some are already at work attempting to find out how much money can be raised toward rebuilding the bridges."

Money was raised and the Midland Erection Company of Kansas was contracted to do the work. Early in the project, county officials discovered that the contractor was pouring a flooting for the west tower in mud and not on bedrock, and promptly stopped the work and dismissed the contracting company. Following this incident, the contract was awarded to Joe Dice. The bridge was completed, this time with steel towers, and reopened, but Missouri Highway Department Engineers later reinforced the bridge because they considered it unsafe.

For more than 40 years this handsome old swinger carried traffic with only one incident -- when a heavily loaded truck broke through the floor of the bridge. In the 1970s, a new bridge for Hwy. 7 was built by the Missouri Highway Department downstream from the Upper Suspension Bridge, which was then taken out of service.

Vernon Cave *(Eldon, Aurora Springs, Miller County)* -

Vernon Cave is located east of old Aurora Springs along the southeast side. The cave was originally called Klinger Cave after William Klinger who owned the property in the 1890s. Around the year 1900, the cave was commercialized by Lynn Tremain who renamed it Ancient Grotto. An earthen dam was constructed at the cave entrance to impound the cave stream and form a small lake so visitors could take an underground boat ride. The flooded section of cave passage has a length of about 210 feet and is 15 to 20 feet wide with a ceiling height about 6 feet above the water's surface. The walls of the passage are beautifully coated with white flowstone and there is an abundance of small stalactites adorning the ceiling. Beneath the water is deep, water-saturated red clay and sediments that form a treacherous mire.

Tremain, then living in Aurora Springs and later a resident of Eldon, was well known locally for his elocutionary and singing talents. He had memorized various compositions of verse and prose and would make presentations on special occasions.

Trips to the cave began at Aurora Springs where his customers would board a wagon, or proceed on their own by horseback or buggy to the cave, which was about one-and-a-half miles from town.

Once seated in the boat and drifting into the cave, Tremain would have them join hands if they were nervous or afraid. Perfect quietness was always requested so the visitors could hear the echoes and strange music produced by drops of water falling from the ceiling into the lake. As the boat proceeded, the lanterns would be turned down and then, after the boat turned the first corner and daylight vanished, Tremain would have the lanterns extinguished. He would then begin reciting, in low, resounding tones, the fate of the last voyage into the unknown depths from which mortal man might not return. Growing more eloquent, he would deliver a recitation that would end "so live that when their summons comes to join the innumerable caravans that move to that myserious realm, each shall take his chamber in the silent halls of death."

Tremain's guests would sometimes become quite unhinged by the alien environment, the total darkness, and his dramatic delivery. Many of his guests came just to listen to him sing funeral dirges in the cave and deliver his recitations. It was spooky, it was fun, and it brought Tremain a steady flow of customers during Aurora Spring's days of glory.

Tremain would, of course, have the lanterns lighted again and continue to the end of the lake where he had constructed a small dock. Braver souls were allowed to disembark and explore a bit beyond the lake to see the beautiful rimstone dams and flowstone draperies hanging from the crevices that lead upward into the cave's upper level.

***Vernon Cave,** Eldon, MO. Photo by H. D. Weaver, 1954.*

In later years, as the underground lakebed silted in more, making the bog beneath the water even worse, the lake became too shallow for a boat. A crude boardwalk was laid over the clay. It was still reasonably intact in the 1950s but the old boardwalk has since rotted and fallen apart, its nail-studded planks and pieces having sunk into the mire. Today's explorer faces the arduous task of getting through the mire, which is several feet deep, while trying not to step on one of the dangerous sunken pieces of debris. It is not a mire to plow through in thin-soled sneakers or tennis shoes.

Vernon Cave, *Eldon, MO. Photo by H. D. Weaver, 1954.*

The entrance to Vernon Cave is 36 feet wide and 12 feet high. The cave probably has about 800 to 900 feet of passage. Beyond the lake on the main level, the cave's stream passage narrows until it is 4 to 8 feet wide. Height decreases until the passage becomes a hands-and-knees crawl over bedrock and then a belly-crawl over and through water-filled rimstone dam impoundments. The water is cold. The full extent of this stream passage is unknown and exploration very difficult. There is an upper level that can be entered in only two places near the rimstone dams.

The cave's upper level is a meandering hands-and-knees crawlway with a winding crevasse in its floor that is generally too narrow to drop through back into the lower level stream passage. The passage is largely barren of cave formations.

Sometime before the 1950s, the property was purchased by the late Edgar Vernon and the cave then became known as Vernon Cave. The cave is still owned by the Vernon family.

Versailles *(Morgan County)* -

First time visitors to Lake of the Ozarks are often unsure how to pronounce the name "Versailles," which is on Hwys. 5 & 52 about nine miles north of Gravois Mills and 20 miles west of Eldon. Although it has the French spelling, the name is pronounced Ver'sales. The name probably originated with Kentucky immigrants who came from Versailles, Kentucky, a town actually named to honor France. But there is still some controversy over how the town got its name.

The birth of Versailles as a settlement dates to 1835 when the town site was platted by Wyan and Galbraith, two pioneer settlers who donated land covering a 36-block area.

When Morgan County was organized in 1933, the settlement of Millville, about six miles south on the headwaters of Little Gravois Creek, was selected as the county seat. The settlement was growing up around a flour mill site. Flour mills and sawmills could once be found up and down the length of the Gravois and Little Gravois creeks, most located at spring sites. All of the old mills are long gone and many of the old springs that powered them have ceased to flow. Some of the old mill sites are now beneath the waters of the Lake.

For reasons unknown, Millville proved unsatisfactory for the county seat. The post office there opened in 1834 and closed in 1835 and immediately afterward, the county seat was moved to Versailles. The Versailles Post Office opened in 1835.

The first courthouse was a log building located on the northwest corner of the public square. It was used for eight years. A two-story brick courthouse replaced it in 1844. This building was replaced in 1889 with the ornate structure that stands as the centerpiece of the downtown square today and it still serves as the Morgan County Courthouse.

Versailles experienced devastating fires in 1886 and 1887 that nearly destroyed the downtown area and it was the second of these fires that destroyed the county's second courthouse. But a number of century-old buildings still survive in the downtown area including the Martin Hotel. It is one of the oldest hotels west of the Mississippi River. The old hotel is now a museum maintained by the Morgan County Historical Society.

The Boonville-Versailles branch of the Missouri Pacific Railroad reached Versailles in 1880, followed by the Rock Island Railroad in 1903. The two railroads brought prosperity to the town.

When Lake of the Ozarks was created, Hwy. 5 was severed in two locations south of Versailles -- at the Osage River crossing, and the Niangua River crossing. Until bridges were built across the Lake at these points -- the Hurricane Deck Bridge and the Hwy. 5 Niangua Bridge -- and opened to traffic in 1938, travelers had to use a ferry to reach Camdenton, or take Hwy. 52 to Eldon and then Hwy. 54 to Camdenton. The newer stretch of Hwy. 5 between Versailles and Gravois Mills was opened in 1965.

Old Hwy. 5, now called Old Five Road, leaves Versailles along the southeast corner of town near the Versailles City Cemetery and becomes Route TT near Jacob's Cave. It is a hilly, winding road and it was along this road that the early resorts and tourist camps associated with the Versailles area developed after the Lake was formed. For a closer look at these businesses, see Dr. Matthew's Cafe & Drug Store.

Versailles, like Eldon, Linn Creek and Barnett, promoted themselves as a "Gateway" to Lake of the Ozarks. Gateway Lodge, an 8-room hotel with about six additional cottages, was built in 1931 in downtown Versailles one block off the square and operated by L. G. McMillen

West Side Of Public Square, Versailles, MO, *Circa. 1950s. Photo by L. L. Cook, Milwaukee.*

and Sons. They also had a financial interest in Trail's End Camp built in 1935 at the 4-mile mark on the Gravois Arm. Trail's End was sold two years later and became Happy Days Resort.

The Versailles Chamber of Commerce was both active and aggressive in promoting the Versailles "sector," a 1910s and 20s newspaper term often used when speaking of the local area. The Chamber's push was hard along Hwy. 5 south of town. Chamber literature described the road south in this manner:

"The Ozark foothills become more rugged as you travel south on No. 5 and only a short time is required to reach the most beautiful bridge in America, over the main channel of the Lake...but make your journey worth while as many points of beauty and interest await you.

"Take time to absorb the beauty of a hillside covered with wild flowers, a peaceful valley -- grazing sheep -- quiet water. As you rush by, the gentle murmur of a waterfall is lost in the roar of your passing, only a glimpse of a magnificent panorama is your reward as you hasten along. These friendly hills and restful waters will linger long in your book of memories. They contain the old Mill on Gravois Creek, the famous trout hatchery, the great heights of Hurricane Deck, the beautiful vista from Sunrise Beach, the mystic art of nature in Jacob's Cave, the historical background of the old Iron works, and the by-ways which lead to secluded nooks and springs.

"The beautiful, serene Gravois Arm with its many spring-fed tributaries is a natural habitat of Bass, Crappie, and Jack Salmon and very popular with fishermen and boatmen.

"All facilities for a successful vacation await you in fishing, sports, boating, or just "vacation."

Even before water filled the Lake basin, the *Versailles Leader* assembled, printed and distributed one of the first booklets to be published on Lake of the Ozarks. It was titled: "*The Open Door to the Center of the $30,000,000 Lake of the Ozarks Created by the Osage Dam Project.*"

The publisher said the purpose of the 32-page booklet was "to give a suggestion of the many things to be seen and done in the Scenic Playground of the Mid-West, to which Versailles serves as a natural doorway; to tell something of its resources, its desirability as a playground, and to give the stranger some of the many reasons why the people of Versailles and Morgan County are proud of the scenic and recreational paradise which is their home."

The booklet touted the fine hotels and cafes of Versailles; praised the town's telephone system, its roads and bridges, its diversified agricultural industry, its railroad connections, the county's mineral resources, carried photos of the major buildings in Versailles, said that Versailles was "the hub for a system of well-kept country roads," and declared Versailles to be a "natural doorway to a veritable angler's paradise."

Now scarce and a collector's gem, this little publication contains some wonderful photos of the valley of the Osage River before Lake of the Ozarks was born.

Ware's Camp *(Osage Beach, Camden County)* -

Ware's Camp, built by Harry & Ella Ware, opened in 1932 adjacent to Supreme View Camp [later Powell's Supreme View Cottages] on the southwest side of Hwy. 54 in Osage Beach near the junction of Hwy. 54 and Bluff Drive and the present day Wal-Mart Super Center.

Ware's Camp had stone cottages and a guest capacity of about 20 people. Their advertising said "Special Attention to Fishing Parties." The camp, they said, had lots of shade and fine well water. It overlooked the Lake with a view just as good as the adjacent camp, Supreme View, who capitalized on the view by using it in their name. Each off season period, Harry Ware would try to add a cottage. His camp was often called a "repeater camp," an expression that early day resort owners dubbed a camp that thrived on repeat business and had good word-of-mouth advertising.

A good example occurred in the summer of 1934 when the Dennis family had a family reunion at Ware's Camp. There were 16 people in the Dennis party and they came from several states. They were at the camp for a week and toward the end of their stay "they unanimously voted Ware's Camp the best." They even put a display ad in the *Lake of the Ozarks News* at their own expense recommending Ware's Camp to vacationists. One of the party is said to have gained 10 pounds during their stay. "They had excellent luck fishing and plenty of fish to eat. Mr. Ware turned his community kitchen over to them and hired Miss Eva McDowell to do their cooking so all they had to do was eat, sleep, fish and swim..."

***Ware's Camp,** Osage Beach, MO, Circa. 1939. Photographer Unknown.*

Later, Flora Belle Dennis wrote an interesting poem titled: "Ware's Camp" and sent it to the local paper. It was not a sophisticated poem and did not rhyme in every instance but is interesting for the insights it provides on the accommodations at Ware's Camp and the hospitality of Harry and Ella Ware:

"From North, from South, from East, from West,
A merry crowd came for a rest.
The place they chose was Osage Beach,
Ware's Camp the place that suited each.

The kitchen with its gravel floor,
And cupboards with their sagging doors,
The cook stove built of native stone,
Stood in the center of the room.

The dining room was long and wide,
All screened in on every side.
Rustic tables with ample room
For the ton of food they did consume.

They brought their appetites
Because they thought would not be wrong.
Down to the beach the bathers ran,
Some could swim while others swam.

Some hung on to the inner tire,
Everyone did his hearts desire.
Fishing was good and boating too,
Lake of the Ozarks, here's to you."

Unfortunately, Harry Ware was in an auto accident in November 1936 and died shortly thereafter at St. Mary's Hospital in Jefferson City. Ella Ware continued to run the camp until she sold it about 1939. The Powell's may have bought her camp and incorporated it into their own.

Warsaw *(Benton County)* -

The Osage River, as an artery of commerce and transportation from the days of settlement until the creation of Lake of the Ozarks, tied communities and their people together along the banks of the river. Warsaw, Linn Creek, Bagnell and Tuscumbia were tightly bound by trade, intermarriage and friendships. On a weekly basis you could find stories in Tuscumbia's *Miller County Autogram* about the happenings in Bagnell, Linn Creek and Warsaw. In the *Warsaw Times* you could learn about the births and deaths, farm sales and politics of Linn Creek and Tuscumbia. In the

Linn Creek *Reveille* you could find stories about floods, fires and celebrations and other happenings in Bagnell, Tuscumbia and Warsaw. But the Lake of the Ozarks changed it all.

Because of the tight meandering of the Osage River, it is not as far between the towns of Tuscumbia, Bagnell and Linn Creek, as it is between these towns and Warsaw. By water, it is more than 100 miles from Tuscumbia to Warsaw. Even from the former site of Old Linn Creek, it is 60 miles to Warsaw by water.

The Lake devastated the agricultural industry of Camden County, the central link between the four impacted counties, changing much of their economic focus from agriculture and mining to tourism and recreation.

Above Bagnell Dam, shipping on the river came to an end and the farming, mining and manufacturing industries of Morgan and Benton counties had to rely upon rail and highway for getting their products to market. The agricultural industries in the river towns of these counties were also impacted when the Chambers of Commerce in the various towns began placing more emphasis upon tourism and recreational promotions than on agriculture.

Gradually, the links between Warsaw and former shipping centers along the Osage River downstream were broken. Warsaw news appeared less and less often in downstream newspapers as the towns along the new Lake began to compete for the tourist dollar.

At first, the Lake of the Ozarks Association held frequent meetings at Warsaw. The merchants of Warsaw advertised in publications and newspapers produced by towns up and down the Lake's extent, particularly in the *Lake of the Ozarks News*, the Lake's only special interest newspaper that was published only during the 1930s. It was headquartered in Miller County.

An example is a half-page newspaper ad that appeared in the *Lake of the Ozarks News* Feb. 1, 1932. It was sponsored by a group of Warsaw merchants: "Warsaw On-The Lake," it said in large, bold type. "Warsaw, the county seat of Benton County, is the only town situated directly on the shores of the great Lake of the Ozarks."

The ad, of course, ignored the fact that Gravois Mills was also on the shores of Lake of the Ozarks, even though it was at the headwaters of the Gravois Arm. The Warsaw ad went on to extol the virtues of its town:

Warsaw, MO, Main Street, *Circa 1950s. Photographer Unknown.*

"Warsaw has many advantages that make it especially attractive to the sportsman and vacationist. Fishing is excellent. Fifteen fishing streams within 15 miles. Duck shooting will always be of the best... Warsaw is equipped to take care of the vacationist' every need. Unusual dock and storage facilities for boats; cabin camps; business houses carrying complete stocks of sporting goods...comfortable hotels; excellent restaurants; everything for the resident or visitor."

But the links were breaking by the end of the 1930s. By 1951, the Lake of the Ozarks Association did not even include the Warsaw area camp and resort ads in their annual tourist guidebook, and very little about the Warsaw area on its annual Lake maps. In fact, it was difficult to find any information in Lake of the Ozarks Association publications beyond the 60-mile mark after this date.

To compensate for this, Warsaw began publishing its own annual tourist guidebook and area maps under the banner of the Headwater's Area Association.

When Truman Dam was built in the 1970s, creating another large lake on the Osage, Warsaw became the centerpiece between these two great lakes.

Warsaw is a historic town and the history of Benton County stretches back to the early 1700s when Phillip Renault and Claude Du Tisne were in the territory trading whiskey and guns to the Shawnee and Osage Indians for furs. The early fur traders named some of the local streams.

Settlement at Warsaw began in the 1820s, the earliest settlers being both French and German. Benton County was organized in 1831 and by the time Warsaw was platted in 1837, it already had a population of nearly a thousand people. The Warsaw Post Office was established in 1839.

The town was named in honor of Polish patriots who fought against the British with American troops during the Revolutionary War.

Warsaw was the highest point [farthest upstream] on the Osage River that steamboats could reach on a regular basis and it became a vital shipping point for merchants who supplied freight wagons and for settlers needing supplies for their wagon trains.

The notoriety of Warsaw during the Civil War was sensational. The town was a major crossroads for both Union and Confederate troops.

A Land Office was located at Warsaw from 1855-1861. The Butterfield Overland Mail, a stagecoach service, had a station in Warsaw from 1851-1861 and other stops in Benton County. The railroad reached Warsaw in the 1870s. The town has seen three county courthouses. The current one was built in 1886-1887. The town is rich in historic sites and the Benton County Historical Society maintains a museum in Warsaw.

The first bridge across the Osage River was constructed at Warsaw in 1895. By the 1920s, eight suspension bridges were crossing streams and rivers in the area. It became known as the "Land of Swinging Bridges."

During the construction of Bagnell Dam, the town saw tremendous growth as it became the focal point for all activities related to the clearing of the upper basin and creation of the Lake. At one point, 133 men associated with the dam work were staying at Warsaw. When ceremonies to dedicate Lake of the Ozarks were held at Warsaw Sept. 22, 23 and 24, 1931, it became a three-day event.

Soon after the Lake filled, G. E. Crosby, an official of Union Electric, cruised from the dam to Warsaw in a 28-foot cabin cruiser. The historic 45-ton Gov. McClurg ferry boat was partially built and then launched at Warsaw, as were other large boats of that day.

Fishing camps, resorts and marinas blossomed on the Lake shores at and near Warsaw. In the 1930s came Shawnee View Camp, established by W. L. Morgan with six cabins, a store and gas station; Swinging Bridge Camp, established by George G. Huse with six cabins; Brill's Hill Resort & Marina, established by T. C. Brill with seven cabins, gas station and marine railway [see Brill's Hill]; Hackberry Camp at the 89-mile mark east of town; Jackson's Beach at the 86-miles mark east of town; Shady Grove Bayou Camp, established by Ernest Hirsch with eight cabins; the Westview Tavern & Hotel north of the Hwy. 65 Bridge, established by A. F. "Turk" West; and the Gateway Cafe south of the Hwy. 65 Bridge, established by Harold Bugeon.

In the 1940s, came Parcell's Cove Camp two miles north of Warsaw; C. G. Scotty's Old Mill Resort at Fairfield; and Ozark Cafe & Modern Cabins.

In the 1950s, came White Branch Resort, White Branch Cafe, Headwater's Motel, Burke's Resort, Paradise Hidden Acres and Wanta Linga Camp north of town; and North Shore Camp, Jackson Beach and the Tip Top all on the south side.

Most of these camps, resorts and businesses no longer exist but a few resorts do still function along Lake of the Ozarks in the Warsaw area.

The upper reaches of the Lake between Warsaw and the 70-mile mark are visually different from those portions of the Lake below the 70-mile mark. There are more sloughs and islands and partially submerged vegetation because the Lake is now shallow here. In fact, silting over the past 70 years has greatly reduced the depth of the water in areas between the 70- and 88-mile marks. As early as 1972, the Lake of the Ozarks Yachting Association began noting on its charts that the Lake here had silted in by as much as 20 feet since 1931.

Times have certainly changed at both ends of the Lake in a number of ways since 1931, and the Lake of the Ozarks itself has also undergone changes.

White House Inn / Hotel *(Lake Ozark, Miller County)* -

Most of the buildings housing businesses along the north side of the Bagnell Dam Strip built in the 1930s have all been lost to fire or demolition, or they have been remodeled to the point that the original structure is no longer recognizable. The White House is one exception.

Standing about mid-way along The Strip on its north side, it looks today almost like it did 50 and 60 years ago. It has lost only the octagonal Italianate cupola that stood atop the tower section at its west end, the small curved roof over the doorway to that section, and the gas pumps that were out front.

The White House was built by G. Riley and Delia DeGraffenreid. Riley was a road construction foreman during the building of the dam. He also built the Riley DeGraffenreid Boat Dock just west of the dam during the same period of time but sold the dock almost as soon as he finished it to Mr. & Mrs. Harry Harrison.

The White House opened for business on May 28, 1932, as the White House Inn, a name it kept for one year and was changed to White House Hotel. The opening was recognized by the *Lake of the Ozarks News* which said:

"This hotel is a welcome addition to the accommodations for visitors to the Lake this season. It is completely modern in every respect, having hot and cold water in every room, tub and shower baths, a large lobby and an inviting dining room. In addition...there is a large dining balcony that overlooks the Lake and which should have a distinctive appeal. The hotel is fully equipped with Frigidaire and a soda fountain is to be added as soon as it can be installed. There is also a five-pump station where the motorist can get every attention without delay."

White House Hotel, *Lake Ozark, MO, Circa. 1940s. Photo by Corwin.*

In 1933, Lawrence M. and Jessie Fry leased the hotel. Lawrence Fry would, in the coming years, become one of the leading citizens and entrepreneurs of Lake Ozark. He was the Lake Ozark postmaster from 1938 to 1973. For a time he owned the Lakeside Casino Restaurant. He built and named the Larry Don Excursion Boat, which is still in business at the west end of the dam but is now called the Captain Larry Don. He was a cofounder of the Lake Ozark Fire Protection District and served as an alderman for Lake Ozark. Fry was instrumental in getting three churches started in the area -- the Community Church, Our Lady of the Lake Catholic Chapel, and the Lake Ozark Christian Church. He died in 1993.

The overnight guest capacity of the White House Hotel was 18, but its dining room facilities could seat large numbers of people. On one occasion in 1934, a banquet was held at the hotel, which was attended by 150 people. The hotel charged $1.50 per person per day for a room in 1934, or $9.00 for a week. Fry came up with a unique slogan for the business -- "The tariff is reasonable."

The Frys sponsored dances at the White House Hotel and engaged live musical entertainment. As it was said in a 1981 history of Lake Ozark: "The White House was THE entertainment center for the whole area. It was known far and wide for its food, dancing and exciting parties. Everybody who was anybody visited the White House."

Dancing got underway at the White House big time in 1933. "The White House Hotel...has inaugurated a series of worthwhile dances for the late winter and they occur every Sunday evening," said a March 1, 1933, article in the *Lake of the Ozarks News*. "The dances are being well attened and are providing clean, wholesome entertainment for both young and old. Mr. Kindle's well known orchestra, formerly of Chicago and the East, is putting up some Cracker-Jack good music and is winning his way with the guests. The lovely, glittering White House dining room is furnishing the dancing space."

Another orchestral group who performed at the White House during this period was the Ozark Ramblers.

White House ads for 1937 said: "Stop awhile. Rest a bit. Everyone else does. Most everything is here for you. Enjoy dancing. Best in liquors. A cool refreshing drink at the fountain and the most appetizing foods." The hotel was also a stop on the Missouri Pacific Bus route.

In 1939, a fire that destroyed most of the businesses between the White House and the west end of Bgnell Dam on the north side, also damaged the north end of the hotel, but did not put it out of business.

Among the proprietors who kept the doors open at the White House Hotel through the 1940s and into the 1950s were John T. McCrory, Clifford Allen, Gary Waters, Fuzzy Adams and Dave Bales.

In 1954, the White House Hotel restaurant was featuring catfish, chicken and steak dinners. They sold fishing tackle, drugstore items, beer, magazines and Standard Oil gasoline.

The building no longer serves as either a hotel or a filling station. For a time in the 1990s it stood vacant. Some renovation work has been done on the building in the past several years and a new business is currently using the building.

Zebra *(Osage Beach, Camden County)* -

Very little has been written about Zebra, a Camden County village with a most unusual name. It was located at the confluence of the Glaize [Grand Glaize Creek] and the Osage River where Lands End Condominiums stand today at the end of Red Bud Road. [see Pla-Port Resort for more information about the history of resorts on the point of this peninsula.]

The village of Zebra appears to have grown up at this location because of the railroad tie industry that began to flourish along the Osage in the 1880s. According to Camden County historian, Lucille Keller Harpham, great stacks of future railroad ties appeared here waiting for suitable river conditions to be rafted to Bagnell.

A steamboat landing and an adjacent warehouse were built on the floodplain about this time as people and merchants began to settle along the ridge road to avoid flooding that occurred frequently in the bottomlands. According to folklore, the name Zebra was given to the town because of the mineral-streaked bluffs nearby, which steamboat pilots said looked like a zebra's hide.

"Uncle Tom Ezard and his wife, Teresa, with his daughter Maud and son-in-law, John McCrory, maintained the Zebra Post Office," said Harpham. The post office was opened in 1886 and located in the Ezard store. The Ezards were also in the tie business.

By the early 1900s, the little town had grown considerably. There were 12 dwellings, a store owned by T. E. Ezard, a store owned by Lloyd and Stevens, a church, the post office, and a grocery store. William Jeffries had the blacksmith shop. Frank Anderson operated the Zebra Hotel. At that time Redbud Road was called HiLow Street. This name is believed to have originated because HiLow Street extended past the point of the peninsula and descended steeply to the river bottom and the steamboat landing. An 1893 map shows a road from Cape Galena that ran down the south side of Shawnee Bend into the Osage River bottom where Frank Anderson kept a ferry. He also owned the ferry that carried people across the Glaize Creek about 1.5 miles upstream from the creeks confluence with the Osage. About the year 1900, a suspension bridge was built across the Glaize at this location. It was replaced in the late 1920s with a steel truss bridge but this bridge had to be demolished when the Lake basin was cleared [see Grand Glaize Bridge]. Before the suspension bridge was built across the Glaize Creek, Frank Anderson also operated a ferry at that location.

A rather troublesome sandbar island existed in the Osage River just above the Zebra steamboat landing. When the river was low the ferry couldn't run and people had to ford the river to reach Zebra. The tapered ends of this island were known as Ray's Shoal No. 1 on the downstream side, and as Ray's Shoal No. 2 on the upstream side.

When the Lake came in, the merchants of Zebra moved their businesses to the new section of Hwy. 54. The post office building was also relocated. It was dismantled in 1935 when the Zebra Post Office was discontinued and renamed Osage Beach [see Osage Beach Post Office].

The last surviving Zebra business was the Zebra Grocery, which stood on the southeast side of Hwy. 54 across from where Shoney's Restaurant is today. It was a small rock building. The business was operated by Ellis & Jessie Scott. It closed in the late 1950s. The building stood vacant until the early 1990s when it was demolished.

Zora / Zora Heights *(Cole Camp, Stover, Benton County)* -

Zora was a settlement that grew up around the Geary Store, which once stood along the Stover and Boylers Mill Road to Duroc and Hastain. It was located at the head of what is today Big Buffalo Cove at the 72-mile mark on the Osage Arm. The Zora Post Office opened in 1887 and closed in 1931.

Zora Heights was a subdivision near old Zora created as soon as the Lake was formed. It was developed by W. F. Geary of Stover. "This historic spot for 50 years was known as Zora, where for that length of time, some member of the Geary family owned and operated a store and post office," said a local newspaper in 1932. "It's scenery is no doubt as beautiful, if not more so, than can be found anywhere on the Lake. This spot is noted as one of the best bass fishing places, it being on the Big Buffalo Creek, where a reputation for game fishing will be vouched for by thousands of anglers.

"Zora Heights is at one of the largest expands [meaning wide places] on the Lake, thereby affording excellent boating facilities for those who love the thrill of riding on the uncrowded water, where traffic blocking is unheard of. Near this site are beautiful rock bluff formations to be explored by boat.

"When Mr. Geary sold his farm to the Union Electric...he retained this picturesque spot and thus far has had 36 lots surveyed and ready for sale..."

SELECTED BIBLIOGRAPHY

A New Map of the Lake of the Ozarks, Points of Interest and the Bagnell Dam. The Ozark Information and Service Bureau, Kansas City, MO. 1932.

Andrews, Elizabeth Riffle. *A History of Soap Creek and Gravois Mills. Bagnell Dam Area of the Lake of the Ozarks, Resort, Entertainment and Service Guides.* Bagnell Dam Chamber of Commerce. Various issues 1960 -1980.

Behymer, F. A. "The Woman Coroner of the Ozarks." *Everyday Magazine*, June 9, 1944.

Benton County Enterprise newspaper. Various early issues.

Bullard, Loring. *Healing Waters: Missouri's Historic Mineral Springs and Spas.* University of Missouri Press, Columbia, MO 2004.

Camden County Historian, Journal of the Camden County Historical Society, Linn Creek, MO. Various issues.

Caves of Miller County, *Missouri Speleology*, Journal of the Missouri Speleological Survey Inc. Vol. 3, No. 2, April 1961.

Cole Camp Area History 1839-1979. Cole Camp Area Historical Society, Cole Camp, MO. 1979.

Dictionary of Missouri Biography. Ed. Lawrence O. Christensen, William E. Foley, Gary Kremer and Kenneth H. Winn, University of Missouri Press, Columbia, MO 1999.

Earngey, Bill. *Missouri Roadsides, The Travelers Companion.* University of Missouri Press, Columbia, MO 1995.

Eldon Advertiser newspaper. Various early issues.

Exploring Missouri's Legacy: State Parks and Historic Sites. Ed. Susan Flader, University of Missouri Press, Columbia, MO 1992.

Fiftieth Anniversary, Bagnell Dam, Lake of the Ozarks 1931-1981. Ed. Lorraine Burke. Lake of the Ozarks Area Council of the Arts.

Funk, John L. *Missouri's Fishing Streams.* Missouri Department of Conservation, Division of Fisheries, Jefferson City, MO 1968.

Gravois Arm Area Lake of the Ozarks Resort, Entertainment and Services Guide. Various issues 1960s and 1970s.

Gravois Mills Centennial 1884-1984. Gravois Mills, MO

Haden, Robert. Historical Resources Mitigations, Vol. II. *Bridges Over The Osage.* U. S. Army Corps of Engineers, Sept. 1980.

Haer Missouri Historic Bridge Inventory, Glaize Bridge. May 4, 1990; Grand Glaize Bridge, 1993; Mill Creek Bridge, 1993. Randy Dawdy, Missouri Department of Transportation, Cultural Resources, Jefferson City, MO.

Harpham, Lucille Keller. *Camden County History.* Camden County Historical Society, Linn Creek, MO

Hawkins, Mabel. *Bank of Brumley.* Miller County Historical Society, Tuscumbia, MO

Hawksley, Oscar. *Missouri Ozark Waterways.* Missouri Conservation Commission, Jefferson City, MO 1965.

Headwaters Association of Lake of the Ozarks Resort, Entertainment and Services Guide & Map. Various early issues.

Headwaters Association of Lake of the Ozarks Vacation Guide Map. Various early maps.

Helbock, Richard W. *United States Post Offices Volume VII - The Lower Mississippi Valley.* 2005

Highway 5 Vacationland Lake of the Ozarks Resort, Entertainment and Services Guide, 1981.

History of Bank of Lake of the Ozarks, The Tradition Continues. Sept. 21, 1987.

Hubbell, Victoria. *A Town On Two Rivers.* City of Osage Beach, MO 1998

Hurley, Frank. "History and Geology of Jacob's Cave." *The Ozark Speleograph,* Vol. 30, No. 2, April-June 2002.

Hurricane Deck Resort Association Entertainment and Services Guide. Various issues 1948-1972.

J Bar H Rodeo Annual. Harry & Jean Nelson. Various issues 1953-1970

Jenkins, Clayton E. *Judge Jenkins History of Miller County, Missouri. Vol. 2, End of Civil War through 1900.*

Jenkins, Clyde Lee. *Judge Jenkins History of Miller County, Missouri, Vol. 1 Through the Civil War.*

Kansas City Journal, newspaper. Various early issues.

Kansas City Journal Post, newspaper. Various early issues.

Kansas City Star, newspaper. Various early issues.

Kansas City Times, newspaper. Various early issues.

Kremer, Gary. "Bagnell Branch Railroad Once Connected Cole, Moniteau, Miller Counties." *Jefferson City, Missouri, News Tribune,* Oct. 10, 1999.

Lake Area News Focus. Various issues.

Lake Life News. Various issues.

Lake of the Ozarks Business Map 1984. Business Maps Ltd., Camdenton.

Lake of the Ozarks Country of Missouri, A Vacation Guide Map. Missouri State Department of Resources and Development Map for Recreational Booket No. 2.

Lake of the Ozarks Life. Various issues.

Lake of the Ozarks News. Eldon, MO. Various issues 1932-1938.

Lake of the Ozarks State Park Coakley Hollow Self-Guided Trail. Brochure. Missouri Department of Natural Resources.

Lake of the Ozarks Yachting Association Navigation Chart 1975. Yachting Association Yearbook Committee 1975.

Lake of the Ozarks, The Niangua Arms Resort Entertainment and Services Guide. Camdenton Chamber of Commerce. Various issues. 1960-1970. *Lake Sun,* newspaper. Various issues.

Long, Carrie. *History of Central Bank of Lake of the Ozarks.* Feb. 26, 1997.

Map of Morgan County. R. Thornton Higgins, 1880.

Marbut, C. F. *The Geology of Morgan County.* Vol. VIII 2nd Series, Missouri Bureau of Geology & Mines.

McCanse, Keith. *Where To Go In The Ozarks, 1932.*

Mehrer, Jim. *Missouri Post Offices.*

Miller County Autogram, newspaper. Tuscumbia, MO. Various early issues.

Missouri Department of Transportation, Cultural Resources. Randy Dawdy. *Bridge Plans for Grand Glaize Bridge, U. S. Hwy. 54, Camden County; Niangua River, U.S. Hwy. 54 Bridge, Camden County.*

Missouri's Lake of the Ozarks, Annual Vacation Guide Map. Lake of the Ozarks Association, Lake Ozark, MO. Various maps 1934-1981.

Missouri's Lake of the Ozarks, Annual Resort and Entertainment Guide. Lake of the Ozarks Association, Lake Ozark, MO. Various issues 1951-1980.

Missouri Landing Facilities. Missouri Division of Resources and Development, Jefferson City, MO 1957

Missouri: The WPA Guide to the "Show Me" State. Missouri Historical Society Press, St. Louis, MO 1998.

Morgan County History, Volume One. Morgan County Historical Society. Versailles, MO 1979

Official Lake of the Ozarks 1937 Map Guide. Milton Oil Company.

Osage Beach Area of Lake of the Ozarks Resort, Entertainment and Services Guide. Various issues 1960s and 1970s.

Points of Interest, Gravois Arm Area, Lake of the Ozarks, A Reminder of Your Visit. Osage Heritage Days brochure 2000.

Ramsay, Robert L. *Our Storehouse of Missouri Place Names.* University of Missouri Press 1973.

Raynor, Tina. *Eldon, A Look Back 1882-1982.* Eldon Centennial Inc. 1982.

Resort Guide and Map, Lake of the Ozarks 1938. Mid-West Map Company.

Schultz, Gerard. *A History of Miller County, Missouri.* Midland Printing Company, Jefferson City, MO, 1933.

Skinner, Glenn Goone. *The Big Niangua River.* 1979.

Stevens, Walter B. "The Missouri Tavern." *The Missouri Historical Review*, Vol. XV, No. 2, Jan. 1921.

Stover Missouri 1903-2003. Stover 2003 Centennial History Book Committee. City of Stover, 2003.

The Reveille, newspaper. Linn Creek and Camdenton. Various early issues.

Twenty-Sixth Anniversary, Camdenton, Hub City of Lake of the Ozarks Resort, Entertainment and Services Guide. Camdenton Chamber of Commerce. 1957.

Union Electric Magazine. Employees Mutual Benefit Association. Union Electric Light & Power Company, St. Louis, MO. Various issues 1929-1943.

"Upper Bridge, Benton County." *National Register of Historic Places.* Report by Lee Gilleard, Steve Mitchell, Scott Myers. Missouri Department of Natural Resources, Historic Preservation Program.

Vacation In The Heart of Missouri. Lake of the Ozarks Association 1939.

Vacation News. Various issues.

Versailles Leader, newspaper. Versailles, MO. Various early issues.

Versailles, Missouri, It's First 150 Years 1835-1895. Versailles Commerce League 1985.

V*ersailles, Missouri: The Open Door to the Center of the $30,000,000 Lake of the Ozarks Created by the Osage Dam Project.* Versailles Leader, 1931.

Vineyard, Jerry D. and Gerald L. Feder. *Springs of Missouri.* Missouri Department of Natural Resources, Division of Geology and Land Survey, 1982.

Vogel, Robert S. Climax Springs. *Missouri Geographer*, Fall 1971.

Weaver, H. Dwight and Paul A. Johnson. *Missouri, The Cave State.* Discovery Enterprises, Jefferson City, MO 1980.

Weaver, H. Dwight. "A History of the Caves of Camden County, Missouri." *Missouri Speleology*, Journal of the Missouri Speleological Survey Inc., Vol. 11, No. 1-2, January-April 1970.

_____. *Lake of the Ozarks: The Early Years.* Arcadia Publishing, 2000.

_____. *Lake of the Ozarks: Vintage Vacation Paradise.* Arcadia Publishing, 2002.

_____. "Outlaw Years in the Osage River Basin." *The Ozark Speleograph*, Vol. 5, No. 1, January 1975.

_____. "The Commercial Caves of Camden County, Missouri." *Missouri Speleology*, Journal of the Missouri Speleological Survey Inc. Vol. 27, No. 1-4. January-December 1987.

Williams, Walter. *The State of Missouri.* E. W. Stephens Press, Columbia, MO 1904

MAIN ENTRIES INDEX

A. M. Pope & Sons Hardware & Lumber Company ... 1
Adam's Cafe & Tobacco Shop ... 2
Adkin's Camp / Resort ... 2
Ak-Sar-Ben Resort ... 3
Ammons Boat Dock & Marine Railway ... 3
Anderson Hollow Bay / Party Cove .. 4
Anderson's Cottages ... 5
Arnhold Cave ... 5
Arnhold Mill ... 6
Arrow Point Cave ... 7
Arrowhead Lodge Hotel ... 8
Art Luck's Fishing & Hunting Resort ... 9
Aurora Springs ... 9
Bagnell ... 11
Bagnell Branch Railroad ... 12
Bagnell Dam ... 13
Bagnell Dam Strip ... 14
Bagnell Ferry ... 14
Bagnell Flats ... 15
Bagnell - Linn Creek Road ... 16
Bagnell Timber Company ... 16
Bank of Brumley ... 17
Bank of Lake of the Ozarks ... 17
Baptism in the Lake ... 18
Barber's Camp ... 20
Barnes Hollow Cove ... 20
Barnett ... 21
Berry's Lodge ... 22
Big Bend Acres ... 23
Boat Shelter Cave ... 24
Boot's Tavern, Super Service Station & Cafe ... 25
Boyler's [Byler's] Mill & Spring ... 26
Bridal Cave ... 27
Brill's Hill Resort & Marina ... 29
Brockman's Island ... 30
Brumley ... 30
Camdenton ... 31
Campbell's Lake House ... 33
Cannady's Cafe & Grocery Store ... 34
Cape Hollow Cove / Moonlight Bay . 35
Caves ... 36
Chet's Anchor Inn ... 36
Chief Ne-Ong-Wah / Stone Face ... 38
Chimney Rock ... 38
Chimney Rock Cave ... 38
Christmas Tree Court ... 38
Cleland's Cottages ... 39
Climax Spring ... 39
Climax Springs ... 39
Climax Springs Cave ... 41
Coakley Hollow & Coves ... 41
Coakley Spring ... 42
Coelleda ... 44
Cole Camp ... 45
Cole Camp Creek & Hollow ... 46
Cole Camp Hollow Cove ... 46

Collin's Spring & Lake 47
Cove Lodge Modern Cottages 47
Damsel 49
Damsel Cafe 49
Dogpatch Cafe / Village 50
Dogwood Festival 52
Dr. Matthew's Cafe & Drug Store ... 53
Drum Rock 54
Dry Branch Cave 55
Duck Hunting on the Lake 1932 56
Duckworth's Camp 57
E. R. Smith Ice Plant 59
Easterville 59
Ebert's Beach Resort 60
Echo Valley Camp 60
Edgewater Beach Resort 60
El Donna Motel / Eldon Inn 61
El Kay Motel 61
El Rancho of the Ozarks 62
Eldon 63
Fish Haven Camp / Resort 65
Flanders Cave 66
Fleetwood Lodge & Boat Dock 67
Flood of 1943 68
Folded Hills Dining Room 70
Forrester's Beach Resort 70
Forth View Resort / Marine 72
Frack's Acre 72
Frank's Resort / Motel / Peaceful Valley Hatchery 74
Gladstone 75
Glaize Bridge 76
Gore's Boat Yard 77
Gov. McClurg Ferry 78
Gov. McClurg Mansion 81
Gov. McClurg Showboat 82
Grand Glaize Arm of the Lake 83
Grand Glaize Bridge 84
Grand Glaize Cafe 86
Gravois Arm of the Lake 87
Gravois Beach Resort 89
Gravois Mills 90
Happy Days Resort 91
Hastain 92
Hawkeye Modern Cabins 92
Heckerman's Cottage Camp & Service Station 92
Hildebrand's Camp / Resort 93
Holiday House 95
Hopi Camp / Cottages / Motel 97
Horseshoe Bend 98
Horseshoe Bend Road 100
Hymes Kottage Kamp One & Two 102
Idle Days & Gala Resort 103
Idlewild Court / Cabins 104
Indian Burial Cave 105
Iron Smelter / Furnace 106
Irontown 107
Irontown Ferry 107
J Bar H Rodeo 109
Jack Salmon 110
Jacob's Cave 110
Jeffries Boat Dock, Fishing Barge & Cottages 113
Jeffries Ozark Cafe 115
Jenn's Point Comfort 115
Jester's Camp 116
Johnson's Snug Harbor 116
Joyce Motel 117
Kaiser 119
Kalfran Lodge 120
Kavanaugh's Gravois Beach Resort 121
Kaysinger Bluff 121
Kellerstrass, Ernest 122
Kinds 'O Fishin' 123
Kirkwood Lodge 123
Klinger Cave 124
Lake Benton 125
Lake Fork Heights 125
Lake McClurg 125
Lake of the Ozarks Improvement & Protective Association 125
Lake Ozark 128
Lakeside 131

Lakeside Casino Restaurant 131
Lakeview Heights 132
Lazy Days Resort 134
Lick Branch Cove 135
Linn Creek 136
Lowell's Niangua Bridge
Boat Dock 137
Malibu Beach Resort 139
McClurg, Joseph Washington 140
Mel Adkins Airplane Landing
Facility 141
Mill Creek Bridge 141
Mining Port 142
Mountain Terrace Court 143
Musser's Ozark Tavern / Resort 143
Naming Lake of the Ozarks 147
Navajo Beach Resort 151
Navy Plane Lands On Lake,
1942 151
Niangua Arm of the Lake 151
Niangua Bridge Camp & Boat
Dock 154
Niangua River 154
Oak Grove Beach Resort 155
Osage Beach Post Office 155
Osage Beach Tavern / Hotel 156
Osage Iron Works / Smelter 158
Our Lady of the Lake Catholic
Chapel 160
Ozark Caverns 163
Ozark Inn / Cafe 165
Ozark Tavern Hotel 167
Palisades 169
Pioneering Spirit 170
Pla-Port Resort 170
Pooler's Modern Cottages, Store &
Bus Stop 173
Powell's Supreme View Cottages /
Court 174
Prairie Hollow Cave 175
Purvis Beach Resort 176
Racetrack Hollow & Cove 179
Ranch House Grill 179
Red Feather Cafe & Camp 179
Riverview 180
Roaring Oaks Camp / Resort 182
Rock Hill Camp 182
Rockway Cabin Court /
Motor Court 183
Rocky Mount 184
Sagrada 185
Sagrada Bridge 185
Salt Road 187
Shady Slope Camp / Resort 188
Shawnee Bend 190
Sherwood Resort / Restaurant 192
Show Caves 193
Stark Caverns / Fantasy World 194
Sunrise Beach / Sunrise Inn 196
Ti-Sun Terrace Resort 199
Tonka Villa Resort 199
Trail's End Camp 200
Tuxhorn Resort 200
Twin Bays Camp 202
Two Waters Resort 203
Uncle Jim's Camp 205
Union Electric Land & Develop-
ment Company 205
Union Electric Light & Power
Company 206
Upper Suspension Bridge 207
Vernon Cave 209
Versailles 210
Ware's Camp 213
Warsaw 214
White House Inn / Hotel 217
Zebra 219
Zora / Zora Heights 220

BUSINESS & COMPANY INDEX

A. M. Pope Hardware & Lumber Company 1-2
Aaron Crain Ferry 19
Adam's Cafe & Tobacco Shop 2
Adam's Star Restaurant 2
Adkin's Camp 2-3, 90, 91, 141
Ak-Sar-Ben Resort 3
American Sales Co. 35
Ammon's Boat Dock 3-4, 36
Anchor Inn 37
Anchorage Pub & Grill 90
Anchorage Resort Park 89
Anderson's Cottages 5
Angus Steakhouse 62
Arnhold Mill 6-7, 21, 38
Arnold' Country Corner 35, 70, 156
Arnold's Gift Shop 35
Arrow Point Cave 7-8, 194
Arrowhead Lodge Hotel 8-9, 160
Art Luck's Resort 9, 10, 56
Arthur M. Pope Hotel 1, 123
Atteberry Cafe 160
Atteberry Grocery 160
Aurora Springs Sanitarium 9-10
Baby Beef Market 73
Bagnell Branch Railroad .. 11, 12-13,15, 85
Bagnell Brothers Construction Company 11
Bagnell Dam Gift Shop 165
Bagnell Ferry 11, 12, 14-15
Bagnell Post Office 11, 12
Bagnell Timber Company 11, 16-17
Baker's Grand View Lodge 161
Ballenger Cabins 160
Bank Building Corp. 18
Bank of Brumley 17, 30
Bank Star One 101
Bank of Lake of the Ozarks 17-18, 30
Barber's Grand Glaize Camp ... 20, 102, 161, 182, 192
Barker's Cottages 5
Barnett Hotel 21
Barnett Post Office 21
Bashore's Antiques 54
Baska's Peaceful Valley Resort 89
Bass Head Tavern & Grocery .. 89,121
Beabout's Archery, Bait, Tackle ... 156, 174
Beach Combers 54
Berry's Lodge 22, 115, 161
Bert's Inn 54
Bickel Contracting Company 13
Big Bend Acres 23-24, 181
Big Buffalo Beach 24
Blair Hotel 162
Blue Dolphin Resort 21, 60
Blue Herron Restaurant 87, 101
Blue Waters Resort 53, 89
Bob's Place Souvenirs 93
Bodie's Rondavo, ... 3, 91
Bond's Grand Glaize Camp ... 182, 183
Boot's Cafe, Motel 25-26
Boot's Cottage Court 26
Boot's Service Station 25-26
Boot's Tavern 25-26
Bott's Printing, Engraving 157
Boyer's Market 204
Boyler's Mill 26-27
Breckenridge Resort 173
Bridal Cave Development Co. 165
Bridal Cave 27-29, 152, 164, 193, 196
Bridge View Resort 161
Bridgeport Boat Rentals 82, 183
Brill's Hill Resort 29-30, 56, 79, 217
Briney's Cove Yacht Club Resort ... 155
Brockman Camp, Grocery 161
Brownie's Camp 60
Bruce's Ozark Inn 166
Brumley Post Office 30
Bruner's Camp 67
Brush Electric Association 206
Buehler's Drug Store 161
Buena Vista Hotel 161

Burke's Resort 217
Burns-McDonnell Engineering
Company 13
Bush & Knickerbocker 24
Byler House 27
C & R Saloon 9
C. P. O'Reilly Construction Company .. 85
Cahill's Phillips 66 Station 144
Cairn's Wayside Inn 54
Camden County Bank 162
Camdenton Boat Dock 138
Camp Wah-Kon-Dah 136
Campbell's Lake House 33-34
Cannady's Cafe 34-35, 70, 104, 161
Cannady's Grocery 34-35, 104, 161
Cape Galena Post Office 35
Cape View Resort 3
Captain's Fancy Resort, 116
Carl's Oil Company 4
Carpenter Developments 182
Casino Pier Cruises 131
Cedar Crest Resort 21
Cedar Dale Springs 90
Cedar Green Resort 200
Central Bancompany 18
Cental Bank, Lake of the Ozarks ....
17-18, 30
Charlie's Resort 65
Char-Mar-Cove Resort 116
Chatterton's Cottages 56
Chet's Anchor Inn .. 36, 37, 38, 82, 102
Chet's Fun Spot 38
Chet's House of Gifts & Eats 37
Chet's Restaurant 37
Chinquapin Cottages 200
Christmas Tree Court 38-39, 54
Churchill's Bridgeport 82, 183, 192
Claud White's Store 162
Clear Water Beach 182
Clear Water Camp 90
Clearwater Resort 203
Cleland's Cottages 39, 174
Cleman Mill 6
Cliff Haven Resort 3
Climax Springs Hotel 40
Coakley Mill 164
Coakley Springs Hatchery Resort 43, 44
Cobb's Wayside Inn 54
Coelleda Post Office 45
Coffman Beach Resort 56
Cole Camp Post Office 45
Collins Oakwood Resort 36
Compass Point Resort 173
Conard Drug Store 162
Condee & Campbell Company 107
Conrad's Anchor Inn 37
Conrad's Cabin Court 93, 160
Cooper's Antiques 54
Cooper's Camp 60, 136
Copper Kettle Cafe 93, 161
Corwin News Agency 55
Cove Lodge Cottages 47-48
Cowan's 5-Acre Resort 178, 205
Crestwood Cottages 5, 36
Crestwood Resort 3
Cromer's Meat Market 73
Cunningham Barber Shop 161
Cunningham Souvenirs 93, 161
Curtright Springs Camp 90
Damsel Cafe & Club 49-50
Damsel Dry Cleaners 49
Damsel Post Office 49
Deer Motel 117, 143
DeGraffenreid Boat Dock 217
Delaney Boat Yard 178
Devall's Lakeview Camp 183
Diamond Filling Station 165, 166
Digger O'Dell's Resort 21
Dillon, Read & Company 14, 206
Dixcel Service Station 161
Dixon's Oak Grove Beach 155
Doe Run Lead Company 207
Dog 'n Suds 143
Dogpatch Cafe 50-51
Dogpatch Village 50-52
Dogpatch 50-52

Dogwood Hills Golf Course 188
Domenico's Restaurant 38
Down-Town Mini Golf 64
Dr. Kaiser's Cottages 5, 52-53
Dr. Matthew's Cafe, Drugs 53-54
Drift-In Resort 200
Duckworth's Camp 57-58, 72, 92
Duncan Hines Company 61
Dunn's Bottling Works 162
E. R. Smith Ice Plant 59
Ebert's Beach Resort 21, 60
Echo Valley Camp 60, 136
Edgewater Beach Resort 60-61
Edgewater Boat Dock 61
Edison Illuminating Company 206
Edmond's Theater 23
EEBCO Marine 116
El Donna Motel 61
El Kay Motel 61-62, 125
El Rancho of the Ozarks ... 62-63, 146
Eldon Advertiser 111, 129, 195
Eldon Bakery 161
Eldon Cheese Company 161
Eldon Hardware, Lumber Company 161
Eldon Inn 61
Elliott Construction Company 196
Ellis Rod & Gun Club Resort . 53, 199
Evelyn's Rathskeller 183
F. C. Arnold Realty 35, 70
F. R. Dutton & Associates 6
Fajen Lumber Company 24
Fantasy World Caverns 193, 194-196
Farmers Fund Inc. 13
Faylor's Lake Trailer Court 200
Fender's Snug Harbor 117
First National Bank 97
Fish Haven Camp 65-66, 161
Flack Resort 22, 115
Flanders Cave 66-67, 193, 195
Fleetwood Lodge & Dock 67, 161
Folded Hills Dining Room 35, 70, 156
Forrester's Beach Resort 70-72, 102
Forth View Resort 72, 92
Frack's Acre 61, 72-73, 161, 183
Frack's Barber Shop 73
Frack's Cafe 73
Frank's Minnows 74
Frank's Motel 74
Frank's Resort 74, 161
Frazee's Modern Cabin 117
Fred Cossey Camp 39, 161, 174
Freidrich Resort 136
Frick & Frack 165
Fulton Iron Works 93
Fun City USA 167
Gambles Store 35
Gateway Cafe 217
Gateway Lodge, Cottages 200, 211
Gatlin's Boat Yard 203
Gay's Tavern 144
Gensert's Texaco Station 161
Glaize Bridge Liquors 183
Glaize Rathskeller 86-87
Globe Mining, Smelting Works 88
Golden Rule Resort 65
Golden Sunset Cafe, Cabins 161
Gordon's Drug Store 92, 93
Gordon's Restaurant 93
Gore's Boat Yard 22, 77-78, 82, 161
Gore's Marine 78
Gov. McClurg Ferry Lines 80, 82
Gov. McClurg Ferry 29, 78, 79-81, 217
Gov. McClurg Showboat 78, 82-83
Grace Lin Resort 203
Grafton Boat Works 79
Grand Glaize Cafe 86-87, 183
Grand Glaize Resort 183
Grand View Camp 151
Gravois Beach Anchorage 89
Gravois Beach Resort 53, 89-90, 121
Green & White Camp 205
Greer's Resort 4, 36
Grewell's 5-Acre Resort 178
Guy Houston Company 14
H. B. Hart Fishing Pier 90
Hackberry Camp 217

Ham's Kottage Kamp 136, 184
Happy Days Resort 90-91, 116, 200, 212
Hare & Hare 127
Harland Bartholomew & Associates 127
Harmony Cove Resort 202
Harrico Cabin Camp 161
Harwood Motor Lodge 168
Hastain Post Office 92
Hawkeye Cabins, Service 92, 161
Hazelcrest Resort 161
Headwater's Motel 217
Heckerman's Cottage Camp 92-93
Heckerman's Service Station 92
Heritage Inn 62
Hickory Point Resort 178
Hildebrand's Camp, Resort ... 93-95, 161
Holiday House 95-97, 99, 129, 131, 161, 205
Holsman's Paradise Beach 67
Hopi Camp, Cottages 97, 162
Hopi Motel 97
Hot Fish Cafe 86
Hultsman Oil Company 86
Hymes Kottage Kamp # 1 .... 20, 37, 102, 161, 182, 192
Hymes Kottage Kamp # 2 .... 37, 102
Idle Days & Gala Resort 103-104
Idle Time Excursion Boat 82
Idlewild Court 1, 104-105
Imperial Electric Light & Power Company, ... 206
Indian Burial Cave 105-106, 194
Indian Creek Mines 88
Indian Creek Resort 56
Irontown Ferry 107-108
Irontown Post Office 107
Island View Resort 36
J Bar H Rodeo 33, 109-110
Jackson's Beach 217
Jacob's Cave 38, 53, 54, 66, 110-113, 193, 212
James House 198
Jeff's Anchorage Resort 89
Jeff's Mobile Home Park 89
Jefferson City Daily Tribune 194
Jeffries Boat Dock, Barge 86, 113-115
Jeffries Camp 114
Jeffries Cottages 114
Jeffries Ozark Cafe 115, 183
Jenn's Point Comfort 115
Jester's Camp 3, 91, 116
Jo Jo's Restaurant 180
Jock Reeder's Resort 199
Johann Service Station, Camp 161
John Pepper's Cabin Camp 23
Johnson's Snug Harbor 116-117
Joyce Motel 117-118
Kaiser Post Office 119-120
Kalfran Lodge 120-121, 124
Kansas City Finance Co. 13
Kansas City Joint Stock Land Bank 13
Kansas City Journal Post 99
Kansas City Star 197
Kapilana Resort, 124 182
Kavanaugh's Gravois Beach 121
Kelly's Modern Cottages 3, 116
Kepner's Cottage Camp ... 161, 182, 183
Keys Resort 91
KFRU Radio Station 146
Kirkwood Lodge 2, 121, 123-124, 156
Knifebird Indian Shop 161
KRMS Radio Station 132
Lake Breeze Resort 136, 184
Lake Center Resort 49-50, 56
Lake Chateau Best Western 182
Lake Edge Resort 102
Lake Fork Heights 61, 125
Lake Lumber Company 2, 105, 183, 213, 215, 218
Lake of the Ozarks News ... 22, 23, 32, 56, 80, 110, 114, 123, 130, 145, 150, 156, 166, 170, 172, 186, 197, 201
Lake Ozark Ice & Storage 161

Lake Ozark Post Office 130
Lake Ozark Service Station 92
Lake View Beach Resort 191
Lake Village Resort 136
Lakeside Casino Dock 82
Lakeside Casino Restaurant 67, 99, 129, 131-132, 145, 161, 218
Lakeside Courts 120
Lakeside Resort 47
Lakeview Cafe 115, 183
Lakeview Heights Land Company 126, 132-133
Lakeview Height Post Office ... 133, 134
Land's End Condos 173
Lane's Resort 203
Larry Don Excursion Boat 218
Lazy Days Condos 135
Lazy Days Resort 134-135, 161
Leaches Shoreline Resort 89
Lefty's Little Steak House 87
Lehr's Cafe 161
Lillibridge Camp 60, 136
Link's Landing 37
Little Bohemian Resort 161
Little Niangua Post Office 45
Little Sunrise Lodge 5
Lodge of the Four Seasons 82
Lone Oak Point Resort 191
Longacres Beach 178, 205
Lowell's Boat dock 137-138, 162
Lucas Lodge Camp 30
Lucky Strike Resort 155
Mai Tai Resort 173
Mai Tai Top Deck Restaurant 87
Malibu Beach Resort .. 139-140, 161, 162
Malibu Beach Yacht Basin 140
Manning's Wayside Inn 54
Maples Motel 161
Massman Construction Company 85
McClain's Camp 30, 84
McCoy Resort 36
McDonald's Restaurant 74
Mel Adkin's Camp (see Adkin's Camp)
Mel Adkin's Airplane Landing Facility 3
Mickeyland Resort 178
Midland Erection Company 208
Mill Creek Resort, Marina 91, 116
Millard's Lucky Point Resort .. 136, 184
Miller County Autogram 76, 144, 150, 185, 214
Mills Motel 18
Minder's Grocery 35
Missouri Aquarium 74
Missouri Hydro-Electric Power Company 12-14, 95, 148, 177, 190, 206
Missouri Pacific Railroad 10, 11, 63, 126, 211
Missouri Transit Lines 189
Missouri-Illinois Railroad 207
Mitchell's Resort 205
Moore's Motel 143
Mooring Yacht Club 140
Morgan's Service Station 162
Mountain Terrace Resort 74, 143
Municipal Electric Lighting Company . 205
Musser's Ozark Resort 62, 143-146
Musser's Ozark Tavern 25, 62, 143-146
Nature's Haven Resort 36
Navajo Beach Resort 151
Neely's Cafe 115, 183
Niangua Bridge Camp 19, 20, 154
Night Hawk Tavern 25
Nolan's Country Music Hall 120
North Shore Camp 217
O'Brien Lumber Company 162
Oak Grove Beach Resort 155
Oak Hill Court, Resort 74, 143
Oak Royal Water Ski Show 67
Oakdell Inn 161
Onyx Quarries Company 6
Orchid Motel 74
Osage Beach Post Office 1, 35, 70, 104, 155-156
Osage Beach Tavern, Hotel 25, 123-124, 156-158, 161

Osage Development Company 56
Osage Garage 161
Osage House 173
Osage Inn 79, 81-82
Osage Iron Works 106, 158-160
Osage Marine 47
Otten's Lakeview Camp 182-183
Otto's Gift Shop 73
Overfelt Grocery 161
Ozark Cafe, Cabins 217
Ozark Caverns 41, 42, 163-165, 175, 194
Ozark Central Telephone Company 161
Ozark Inn, Cafe 165-167
Ozark Land Company 200
Ozark Opry 106, 132
Ozark Realty 179
Ozark Tackle, Supply 161
Ozark Tavern Hotel 25, 167-168
Ozark Water Ski Thrill Show 67
Ozark Woodcrafts 78
Paradise Hidden Acres 182, 217
Parcell's Cove Camp 217
Pasta House 174
Payne's Souvenirs 93
Pelican Point Resort 182
Phillips Petroleum Company ... 62, 142
Phone Station 179
Pickett Line Inn 183
Pioneer Construction Company 85
Pistol Club 80
Pla-Mor Beach 184
Pla-Mor Mini Golf 64
Pla-Port Resort, Lighthouse 56, 71, 126, 161, 170-173, 219
Platt Boat & Dry Dock 182
Pleasure Cove Resort 21
Pooler's Cottages, Store, Bus Stop 39, 161, 173-174
Port Arrowhead 78
Porter's Twin Coves 4
Potted Steer 87
Powell's Supreme View Cottages 162, 174-175, 213
Prewitt's Point Development 18
Purvis Beach Cafe 177
Purvis Beach Post Office 177
Purvis Beach Resort 176-178
Quails Nest Motel 143
Quigley's Resort 53, 89
Ranch House Grill 179
Randle's Court, Coffee Shop 26
Red Bird Camp 162
Red Feather Cafe, Camp 179-180,
Red Hollow Resort 203
Reeder's Resort 5
Reveille Newspaper 162, 215
Riffle Inn 75
Riverview Heights Camp 182
Riverview Post Office 180
Roaring Oaks Camp 182
Roberts Rodeo Company Ranch 109
Rock Harbor Resort 36
Rock Hill Camp 182, 183
Rock Island Depot 21, 63, 64
Rock Village Resort 21
Rockwood Court 74, 143
Rockledge Resort 36
Rockway Cabin Court 183
Rockway Center 92, 183
Rocky Mount Post Office 184
Rocky Mount Resort 56
Runners Rest Lodge 201
Sagrada Ferry 23, 181, 186
Schneider's Resort 21
Schreit's Lodge 36
Scottie's Old Mill Resort 217
Seibert Contracting Company 79
Seven Seas Hotel 75
Shady Grove Bayou Camp 217
Shady Point Camp 182
Shady Shore Resort 47, 56,
Shady Slope Camp 182, 188-189
Shawnee Bluff Inn 18
Shawnee View Camp 217,
Sherwood Resort, Restaurant, 20, 102, 182, 192-193

Shoney's Restaurant 171, 220
Sidwell Barbershop 31
Silver Moon Camp 3, 91, 116
Silver Sand Resort 205
Sinclair Gas 162
Singing Hills Resort 21, 60, 162
Snell Groves Resort 91
Spalding Liquors & Gifts 93
St. Joe Lead Company 207
St. Louis Gas Company 132
St. Louis Illuminating Company..... 206
Standard Oil Distributors 162
Stanton Novelty Company 161
Stark Caverns 66, 193-196
Stoecker's Cottages 162
Stone & Webster Engineering, Inc. 14, 84, 207
Stone House Post Office 21
Stover Coal Mine 88, 184
Stover's Shady Rest Resort 182
Strickland's Cottages 105
Strickland's Texaco Service 105
Stults-Drummond Camp 205
Stupp Brothers Bridge & Iron Company 85
Sunrise Beach Corp. 196-198
Sunrise Inn 196-197
Sunrise Lodge 199
Sutton Refrigeration 161
Sverdrup & Parcel Engineering Inc. 84, 85
Swinging Bridge Camp 217
Tal Gorer Refreshment Stand 161
Tanner's Station & Garage 23
Taylor's Grocery 204
Teeter's Hill Resort 30
Temple Resort 124
Thickstun's Store 5, 199
Thomas Cabins & Cafe 161
Thomas Ozark Inn 166
Timberline Motel 54
Tip Top 217
Ti-Sun Terrace Resort 5, 199
Tonka Villa Resort, Restaurant 154, 199
Top O'The Hill Grocery 54
Tracey's Shoreline Resort 53, 89
Trail's End Camp 91, 200, 212
Trammell's Redwoods Resort 136
Troutdale Ranch 47, 90
Turrin's Cafe 115
Tuttle, Ayers, Woodward Engineering Company 126
Tuxhorn Airway Lodge 200-202
Tuxhorn Resort 200-202
Tweedie's Cottages 136
Twin Bays Resort 90, 202-203
Twin Beach Resort 182
Two Waters Resort 56, 90, 91, 203-204
Union Electric Boat Dock 67, 99, 129, 205
Union Electric Land & Development Company 96, 97, 98-101, 128, 129, 131, 132, 190, 205-206
Union Electric Light & Power Company 1, 12, 14, 29, 67, 77, 81, 84, 86, 95, 108, 126, 128, 135, 137, 148, 150, 159, 177, 185, 190, 206-207, 216, 220
Uncle Jim's Resort 178, 205
Urlaub's Cabin Court 38, 54
V Red Moore Cafe, Novelties 92, 93, 161
Val-E-Vue Resort 21
Van's Motel 166
Versailles Gazette 182
Versailles Leader 108, 122, 195, 212
Versailles Orchard Company 111
Versailles Post Office 211
Versailles Statesman 126
Village Marina Boat Sales 173
W. H. Powell Lumber Company 31
Wagon Wheel Resort 136
Walgreen's Drug Store 18
Wal-Mart Supercenter 18, 39, 92, 173, 174, 179

Walt Reid's Camp 205
Walter's Modern Camp.................... 162
Wanta Linga Camp........................... 217
Ward C. Gifford Realty Company...... 8
Ware's Cabin Camp 162, 213-214
Warsaw Times 208, 214
Washburn's Point 90, 91, 204
Water's Edge Camping 200
Waterfront RV Park 30
Watkin's Ozark Jamboree................. 120
Watson's Niangua Bridge Camp .. 137, 154
Wayham Post Office 135
Wayside Pottery Shop 61, 73
Westview Tavern, Hotel........... 25, 217
Whispering Oaks Resort 3
White Branch Cafe........................... 217
White Branch Resort 217
White House Hotel...... 59, 92, 93, 131, 132,145, 161, 217-219
White Way Beach 178, 205
White's Cash Market........................ 162
Wildwood Resort.............................. 202
Willard Drugs 162
Williams Grocery 162
Wilson's Hill 162
Wilson's Resort 47
Win-Rock Marina 136
Wiseman's Service Station 162
Wonder Bay Resort 182
Wood's Lake Cove Lodge 47, 116, 162
Woodbine Cafe 162
Young's Cafe 161
Zebra Grocery 220
Zebra Hotel 219
Zebra Post Office 49, 155, 156, 170, 219, 220
Zora Heights 24, 220
Zora Post Office 220

LAKE ROADS, COVES & SELECTED GEOGRAPHIC FEATURES INDEX

Adkins Village Road 2
American Legion Drive....................... 3
Anchorage Drive 121
Anchorage Road 89
Ancient Grotto 193, 209
Anderson Hollow Bay 4, 83
Angel's Shower........................... 42, 165
Apple storage, in cave 111
Arnhold Cave 5
Arnhold Natural Bridge 152
Arnhold Onyx Cave.................... 6, 152
Arrow Point Cave.................. 7, 30, 194
Artesian well............................... 10, 42
Auglaize Bridge 76
Aurora Cave 194
Aurora Caverns 194
Aurora Springs Cave 194
Autumn Lane 22
Barnes Hollow Cove.......................... 60
Barnes Hollow 21
Bat guano 176
Beachwood Drive 199
Ben Anderson Hollow..................... 188
Bennett Spring 138
Berry Cave 193
Big Bend 23-24, 186
Big Buffalo Cove....... 26, 180, 181, 220
Big Buffalo Creek 180, 220
Big Gravois Creek 75
Big Mouth Cave............................... 105
Big Niangua Caverns 193
Blue Ridge Road.............................. 119
Big Spring Branch Hollow & Cove 94, 179
Blue Springs 94
Bluff Drive...................... 173, 179, 213
Bluff Spring 10
Bluffs Circle 101

Boat Shelter Cave 24-25, 84
Bogue Bay 87
Bollinger Creek Cove 81, 107
Booger Allen Cave 57
Boyler's Spring 26
Boylers Mill Road 220
Bridal Cave 27-29, 165, 193
Brockman's Island 11, 30
Brown Bend 185
Brush Creek Cove 176, 205
Brush Creek Hollow 178
Brushy Hollow Creek Cove ... 132, 134
Brushy Creek 133
Buffalo Creek 46
Bull Run Bluff 152, 153
Bunch Cave 153, 193
Buried treasure 105
Camp Branch Road 53
Camp Hohn Drive 107
Cape Galena 35
Cape Hollow Cove 3, 35
Carroll (Carrot) Bluff 190
Cartwright Springs 177
Castaway Cove 67
Cedar Creek Cove 87
Chief Ne-Ong-Wah 5, 38
Chiles Island 188
Chimney Cove 115
Chimney Rock Bluff 38
Chimney Rock Cave 5, 38, 152
Chimney Rock 5, 38, 152
Chinquapin Spring 201
Climax Spring 39
Climax Springs Cave 39, 41
Coakley Cave 41, 43
Coakley Hollow Cove 41, 163
Coakley Hollow 41, 84
Coakley Spring Branch 42
Coakley Spring 42-43
Coal mining 88
Cobblestone 81, 95, 157, 203
Cole Camp Creek 46
Cole Camp Hollow & Cove 46-47
Collin's Spring & Lake 47
Community Bridge 101
Cozy Cove Road 200
Crabtree Cove 200
D Road 105
Darby Hollow Cove 70, 120, 121
Deer Creek Hollow Cove 57, 72, 92
Deer Creek 46, 57, 92
Dogwood trees 52
Drum Rock 54-55
Dry Auglaize Creek 76
Dry Branch Cave 55
Eadson's Spring Branch 45
East Fork, Little Gravois Creek 15
El Rancho Junction 62, 143, 144
Enchanted Caverns 194
Endangered bats 24, 165, 176
Fantasy World Caverns 193, 194-197
Fault 152
Fens .... see wet meadows
Flanders Cave 66, 193
Fleetwood Cove 67
Flood of 1943 68-69
Flynn Road 143
Fontana Lane 9
Forrester's Beach Road 70
Fort Leonard Wood Recreation Area 84
Frudeger Road 74
Galena Point 3
Galena 35
Gibson Point 91, 116, 200
Gladstone Cove 75, 87, 142, 184
Gladstone-Linn Creek Road ... 176-177
Glaize Creek 1
Glaize Bridge 76-77
Grand Auglaize Creek 76, 84
Grand Glaize Bridge 36, 37, 47, 76, 82, 84, 86, 102, 103, 113, 115, 116, 182, 188, 192
Grandglaize Creek 76, 84, 141
Gravois Creek 142, 184
Gravois Mills Spring 47, 90
Gulliver's Ridge 44

Gunpowder making 27
Ha Ha Tonka Cove 138, 153
Ha Ha Tonka Spring 137, 153
Ha Ha Tonka State Park 27
Happy Days Road 116
Harmony Mission Trace 75, 184
Harpers Hollow Cove 102, 120
Hawks Nest Road 115, 183
Healing Spring 10
Hidden Acres Road 74, 117, 143
Honey Run Hollow Cove 84
Horseshoe Bend Road 100-101
Horseshoe Bend 4, 98-100, 135, 190
Human remains 112
Humes Spring & Lake 47
Hunter Road 116
Hurricane Deck Bridge 80, 81, 85, 155, 187
Hwy. 5 Niangua Bridge 80, 81, 85, 137, 152, 153, 154, 200
Indian artifacts 7, 8, 105
Indian Burial Cave 105, 194
Indian burial mound 88
Indian burials 105, 197
Indian Creek Cove 87
Indian Creek Mines 88
Indian Creek 21, 22, 46
Indian Hills Road 5
Indian legend 203
Irish Drive 200
Iron mining & smelting 81
Iron smelter 158
Jack Salmon (Walleye) 110
Jacob's Cave 38, 110-113, 193
Jade Road 60
Jeffries Point 42, 84
Jeffries Road 102, 103, 120
Jennings Branch Cove 67, 99
Jo Jo Drive 173, 179
Jones Drive 60
Kaiser Forest Lookout Tower 48
Kaiser Road 119
Kalfran Drive 120
Kansas City Way 199
Kapilana Road 182
Kay's Point 135
Kaysinger Bluff 121-122
Klinger Cave 124, 193, 209
Ladinsky Bend 152
Lake Benton 125, 147-150
Lake Creek 46
Lake McClurg 125, 147-150
Lake of the Ozarks State Park 4, 5, 24, 25, 30, 42, 43, 76, 119, 163
Lake of the Ozarks, Naming of 147
Lake Ozark Forest 47
Large trees 88
Lazy Days Road 134
Lick Branch Cove 60, 135, 136
Lighthouse Road 71, 170
Linn Creek Bend 190
Linn Creek Cove 9, 136
Linn Creek Hollow 31, 59
Linn Creek Road 135
Linn Creek Toll Bridge 19, 79, 152
Little Boat Shelter Cave 84
Little Buffalo Creek 27, 46
Little Gravois Cove 53, 87, 89, 121
Little Gravois Creek 11, 15, 210
Little Mouth Cave 105
Lost Boys Cave 57
Lovers Leap Bluff 152
Lovers Leap 79
Malibu Beach Road 139
Matt's Hill 53
McClain's Point 84
McDowell Cave 24
Mel Adkin's Airplane Landing Facility 141
Mill Creek Bridge 77, 141-142
Mill Creek Cove 2, 87, 88, 91, 141
Mill Creek Marina Road 116
Mill Creek Hollow 30
Mill Creek 75, 141
Miller County Cave 194
Miller Creek Cove 116

Miller Hollow Cove 22, 115, 188
Mineral springs 39, 40, 41
Mining 4, 88, 107, 110, 142, 158
Missouri Geological Survey 47
Moonlight Bay 3, 35
Mount Alfter 181
Mystery Lake, 28 29
Mystic River Cave 193
Natural bridge 4, 83
Neongwah Bear Cave 29, 152
Niangua River 154
Nichols Road 188
Normandy Road 156
North Mill Creek 88
Oak Bend Road 200
Oak Bluff 152
Observation Heights 170, 171, 172
Old Bagnell Road 66
Old Five Road 53
Old Salt Road 187
Onyx Cave 6, 153
Onyx mining 6
Osage Beach Road 70, 74, 75, 92, 104, 123, 134, 156, 183
Osage Indian Trail 75
Osage River Breaks 46
Osage Trails Drive 107
Owens Point Road 60
Ozark Caverns..... 24, 41, 43, 163-165, 194
Palisades 93, 94, 169
Paradise Cove 67
Party Cove 4, 83
Passover Road 156
Pelican Point 182
Perched water table 42
Picnic Hollow 92
Pogue Hollow Cove 77
Porter Mill Cove 205
Possum Trot Hollow Cove 180
Prairie Hollow Cave........... 44, 175-176
Prairie Hollow Spring Cave 44, 45
Prehistoric bones 113
Public Beach No. 1 163
Purvis Beach Road 178
Raccoon Hollow Cove 87
Racetrack Hollow Cove 179
Ray Shoal No. 1 220
Red Arrow Road 60, 135
Red Bud Road 38, 71, 156, 170, 219
Red Hollow Cove 151
Region Recreation Area 48
River Cave 193
Riverview Bridge 181
Road P 91
Rocky Cliff 132
Ross Creek 46
Round Spring 10
Route DD 23
Route F 79, 200
Route FF 23, 185
Route HH 87
Route KK 22, 49, 93, 115
Route MM 191
Route O 182
Route P 116, 200
Route RA 107
Route TT 53, 110
Route V 92
Route W 88, 184
Route Y 184
Sagrada Bridge 23, 181, 185-187
Saline Creek 9, 124
Salt Hollow Cove 188
Salt Hollow 187
Salt Ridge 4, 187
Salt Shoal No. 1 188
Salt Shoal No. 2 188
Saltpeter 27
Santa Fe Road 203
School of the Osage 119, 120
Shawnee Bend Preserve 191
Shawnee Bend 98, 190-191
Shelida Hill 21, 80
Shoop Hollow Cove 169
Soap Creek Cove 87, 91
South Mill Creek 88

Spirit Lake 29
Spring River 38
Springs 9, 39, 90, 94, 210
Stark Caverns 193-196
Stephen Houser Shoals 135
Stephen's Island 135
Stone Face 5, 38, 152
Stover Coal Bank 184
Swiss Village Road 93
Sycamore record tree 88
Tan-Tar-A Island 169
The Rock 101
Three Seasons Road 22, 188
Thunder Mountain 28, 152
Tunnel Dam 99, 154, 216
Turkey Bend 115, 190
Turkey Creek 46
Turkey Hollow 92
Tuxhorn Air Port 201
Twin Bays Road 151, 202
Twin Islands 3, 35
U. S. Geological Survey 47, 76
Underground lake 28, 29
Upper Suspension Bridge 18, 29, 207-208
Upside Down Bridge 85
Utica Drive 155
V Road 11
Vernon Cave 193, 209-210
Washburn's Point 91
Welcher Hollow Cove 155
Wet Glaize Creek 76
Wet meadows 42, 165
Williams Creek 45
Willow Springs & Cave 4
Willow Springs Hollow 4
Wilson Bend 47
Winn Road 182
Wright Cave 7, 30, 194
Wrights Creek 15
Y Road 9
Zebra Bridge 84, 85

TOWNS & VILLAGES INDEX

Aurora Springs 9, 13, 209
Bagnell 1, 11, 14, 16, 88, 126, 148
Barnett 21, 56
Barnettsville 21
Blakey Town 45
Bonds Mines 88
Boyler's Mill 27, 181
Brumley 7, 17, 30, 76, 141
Camdenton 2, 5, 6, 18, 20, 25, 31, 38, 52, 60, 61, 97, 109, 125, 137, 154, 162, 163, 167, 199
Cape Galena 35, 75
Capps 17
Climax Springs 39, 40, 41, 106, 107, 158, 181, 185
Coelleda 44-45
Cole Camp 45, 46, 132, 220
Conner's Camp Ground 128
Crest 46
Crockerville 46
Damsel 49, 56, 188
Damsite 23, 128
Easterville 136-137
Edmonson 46
Eldon 9, 13, 18, 25, 26, 30, 33, 56, 61, 62, 63, 124, 126, 143, 161, 194, 209
Gladstone 75, 87, 142
Gravi Mills 89, 184
Gravois Mills 38, 47, 53, 89, 90, 91, 110, 116, 121, 122, 141, 151, 200, 202, 203
Hastain 57, 72m 92
Irontown 107
Kaiser 119
Lake Ozark 8, 14, 17, 18, 30, 33, 50, 59, 60 65, 66, 67, 68, 74, 77, 82, 92, 95, 98, 100, 117, 128, 131, 143, 151, 160, 165, 217
Lakeside 131
Lakeview Heights 133

Laurie 18, 75, 182
Linn Creek 1, 9, 16, 18, 19,31, 41, 42, 59, 81, 108, 134, 136, 140, 163, 169, 188
Little Niangua 44
Lively 181
Mining Port 87, 142
Mt. Hulda 46
Olean 13
Osage Beach 1, 4, 17, 18, 20, 22, 25, 30, 34, 36, 39, 47, 61, 70, 72, 74, 82, 84, 86, 92, 93, 102, 103, 104, 113, 115, 116, 120, 123, 134, 139, 155, 156, 161, 170, 173, 174, 179, 182, 192, 213
Passover 1, 119
Poplar 46
Raymond 46
Riffletown 75, 87, 142
Riverview Heights 46
Riverview 23, 181
Roach 19, 175
Rocky Mount 60, 80, 135, 184
Sagrada 23, 181, 185
Spring Camp 128
Spring Valley 181
Stover 23, 26, 132, 180, 220
Sunrise Beach 3, 5, 35, 52, 155, 176, 196, 199, 200, 205
Tahoma 46
Todd 181
Tuscumbia 17, 68
Versailles 38, 53, 56, 110, 126, 191, 210
Victor City 128
Warsaw 18, 25, 29, 56, 79, 121, 126, 132, 207, 214
Wayham 135
Zebra 56, 85, 126, 156, 219
Zora 46, 181

PEOPLE INDEX

Ackerman, Mr. & Mrs. Louis 67
Adams, Fuzzy 219
Adams, L. L. 197
Adkins, Mel 2-3, 91, 141
Alfter, Judge John H. 181
Allee, Dr. W. L. 126
Allen, Clifford 219
Allen, Ed 61
Allen, Mary Ann 61
Alton, John 79, 82
Alton, Tom 79, 82
Amick, Dr. A. J. 124
Ammons, Ben 3-4
Anderson, C. P. 5
Anderson, Frank 219, 220
Anderson, George 191
Andrews, Elizabeth Riffle 201, 203
Andrews, Frank V. 130
Anthony, Gov. George 10
Arnhold, Dorotha 7
Arnhold, George 6-7
Arnold, F. C. 35, 70
Arnold, Mercer 197
Arnold, Mr. & Mrs. E. A. 98
Atkinson, John M. 198
Atkinson, M. E. 202
Atkisson, J. A. 105
Atkisson, James F. 105
Atteberry, Magnus 160
Atteberry, W. W. 17
Atteberry, Ward 160
Ayers, Dean 132
Ayers, Ruby 132
Baden, Elihu 27
Bagnell, Robert 11, 13, 16
Bagnell, William 11, 13, 16, 148
Bailey, C. E. 79
Bailey, Rev. Morris 111
Baker, Louis I. 126
Bales, Dave 219
Ballenger, Harry 160

Bankson, Abbie Woolery 31-32
Banner, Jim 28, 31, 165, 196
Barnes, J. H. 20
Barnes, Judge C.A 198
Barry, I. N. 133
Barry, Robert D. 133
Bashore, Glen 196
Bass, C. B. 17
Baulicault, Marcel 162
Bedford, Thos. P. 198
Behymer, F. A. 221
Belcher, Donald D. Jr. 47
Bemis, Tex 67
Benne, Betty 116
Benne, Harry 116
Bennett, Phil A., 196
Benton, Thomas Hart 147, 148
Berry, Lester 22, 161
Biggs, V. M. 134, 161
Biley, Arthur 108
Billings, Judge James V. (Josh) 145
Biselx, Francis 62-63, 146
Blair, John 162
Blakely, Vic 124
Boer, Joseph H. 87
Bollinger, Stephen 159
Bollinger, William 159
Boots, Lloyd A. 25-26
Boulden, Mr. & Mrs. H. H. 91
Bowman, Deane 200
Bowman, Don 200
Boyd, Judge J. M. 145
Boyer, Clarence 204
Breden, Maynard W. 199
Brill, T. C. 217
Brinkman, Silvia 95
Brockman, C. E. 161
Brockman, John N. 14
Brockman, W. S. 14
Brockman, W. W. 30
Brown, Aaron 3
Brown, Leah 3
Brown, Moreland 126, 160
Buckhart, William E. 146
Buehler, Carl 161
Buehler, Henry A., Ph.D. 13
Buehler, Kent 196
Buell, W. A. 196
Bugeon, Harold 217
Bunch, J. W. 162
Bunker, William 194
Burd, Les 92
Burke, Lorraine 221
Butts, Elmer 203
Butts, Helen 203
Bybee, W. A. 157
Byler, Jacob 26
Byler, Mary Maree 27
Cahill, William 144
Calfee, Dr. J. W. 35
Campbell, Alex J. 107, 159
Campbell, Jewel Marshall 33-34
Campbell, Joseph Audell 33-34
Campbell, Margaret 34
Campbell, William, 34
Cannady, Mr. & Mrs. A. B. 34-35
Capps, Lindsey 108
Carlson, Elom F. 47
Carmack, P. M. 14
Carnes, W. R. 17
Carrington, Ed 204
Carrington, Marge 204
Caruthers, J. Henry 197
Caufield, Gov. Henry S. 149
Christensen, Lawrence O. 221
Claiborn, B. O. 1
Claiborn, Dr. E. G. 162
Clark, C. B. 161
Clark, John 130
Clayton, Ross 161
Collins, Andrews 47
Condee, Dr. A. 107, 159
Conrad, Fr. William J. 160, 162
Conrad, Herb 37
Conrad, Mabel 37
Cook, L. L. 86, 99, 118, 157, 211

Cossey, Fred 39, 161, 174
Costa, Damian 200
Cox, A. D. 189
Cox, W. L. 66
Craft, Len 3
Craft, Ruby 3
Crain, Aaron 152
Crane, Kent 17
Cravens, Walter 13, 190
Craycraft, Jacob 110
Critton, Keith 23, 181
Cromer, Francis 61
Cromer, Shirley 61
Crosby, G. E. 29, 126, 216
Crow, Charley 4
Cunningham, Bob 93
Cunningham, C. J. 161
Cunningham, George 15, 161
Davenport, John 66
Davis, H. L. 72
Davis, Opal 103
Dawdy, Randy 222, 223
Dean, Bill 60-61
Dean, Clara 60-61
Dean, Mike 60-61
Dech, Fred 143
Dech, Lena 143
DeGraffenreid .... Delia, 217
DeGraffenreid .... G. Riley, 217
DeLozier, Abram E. 107
Dennis, Flora Belle 214
Depping, Henry 197
DeShetley, Dr. William 197
Dice, Joseph A. .. 77, 141-142, 207, 208
Dixon, E. W. 155
Dolby, Matt 161
Donnelly, Gov. Phil M. 109
Downing, Rev. William C. 9
Drenon, Roy 57, 92
Duckworth, J. W. 57
Dudley, Dan D. 188
Duffy, Mr. & Mrs. Bruce J. 166
Earngey, Bill 63, 221
Eastwood, Clint 109
Edmonds, Chester "Chet" 23-24, 181, 186-187
Edwards, Samuel 79
Egan, L. H. 207
Elam, Al G. 17
Elmer, William P. 150
Ernst, Betty 60
Ernst, Marty 60
Estes, J. K. 162
Ester, Lester 117
Evans, Bill 161
Evans, Hazel 161
Ezard, Maud 219
Ezard, Teresa 219
Ezard, Uncle Tom 219
Firoved, Don 91
Firoved, Iris 91
Fleener, Jay 203
Fleener, Nina 203
Fleetwood, Charles "Charley" 67
Fletcher, Gordon C. 117
Flippin, Tip, ... 23, 181
Flippo, Marshall 124
Foley, William E. 221
Forrester, Ida May 71
Forrester, Thomas "Tommy" H. 70, 171
Forrester, Thomas Sr. 71
Forth, G. J. 72
Foster, Joe V. 162
Fowler, Phil 198
Frack, Harry 61, 72-23, 161
Franklin, B. Ray 25, 123, 156
Franklin, Charles 189
Franklin, Dee 189
Franklin, J. S. 17
Franklin, James A. Sr. 17
Franklin, Jimmy 157
Frederich, J. H. 126
Fremont, Gen. John C. 207
Frudeger, Frank 74, 161
Frudeger, Margaret 74

Fry, Harvey 196
Fry, Jessie 218
Fry, Lawrence M. 132, 161, 218
Fry, Vivian 196
Fuller, Ilse 62
Fuller, Floyd 62
Funk, John L. 221
Gabriel, Judge D. 196
Gampher, Loyd 162
Garvey, Dot 35, 70
Garvey, Harvey 35, 70
Gates, Allen A. 47
Geary, W. F. 220
Gerhard, Fredrick 44
Gibson, Bill 91
Gibson, Viola 91
Gier, Jacob "Jake" 66
Gifford, Romney R. 8
Gifford, Ward C. 8, 126-128
Gill, Don 146
Gilleard, Lee 224
Goering, Lorett 89
Goering, Vic 89
Gordon, Paul 92
Gore, Florence 77, 78
Gore, G. W. "Jud" 77, 78, 161
Gore, W. W. 77
Greer, Harry 161
Gulager, Glu 109
Gunnison, Lee 104
Haar, Clara 192
Haar, George 192
Haden, Robert 221
Hagadorn, Al 123
Hagadorn, Amy 123
Hagadorn, Betty 123
Hagadorn, Bill 123, 124
Hall, Russell P. 113
Halloman, Curley 103
Halloman, Vi 103
Hamlin, Ray 198
Hammitt, F. L. 196
Hanks, Fernando 19, 154
Hannaford, James 62-63, 146
Hansen, C. F. 162
Hansen, Mr. & Mrs. C. Fred 97-98
Harpham, Lucille Keller .. 137, 219, 222
Harris, K. R. 161
Harrison, Marshall 144
Harrison, Mr. & Mrs. Harry 217
Hart, H. B. 90
Harvey, R. S. 17
Harwood, Boyd H. 167-168
Harwood, Boyd W. Jr. 167-168
Hatcher, R. B. 116
Hauenstein, George T. 17
Hawkins, Chas. R. 17, 145
Hawkins, James M. 17, 30
Hawkins, Lena C. 17
Hawkins, Mabel 17, 222
Hawksley, Oscar 222
Hayes, Mr. & Mrs. C. E. 183
Hayes, Mr. & Mrs. Eli 111
Heckerman, Howard H. 92
Heckerman, Mrs. Howard 93
Helbrock, Richard W. 222
Henderson, Bud 117
Hensiek, Ed H. (El) 91
Hensiek, Jo 91
Higgins, R. Thornton 223
Hildebrand, Reinhard 93-95
Hilton, Mr. & Mrs. Bob 135
Hirsch, Ernest 217
Hobson, H. B. 27
Hockman, James T. 40
Hockman, Milton C. 40
Hockman, W. W. 39
Hoffman, Bert 54
Hoffman, Dale 197
Hohn, Clara 95
Hohn, John 95
Howard, Joe M. 142
Howser, J. L. 14
Howser, R. P. 14, 15
Hubble, Victoria 174, 222
Huffman, Alfred 151

Huffman, Letta 151
Hultgren, J. H. 167
Humes, Joseph 47
Humes, Thomas 47
Humm, C. A. 161
Hunter, John H. 27, 180, 181
Hunter, Quillie O. 49-50
Hunter, William A. 49
Hurley, Frank 112, 222
Hurley, J. F. Jr. 43
Hurley, Jane 113
Huse, George G. 217
Hutchinson, Don 183
Hutchinson, Lee 183
Hymes, "Chet" Mason 37, 102
Hymes, Charles M. 20, 102, 192
Hymes, Hazel D. 20, 102, 192
Imbrie, George H. 133
Jackson, Alexander R. 40
James, W. B. 17
Jasinsky, Dick 120
Jeffrey, Jeff 89
Jeffrey, Lavonne 89
Jeffries, Frank 114
Jeffries, J. P. 81
Jeffries, Leland 114
Jeffries, N. D. 86
Jeffries, Nellie 114
Jeffries, Robert 115
Jeffries, Roy 86, 87
Jeffries, Tolliver 114
Jeffries, Valonia 114
Jeffries, William Derrick 114, 219
Jeffries, Wilma 114
Jenkins, Judge Clayton E. 222
Jenkins, Judge Clyde Lee 222
Jester, Harry G. 116
John, Mr. & Mrs. E. J. 145
Johnson, M. P. 116-117
Johnson, Mary 140
Jones, Gordon 72
Jordan, Eddie 9
Kaiser, Dr. A. A. 5, 52
Kavanaugh, C. W. 89, 121
Kehr, J. E. 14
Kehr, Lewis 11
Kehr, Perry O. 11, 14
Kellerstrass, Ernest 122
Kelly, A. L. 161
Kelly, Arthur J. Jr. 8, 160
Kelly, Bette 199
Kelly, L. A. 126, 171
Kelly, Leonard 199
Kelly, Orville 36, 172
Kelsay, S. 156
Kirby, G. M. 110
Kirkman, Lawrence 124
Klinger, William 124, 209
Knox, B. D. 162
Koopman, Carl A. ... 139-140, 161, 162
Krehbeil, B. F. 28, 165
Kremer, Gary 16, 221, 222
Kuhn, Richard 62
Kuhn, Susan 62
Kumpf, Ernest 41
Lapp, George H. 111-112
Laurie, John 17
Lawrence, James 62-63, 144, 146
Lawrence, Martha 63
Leatherman, Ora 196
Lechner, Al 106
Lehr, W. E. 161
Lesem, Mark 30
Libby, Joe Sam 109
Loeffler, H. H. 161
Logan, Arthur "Slim" 165
Logan, Eva 165
Logan, James A. 125, 148, 149
Long, Carrie 223
Long, Ralph 17
Lowell, Elmer C. 137-138, 154, 162
Luck, Art 9
Mace, Lee 17, 106, 132
Malloy, Madeleine 200
Malloy, Raymond 200
Mara, Mrs. Tomy 200, 201, 202

Marbut, C. F. ... 142, 223
Marose, David ... 196
Marr, Dorothy ... 203
Marr, Jim ... 203
Martin, Hiram ... 197
Martin, W. P. ... 14
Mason, Robert E., D.O. ... 17
Massie, Gerald R. ... 118
Matthew, Dr. A. A. ... 53-54
Matthey, V. J. ... 205
Mattinson, S. T. ... 197
McCanse, Keith ... 197, 223
McClure, Doug ... 109
McClurg, Gov. Joseph W. ... 81, 125, 140-141, 149, 150, 152, 187
McCrory, John T. ... 219
McDonough, Peter J. ... 177
McDonough, Pricilla ... 177
McDow, Hiram ... 21
McDowell, Eva ... 213
McGinnis, Wiley ... 177
McGuire, Helen ... 103
McGuire, Paul ... 103, 135
McKee, Raymond ... 198
McMillen, L. G. ... 212
McNiel, Daniel T. ... 40
Mcquerter, H. C. ... 47
Mead, Johnnie ... 15
Mehrer, Jim ... 223
Merwin, H. B. ... 17
Miles, Frank, 79 ... 82
Millen, G. S. ... 196
Miller, Clarence ... 80
Miller, James W. ... 145
Miller, W. A. ... 9
Minder, Mr. & Mrs. Melvin ... 35
Mitchell, Mr. & Mrs. Jefferson W. ... 62, 146
Mitchell, Steve ... 224
Mitchell, Silvia J. ... 62
Moles, H. L. ... 14
Monte, Alta ... 86, 87
Moore, Dr. George M. ... 32
Moore, Red V. ... 92, 93, 132
Moore, Ted ... 145
Moreland, Fern ... 31
Morgan, Gib ... 54
Morgan, L. W. ... 162
Morgan, Ralph L. ... 162
Morgan, Scottie ... 54
Morgan, W. L. ... 217
Moulder, Dave ... 81
Musser, Clarence W. ... 144-146
Musser, L. N. ... 144
Myers, Scott ... 224
Nance, El ... 61, 125
Nance, Kay ... 61, 125
Nellans, Floyd ... 98
Nellans, Vera ... 98
Nelson, A. W. ... 201
Nelson, Harry B. ... 109, 110, 222
Nelson, Jean ... 109, 222
Newman, Alfred E. ... 52
Nichols, H. W. ... 182
Nichols, L. O. ... 18, 191
Nolan, Bob ... 120
Norquist, E. E. ... 197
O'Hara, Bishop Edwin V. ... 160, 162
Oechlc, Paul ... 161
Ohlson, Mary P. ... 165
Ohlson, Ralph H. "Ollie" .. 42, 165, 175
Olendorf, George ... 197
Owings, Mr. & Mrs. Kenneth ... 117
Paradise, Leo ... 182
Parker, Fess ... 109
Parrick, Rev. Gentry ... 19
Payne, Oliver ... 93
Perry, Miss Gene ... 108
Petts, R. B. ... 126
Pike, Zebulon ... 75, 87, 142
Plemmons, Earl A. ... 17
Pooler, J. W. ... 39, 161, 173-174
Poor, William ... 75
Pope, Arthur M. ... 1
Pope, Greenberry ... 77
Pope, Joe ... 1
Pope, John ... 1

Pope, Lee 1
Pope, Neta 7, 107, 108, 159
Pope, Vernon 1
Pope, Walter 1
Popkess, G. Edwin 8-9
Porter, C. E. 161
Potts, A. B. 178
Powell, W. H. 31
Pruitt, James 66
Purvis, Charley 177
Purvis, Ivy 177, 178
Purvis, Jack 177
Purvis, John 178
Purvis, Ora 177, 178
Rackow, Harry 60
Ramsay, Robert L. 76, 147, 223
Randle, Helen 26
Rastofer, Uncle John 88
Ray, Means 197
Raynor, Bill Sr. 8
Raynor, Tina 223
Rea, D. H. 14
Renault, Phillip 216
Richards, G. T. 162
Rieder, Al 72
Rieder, Vera 72
Riffle, Joseph B. 75
Robb, Gerry 61
Robb, Thomas 61-62
Robinett, Fred 7-8
Rockwell, Helen R. 72
Rogers, W. T. 201
Rutledge, Jack 78
Rutledge, Pee Wee 78
Schmidt, Carl 89, 121
Schopp, Gladys 120-121
Schopp, K. K. 120-121
Schopp, Kym 120
Schopp, Pat 120
Schopp, Steve 120
Schopp, Tom 120
Schultz, Gerard 223
Schwader, Nellie 203
Schwader, Oscar 203
Scott, C. G. 217
Scott, Col. R. G. 27, 81
Scott, Ellis 220
Scott, Jessie 220
Scott, Lucky 198
Shepherd, E. H. 195
Shockley, Donna 18
Shockley, Linda 18
Shockley, Mrs. Claudius 18
Shoemaker, Floyd C. 25
Shull, M. P. 155
Sidebottom, Emeline 75
Sidebottom, Peter 75
Simmons, Mrs. George B. 145
Singleton, Mr. & Mrs. Sheldon, ... 199
Skinner, Glenn Boone 19, 223
Slone, Lloyd 30
Smith, E. R. 59, 161
Smith, Fred L. 161
Smith, Mr. & Mrs. Roy 66
Stanton, Lon 17
Stark, Elisha V. 194
Stark, Gov. Lloyd 146
Stephens, Hugh 126
Stetter, Charley W. 188
Stevens, Walter B. 223
Street, Ralph W. 13, 190
Strickland, George 105
Strickland, Vi 105
Stubblefield, Monte 3
Sutton, L. F. 161
Sutton, Mrs. L. E. 17
Swallow, G. C. 153
Sweet, Kenneth B. 196
Tate, Mr. & Mrs. Alva 151
Teague, B. R. 161
Teeter, Helen 30
Teeter, Ted R. 30
Tettly, Emmit 161
Theison, Mr. & Mrs. Fred J. 199
Thomas, Frank 161
Thomas, Harry 60
Thomas, Lewis B. 92
Thompson, Clyde A. 17
Thompson, Craven 40
Thompson, E. C. 17

Thompson, Elmer 17
Thompson, James 17
Thornsberry, Lee 17
Thornsberry, W. E. 17
Thorp, R. S. 14
Tietmeyer, Ada 50-51
Tietmeyer, Walter 50-52
Tisne, Claude Du 216
Tobias, Arthur B. 133
Tobias, G. E. 133
Todd, Alice B. 14
Towne, M. H. 203
Traber, H. L. 126
Tremain, Lynn 209
Treybal, Joe 161
Tryon, Darvene 140
Tryon, Phil 140
Tuttle, E. 161
Tuttle, Frank W. 126
Tuxhorn, B. M. 200
Ulkus, Bill 72
Ulkus, Del 72
Umpsted, Samuel 11, 14
Vandike, Jim 28
Vernon, Edgar 210
Vincent, J. W. 125, 149
Vineyard, David 5
Vineyard, Jerry D. 224
Vineyard, Mrs. Henry 15
Vineyard, Wayne 15
Vogel, Robert S. 40, 224
Voss, J. A. 162
Waddle, W. H. 14
Ward, Fred M. 89
Ware, Ella 162, 213-214
Ware, Harry 213-214
Warren, James C. 17
Waters, Gary 219
Watkins, Chuck 120
Webb, Clint 31
Webster, Asa 47
Weeks, George 63
Weimar, Bill 155
Welch, Arnold 143
Welch, Don 143
Welch, Harold 143
Welch, Jo 143
Welch, Winna 143
Wells, Red 154, 199
Wells, Stella 154, 199
West, A. F. "Turk" 217
Whaley, Jesse 113
White, John 108
Whitman, Curtis 196
Whitman, Glen 196
Wiley, Prof. H. W. 39
Wilhelmi, Betty 143
Wilhelmi, Jean 143
Wilhelmi, Jim 143
Wilhelmi, John 143
Wilhelmi, Richard 143
Wilkerson, R. L. 28, 165, 196
Williams, Carl 17
Williams, Ezekiel 45, 46
Williams, J. T. 162
Williams, L. O. 202
Williams, Walter 224
Williamson, Mrs. Merle 96
Willmore, Cyrus 206
Willuhn, John 183
Willuhn, Mary Ann 183
Wilson, Edgar 162
Winn, Kenneth H. 221
Wisdom, Carroll 198
Witman, Elsi 203
Witman, Larry 203
Witt, Ab 81
Witt, Mrs. Myrtle 161, 196, 198
Woodmansee, John D. 124
Woods, Chas L. 197
Woolery, Abbie 31-32
Woolery, B. E. 32
Wright, Frank 7
Young, Nathan 126
Ziska, Col. Theodore 198

ABOUT THE AUTHOR

Dwight Weaver is the author of seven previous books, two of them on Lake of the Ozarks. Between 1971 and 1992, he authored five books on Missouri caves. Since his retirement in 2000 from the position of Public Information Officer for the Missouri Department of Natural Resources' Division of Geology and Land Survey, he has devoted his time to studying the history and geography of the Lake of the Ozarks region, where he and his wife, Rosie, have lived for more than 40 years.